NEW ENGLAND
MAP KEY

MAINE

1. BAXTER STATE PARK
2. BLACKWOODS CAMPGROUND
3. BRADBURY MOUNTAIN STATE PARK
4. COBSCOOK BAY STATE PARK
5. HERMIT ISLAND CAMPGROUND
6. LAMOINE STATE PARK
7. LILY BAY STATE PARK
8. MOUNT BLUE STATE PARK
9. MOUNT DESERT CAMPGROUND
10. PEAKS-KENNY STATE PARK
11. RANGELEY LAKE STATE PARK
12. SEAWALL CAMPGROUND
13. WARREN ISLAND STATE PARK

NEW HAMPSHIRE

14. BEAR BROOK STATE PARK
15. BIG ROCK CAMPGROUND
16. BLACKBERRY CROSSING CAMPGROUND
17. COVERED BRIDGE CAMPGROUND
18. CRAWFORD NOTCH CAMPGROUND
19. DOLLY COPP CAMPGROUND
20. DRY RIVER CAMPGROUND
21. HANCOCK CAMPGROUND
22. JIGGER JOHNSON CAMPGROUND
23. LAFAYETTE CAMPGROUND
24. MONADNOCK STATE PARK
25. PASSACONAWAY CAMPGROUND
26. PAWTUCKAWAY STATE PARK
27. PILLSBURY STATE PARK
28. WHITE LAKE STATE PARK

VERMONT

29. ALLIS STATE PARK
30. BRANBURY STATE PARK
31. CHITTENDEN BROOK RECREATION AREA
32. COOLIDGE STATE PARK
33. EMERALD LAKE STATE PARK
34. GIFFORD WOODS STATE PARK
35. GROUT POND RECREATION AREA
36. HALF MOON STATE PARK
37. JAMAICA STATE PARK
38. MOUNT ASCUTNEY STATE PARK
39. MOUNT MOOSALAMOO CAMPGROUND
40. QUECHEE GORGE STATE PARK
41. SMUGGLERS NOTCH STATE PARK
42. UNDERHILL STATE PARK

MASSACHUSETTS

43. BEARTOWN STATE FOREST
44. BOSTON HARBOR ISLANDS
45. CLARKSBURG STATE PARK
46. GRANVILLE STATE FOREST
47. HAROLD PARKER STATE FOREST
48. MOHAWK TRAIL STATE FOREST
49. MOUNT GREYLOCK STATE RESERVATION
50. NICKERSON STATE PARK
51. SAVOY MOUNTAIN STATE FOREST
52. TOLLAND STATE FOREST
53. WAQUOIT BAY NATURE PRESERVE
54. WOMPATUCK STATE PARK

CONNECTICUT

55. DEVIL'S HOPYARD STATE PARK
56. HOUSATONIC MEADOWS STATE PARK
57. MACEDONIA BROOK STATE PARK
58. SELDEN NECK CAMPGROUND

RHODE ISLAND

59. FORT GETTY RECREATION AREA
60. GEORGE WASHINGTON MANAGEMENT AREA

Other titles in this series

THE BEST IN TENT CAMPING

A GUIDE FOR CAR CAMPERS WHO HATE RVs,
CONCRETE SLABS, AND LOUD PORTABLE STEREOS

NEW ENGLAND

THIRD EDITION

LAFE LOW

MENASHA RIDGE PRESS
BIRMINGHAM, ALABAMA

*This book is for my son, Devin, my best camping buddy ever,
and for Douglas W. Low (1947–2008).*

Copyright © 2008 by Lafe Low
All rights reserved
Printed in the United States of America
Published by Menasha Ridge Press
Distributed by Publishers Group West
Third edition, second printing 2009

Library of Congress Cataloging-in-Publication Data

Low, Lafe, 1962—
    The best in tent camping. New England : a guide for car campers who hate
    RVs, concrete slabs, and loud portable stereos / Lafe Low. — 3rd ed.
        p. cm.
    Includes bibliographical references and index.
    ISBN-13: 978-0-89732-666-7 (alk. paper)
    ISBN-10: 0-89732-666-0 (alk. paper)
        1. Camping—New England—Guidebooks. 2. Camp sites, facilities, etc.—
    New England—Guidebooks. 3. Automobile travel—New England—Guidebooks.
    4. New England—Guidebooks. I. Title.
      GV191.42.N3L69 2008
      917.406'844—dc22

                        2007049418

Cover and text design by Ian Szymkowiak, Palace Press International, Inc.
Cover photo by Danita Delimont / Alamy
Cartography by Steve Jones and Lafe Low

Menasha Ridge Press
P.O. Box 43673
Birmingham, Alabama 35243
www.menasharidge.com

TABLE OF CONTENTS

VERMONT 111

MASSACHUSETTS 163

CONNECTICUT 207

RHODE ISLAND 221

APPENDIXES & INDEX 229

ACKNOWLEDGMENTS

WHILE I WROTE THE WORDS and drove the miles in preparing this book, I enjoyed the tremendous benefit of support and inspiration from many people. Most of all, I would like to thank my family and my parents (all three of them!), Douglas and Linsey Low, and Larry Howard, for their endless encouragement, understanding, love, and patience, especially while I dragged them around to these campgrounds.

To the innumerable state park rangers and volunteers I chatted with at campgrounds all over New England, and to the friendly folks at the private campgrounds I visited: I tip my hat to you. I'll be back soon, when I can stay a few days and relax!

PREFACE

NEW **E**NGLAND **IS A REMARKABLE REGION.** Nowhere else in the United States are you simultaneously so close to an ocean, mountains, lakes, and rivers. Drive a few hours and the landscape and the scenery change as rapidly and dramatically as the weather.

I have lived in New England all my life, moving around and experiencing almost all of the six New England states. (Rhode Island is the only New England state whose license plate hasn't graced my vehicle at one point or another.)

I am also somewhat of a creature of habit. Over the years, I have found spots where I can experience the solitude, wonder, and awesome beauty of the wilderness, and I keep going back to those same spots. There's a comfortable cloak of familiarity, but in cruising back to familiar territory, I've inadvertently blown by some incredible areas.

By traversing New England to research this book, I discovered some magical spots I might never have found otherwise, and for that I am thankful. The beachfront solitude of the Washburn Island, the isolation and deep wilderness beauty at several of Pillsbury State Park's campsites, the natural cathedral of site 21 at Branbury State Park—these are places that gave me chills when I first found them. Now I'll return to these spots for longer visits. When you have the chance to visit here, I hope you have an equally memorable experience. Enjoy the ride.

ABOUT THE AUTHOR

A **LIFELONG NEW ENGLANDER,** Lafe Low spends nearly all of his free time outside—skiing, camping, skiing, mountain biking, skiing, kayaking, and skiing. You get the picture. He first started camping in grade school, when he and his best friend, Dan Quagliaroli, would head off into the woods of southern Connecticut every Saturday afternoon with lofty ideals, indomitable spirit, and ridiculously heavy backpacks.

On the professional side, Lafe earned a bachelor of arts degree in journalism from Keene State College in 1984. From there, he immediately went to work in the magazine world. After working for a variety of computer magazines, he decided to launch his own magazine, *Explore New England,* in 1995. This was truly the crossroads of his personal and professional passions. After *Explore New England,* he went on to be the editor of *Outdoor Adventure* and an acquisitions editor for the Globe Pequot Press. He is now an editor with *Redmond* magazine. *The Best in Tent Camping: New England* is his first book, but probably not his last. He currently lives in the Boston area.

INTRODUCTION

WELCOME TO THE THIRD EDITION OF *The Best in Tent Camping: New England.* This represents what I think are 60 of the greatest campgrounds in New England. There are literally hundreds of campgrounds in New England. Winnowing the list down to 60 was no easy task. That said, this book is a guide to 60 of the current best for tent camping.

There are five new campgrounds in this edition that truly capture the solitude and sense of wilderness that define the very best in tent camping, including Hermit Island in Maine and Tolland State Forest in Massachusetts. These are two spots that offer that magic combination of woods and water.

There are plenty of wonderful campgrounds and campsites out there that didn't make it into the book but are still well worth checking out. In developing the list of campgrounds to explore here, I took into account numerous factors, one of which was accessibility. I wanted to profile campgrounds that offer a peaceful wilderness experience and are also accessible enough for a quick escape.

Of course, there are some pristine, incredibly remote campsites carved out of the wilderness of northern Maine and northern New Hampshire, or tucked away on islands in several New England lakes that aren't included in this book—yet. They may be in future editions, so stay tuned.

One other thing you'll no doubt notice is that most of the campgrounds profiled here are either state park or national forest campgrounds. That's no accident, as these campgrounds tend to provide much more of a wilderness experience. It's probably a simple matter of economics. Many private campgrounds cater to the RV crowd because, quite frankly, they spend more money when they visit. RV campers need hookups, which cost money, and they tend to stay for long periods of time.

In researching campgrounds for this third edition, I came across one private campground that was closing down for good because of economic hardship. Another private campground that was featured in the first two editions has been removed from this edition because it has gone all RV.

There are some notable exceptions, however. The Mount Desert Campground leaps to mind. While it neither excludes nor bends over backward to bring in the land yachts, the simple fact of its rugged, waterfront topography will limit the size and quantity of RVs. Another exception: the Hermit Island Campground, which is new to this edition. Both Mount Desert and Hermit Island are fabulous spots that you should make time to discover. I hope you'll be able to visit many of the other campgrounds profiled in this book and will agree that they are among the region's best.

THE OVERVIEW MAP AND OVERVIEW-MAP KEY

Use the overview map on the inside front cover to determine the exact location of each campground. The campground's number appears not only on the overview map but also on the map key facing the overview map, in the table of contents, and on the profile's first page.

The book is organized by state, as indicated in the table of contents. A map legend that details the symbols found on the campground-layout maps appears on the inside back cover.

CAMPGROUND-LAYOUT MAPS

Each profile contains a detailed campground-layout map that provides an overhead view of campground sites, internal roads, facilities, and other key items. Each campground entrance's GPS coordinates are included.

THE CAMPGROUND PROFILE

In addition to maps, each profile contains a concise but informative narrative of the campground and individual sites. This descriptive text is enhanced with four helpful side-bars: Ratings, Key Information, and Getting There (accurate driving directions that lead you to the campground from the nearest major roadway). On the first page of each profile is a Ratings box.

THE RATING SYSTEM

For each campground, there's a rating from one to five for each of the following categories: beauty, privacy, spaciousness, quiet, security, and cleanliness. This was often a tough call because each section within each campground might warrant different ratings. So the ratings you'll see at the beginning of each profile are representative of the campground as a whole. While you may see a three or four for privacy overall, you can probably bet there are a couple of sites tucked in the far reaches of the campground that clearly rate at least a five.

BEAUTY This factor may seem obvious but is often elusive, or at the very least, subjective. What appeals to one camper may not appeal to another. I prefer campgrounds and campsites that are set deep within the woods. The greater the sense of natural solitude a campsite provides, the better it is, at least in my view.

Speaking of views, many of the campgrounds profiled here, and certainly many of the individual sites within these campgrounds, are perched right along the shores of a lake, a pond, or even the ocean. These campsites are off the charts when it comes to site beauty. If there were a six-star rating, sites like those situated along the waters of Moose-head Lake, Half Moon Pond, and Somes Sound would easily deserve it. There are also many sites at campgrounds close to the water that, while they may not be right on the shore, provide dramatic water views. These sites too are among some of the most spectac-ularly scenic.

PRIVACY When you set up your campsite, the last thing you want is to feel as if you're piled up on top of your neighbors. Even in campgrounds where the sites aren't huge, if they are encircled by a relatively dense forest and arranged with an eye toward privacy, you can find a site that puts you in your own slice of the woods.

SPACIOUSNESS Some of the campsites I've seen in New England are just barely big enough for your tent, a picnic table, and a fire ring. Others are large enough to accommodate a house. I don't typically need a lot of room when I'm camping, but I don't want to pitch my tent right next to the picnic table. This rating will give you an idea of how much elbow room you can expect when you set up camp.

QUIET This is another factor that is particularly important to me. I like campsites that are very well isolated, secluded from neighboring sites and the rest of the campground. So I find it especially distracting if there is a persistent drone of cars and trucks blasting by on a nearby road, the steady whine of powerboats zipping by on a lake, or (worse yet) the sounds of portable TVs and radios.

You can rest assured I paid close attention to the noisiness of these campgrounds. In some cases, there are parts of a campground that are close to a main road, while the rest of the campground is separated by enough distance and enough forest to block out the road noise.

SECURITY It's a shame that this even has to be a factor, but you have to be practical. I've never had anyone steal or rummage through my stuff at any of the campgrounds mentioned here, but there are some that feel "safer" to me than others. The size of the campground and proximity to urban areas are the primary aspects I considered when making my security determinations. Be prudent, even when it looks like there's no one around. It's not a bad idea to lock up your car and your bike when you retire to your tent for the night. A little bit of precaution can go a long way toward making sure you return home with all your gear.

CLEANLINESS Most of the campgrounds profiled here scored highly on the cleanliness scale. This is true for a couple of reasons. First, I think that most people who enjoy the idea of spending a night in the woods are also inclined to take good care of the forest and their campsites. Second, many state parks make extraordinary efforts to keep their campsites well maintained. When you see the park rangers or other staff about the campground, take a moment to say "hi" and thank them for keeping the campground clean.

Of course, all of this depends on you doing your part as well. Even though campgrounds are heavily traveled and well-worn spots, do what you can to leave no trace. Pack out everything you packed in (and even a little more). Please don't pile your trash in the fireplace or try to burn things that won't burn or that emit dangerous fumes.

Even at the cleanest of campgrounds and campsites, whenever I find a stray piece of paper, a bottle cap, or a cigarette butt (especially the latter), I always take a moment to reach down and pick it up to dispose of it properly. If everyone is mindful to be as gentle with the forest as possible, it will remain pristine for generations to come. Every time you pick up a bit of trash in the woods, consider it doing a favor for your children or grand-children, even if you don't have any yet!

NEW ENGLAND WEATHER

Even during the summer, it's prudent to pack a fleece jacket and a waterproof jacket. It seems like on at least half of the occasions where I find myself camping outside, it rains. I think the camping gods start chuckling every time they see me grab my tent.

Anyway, it's a good idea to be prepared for any kind of weather. That doesn't mean bring your snowshoes in August, but by all means do bring a warm jacket and something water-resistant. The weather in New England can and does change faster than the scenery as you drive from Cape Cod to the Berkshires. Have something warm, have something dry. You'll be much more comfortable and safer.

Also, even if it has been a bright, sunny day, foul weather can blow in at any time, and frequently does. I've been tempted on many nights to ignore the rainfly on my tent and just leave it in the car. This can be a bad idea, especially if it starts raining at 2 a.m. Be ready and you'll be happy.

CANOE AND KAYAK CAMPING

Several of the campgrounds profiled here are accessible only by canoe or kayak. While this poses several logistical and packing challenges, the rewards of absolute solitude and camping right on the water are well worth the extra effort.

There are a few important safety factors to consider when canoe or kayak camping. First and foremost, you need to be comfortable with your paddling skills before you add the weight of camping gear to your boat. Don't plan a camping trip the first time you try paddling a canoe or kayak.

With a sea kayak, try to stow all your gear in the sealed bulkheads. It may be tempting to strap your tent or sleeping pad to the deck, but anything protruding above deck level will make your kayak less stable. Besides catching the wind, it also raises the boat's center of gravity. Keep all your gear below decks.

Most touring kayaks have a fore and aft storage compartment. Try to spread your gear out evenly. Even if all your gear will fit in the aft compartment, spread it out among both to ensure that your kayak floats level. Once you've packed your boat, take it for a test float. Get it into water deep enough that it floats freely. If it looks like you're riding a wheelie or about to do a nose dive, you need to redistribute your gear. The same goes for side-to-side balance. Keep those same principles in mind when stowing gear in a canoe. Try to balance to load in the center of the canoe and evenly distributed fore and aft.

Having said all that, you can pack an amazing amount of gear in a canoe or kayak. Prior to packing up for the first group trip I ever went on, we divided the group gear. I stowed the group gear in my aft compartment and my personal gear in the forward compartment and still had plenty of room in each.

There are a few things you can do to make your canoe or kayak camping trip a bit more convenient. For your first dinner at your island campsite, prepare something in advance, freeze it in a Tupperware container, then when dinnertime arrives, all you have to do is heat it up and you're ready to eat. Also, you should wrap any gear that you haven't been able to store in a dry bag, tightly in a large, plastic garbage bag. Anything you store in the bulkheads or open in your canoe can and most likely will get a bit wet. There's nothing worse than reaching for a jacket or vest to wear and finding it damp and soggy.

THE CAMPFIRE AWAITS

There's nothing like a night spent outside. The soft crackle of a campfire, the flickering light thrown about the forest, the satisfaction of the day's travels, and the anticipation of tomorrow's adventures—it's a potent combination.

Hopefully, the camping tips provided here and the descriptions of the campgrounds that follow will steer you to a memorable experience. Pick a state, read the profiles, pack the car, and hit the road! New England is a vast and diverse region. There are campgrounds profiled here from the farthest northern reaches of Vermont, New Hampshire, and Maine to the seashores of Connecticut and Rhode Island, and everything in between. Some are familiar haunts, some are unexpected hidden gems; all are spectacular.

Wherever you choose to go camping in New England—from the sandy bluffs of Nickerson State Park to the deep woods of Clarksburg State Forest, from the absolute solitude of Warren Island to the cool, crisp mountain air of the Crawford Notch Campground—you're in for a memorable and magical trip.

GET OUT AND GET ACTIVE WITH THE APPALACHIAN MOUNTAIN CLUB

With the AMC, you can participate in a wide variety of outdoor activities, connect with new people, and help to protect the natural world you love. Join us and each year you'll receive ten issues of our member magazine, *AMC Outdoors,* which will keep you informed of environmental issues and outdoor recreation opportunities—including hiking, paddling, biking, and snowshoeing—across the Appalachian region. You'll receive discounts on AMC's guided adventures, courses, lodging, and books. You can also join our Conservation Action Network (CAN) to help increase public influence regarding critical conservation issues today at **www.outdoors.org/conservation/can.**

LEARN SOMETHING NEW: AMC OUTDOOR ADVENTURES

Develop your outdoor skills and knowledge through AMC Outdoor Adventures! Learn to rock-climb, snowshoe, or navigate by map and compass. From beginner backpacking and family canoeing to dogsledding and guided winter camping trips, you'll find something for any age or interest at spectacular locations throughout the Appalachian region, including the Maine Woods, White Mountains, Adirondacks, Catskills, and Delaware Water Gap. For a full listing and to sign up, go to **www.outdoors.org** and click on "Education."

BE OUR GUEST: AMC DESTINATIONS AND ACCOMMODATIONS

From the North Woods of Maine to the White Mountains to the Delaware Water Gap, AMC offers a wide variety of accommodations, from full-service lodges to backcountry huts, shelters, and campsites. Experience outdoor adventure at its best as our guest. Get trip suggestions, check lodging availability, and make reservations through our Web site, **www.outdoors.org.**

Contact Us Today
    Appalachian Mountain Club
    5 Joy Street
    Boston, MA 02108
    www.outdoors.org

FIRST-AID KIT

A useful first-aid kit may contain more items than you might think necessary. These are just the basics. Prepackaged kits in waterproof bags are available (Atwater Carey and Adventure Medical make them.) As a preventive measure, take along sunscreen and insect repellent. Even though quite a few items are listed here, they pack down into a small space:

- Ace bandages or Spenco joint wraps
- Adhesive bandages, such as Band-Aids
- Antibiotic ointment (Neosporin or the generic equivalent)
- Antiseptic or disinfectant, such as Betadine or hydrogen peroxide
- Aspirin or acetaminophen
- Benadryl or the generic equivalent, diphenhydramine (in case of allergic reactions)
- Butterfly-closure bandages
- Epinephrine in a prefilled syringe (for people known to have severe allergic reactions to such things as bee stings)
- Gauze (one roll)
- Gauze compress pads (six 4 x 4-inch pads)
- Matches or pocket lighter
- Moleskin/Spenco "2nd Skin"
- Waterproof first-aid tape
- Whistle (it's more effective in signaling rescuers than is your voice)

ANIMAL AND PLANT HAZARDS

Ticks

Ticks are often found on brush and tall grass waiting to hitch a ride on a warm-blooded passerby. Among the local varieties of ticks, the nymph deer tick is the primary carrier of Lyme disease. You can use several strategies to reduce your chances of ticks getting under your skin. Some people choose to wear light-colored clothing, so ticks can be spotted before they make it to the skin. Most important, be sure to visually check your hair, the back of your neck, your armpits, and your socks at the end of the hike. During your posthike shower, take a moment to do a more complete body check. For ticks that are already embedded, removal with tweezers is best. Use disinfectant solution on the wound.

Poison Oak

Poison oak grows in moist areas, favoring shade trees and water sources. Recognizing and avoiding contact is the most effective way to prevent the painful, itchy rashes associated with these plants. Identify the plant by its three-leaf structure, with two leaves on opposite sides of the stem, and one extending from the center. Refrain from scratching because bacteria under fingernails can cause infection. Wash and dry the rash thoroughly, applying a calamine lotion to help dry out the rash. If itching or blistering is severe, seek medical attention. If you do come in contact with one of these plants, remember that oil-contaminated clothes, pets, or hiking gear can easily cause an irritating rash on you or someone else, so wash not only any exposed parts of your body but also clothes, gear, and pets if applicable.

Poison Ivy

Poison ivy occurs as a vine or groundcover, three leaflets to a leaf; poison oak occurs as either a vine or shrub, also with three leaflets; and poison sumac flourishes in swampland, each leaf having seven to thirteen leaflets. Urushiol, the oil in the sap of these plants, is responsible for the rash. Within fourteen hours of exposure, raised lines and/or blisters will appear on the affected area, accompanied by a terrible itch. Refrain from scratching because bacteria under your fingernails can cause an infection. Wash and dry the rash thoroughly, applying a calamine lotion to help dry out the rash. If itching or blistering is severe, seek medical attention. If you do come into contact with one of these plants, remember that oil-contaminated clothes, pets, or hiking gear can easily cause an irritating rash on you or someone else, so wash not only any exposed parts of your body but also clothes, gear, and pets if applicable.

TIPS FOR A HAPPY CAMPING TRIP

There is nothing worse than a bad camping trip, especially because it is so easy to have a great time. To assist with making your outing a happy one, here are some pointers:

- **RESERVE YOUR SITE AHEAD OF TIME,** especially if it's a weekend, a holiday, or if the campground is wildly popular. Many prime campgrounds require at least a six-month lead time on reservations. Check before you go.

- **PICK YOUR CAMPING BUDDIES WISELY.** A family trip is pretty straight-forward, but you may want to reconsider including grumpy Uncle Fred, who doesn't like bugs, sunshine, or marshmallows. After you know who's going, make sure that everyone is on the same page regarding expectations of difficulty (amenities or the lack thereof, physical exertion, and so on), sleeping arrangements, and food requirements.

- **DON'T DUPLICATE EQUIPMENT** such as cooking pots and lanterns among campers in your party. Carry what you need to have a good time, but don't turn the trip into a major moving experience.

- **DRESS FOR THE SEASON.** Educate yourself on the temperature highs and lows of the specific area you plan to visit. It may be warm at night in the summer in your backyard, but up in the mountains it will be quite chilly.

- **PITCH YOUR TENT ON A LEVEL SURFACE,** preferably one covered with leaves, pine straw, or grass. Use a tarp or specially designed footprint to thwart ground moisture and to protect the tent floor. Do a little site maintenance, such as picking up the small rocks and sticks that can damage your tent floor and make sleep uncomfortable. If you have a separate tent rainfly but don't think you'll need it, keep it rolled up at the base of the tent in case it starts raining at midnight.

- **IF YOU ARE NOT COMFORTABLE SLEEPING ON THE GROUND,** take a sleeping pad with you that is full-length and thicker than you think you might need. This will not only keep your hips from aching on hard ground, but will also help keep you warm. A wide range of thin, light, inflatable pads is available at camping stores, and these are a much better choice than home air mattresses, which conduct heat away from the body and tend to deflate during the night.

- **IF YOU'RE NOT HIKING IN TO A PRIMITIVE CAMPSITE,** there is no real need to skimp on food because of weight. Plan tasty meals and bring everything you will need to prepare, cook, eat, and clean up.

- **IF YOU TEND TO USE THE BATHROOM MULTIPLE TIMES AT NIGHT,** you should plan ahead. Leaving a warm sleeping bag and stumbling around in the dark to find the restroom, whether it be a pit toilet, a fully plumbed comfort station, or just the woods, is not fun. Keep a flashlight and any other accoutrements you may need by the tent door and know exactly where to head in the dark.

- **STANDING DEAD TREES AND STORM-DAMAGED LIVING TREES** can pose a real hazard to tent campers. These trees may have loose or broken limbs that could fall at any time. When choosing a campsite or even just a spot to rest during a hike, look up.

CAMPING ETIQUETTE

Camping experiences can vary wildly depending on a variety of factors, such as weather, preparedness, fellow campers, and time of year. Here are a few tips on how to create good vibes with fellow campers and wildlife you encounter.

- **OBTAIN ALL PERMITS AND AUTHORIZATION AS REQUIRED.** Make sure you check in, pay your fee, and mark your site as directed. Don't make the mistake of grabbing a seemingly empty site that looks more appealing than your site. It could be reserved. If you're unhappy with the site you've selected, check with the campground host for other options.

- **LEAVE ONLY FOOTPRINTS.** Be sensitive to the ground beneath you. Be sure to place all garbage in designated receptacles or pack it out if none are available. No one likes to see the trash someone else has left behind.

- **NEVER SPOOK ANIMALS.** It's common for animals to wander through campsites, where they may be accustomed to the presence of humans (and our food). An unannounced approach, a sudden movement, or a loud noise startles most animals. A surprised animal can be dangerous to you, to others, and to itself. Give them plenty of space.

- **PLAN AHEAD.** Know your equipment, your ability, and the area where you are camping—and prepare accordingly. Be self-sufficient at all times; carry necessary supplies for changes in weather or other conditions. A well-executed trip is a satisfaction to you and to others.

- **BE COURTEOUS TO OTHER CAMPERS,** hikers, bikers, and others you encounter. If you run into the owner of a large RV, don't panic. Just wave, feign eye contact, and then walk slowly away.

- **STRICTLY FOLLOW THE CAMPGROUND'S RULES** regarding the building of fires. Never burn trash. Trash smoke smells horrible, and trash debris in a fire pit or grill is unsightly.

VENTURING AWAY FROM THE CAMPGROUND

If you go for a hike, bike, or other excursion into the wilderness, here are some tips:

- **ALWAYS CARRY FOOD AND WATER,** whether you are planning to go overnight or not. Food will give you energy, help keep you warm, and sustain you in an emergency until help arrives. Bring potable water or treat water by boiling or filtering before drinking from a lake or stream.

- **STAY ON DESIGNATED TRAILS.** Most hikers get lost when they leave the trail. Even on the most clearly marked trails, there is usually a point where you have to stop and consider which direction to head. If you become disoriented, don't panic. As soon as you think you may be off track, stop, assess your current direction, and then retrace your steps to the point where you went astray. If you have absolutely no idea how to continue, return to the trailhead the way you came in. Should you become completely lost and have no idea of how to return to the trailhead, remaining in place along the trail and waiting for help is most often the best option for adults and always the best option for children.

- **BE ESPECIALLY CAREFUL WHEN CROSSING STREAMS.** Whether you are fording the stream or crossing on a log, make every step count. If you have any doubt about maintaining your balance on a log, go ahead and ford the stream instead. When fording a stream, use a trekking pole or stout stick for balance and face upstream as you cross. If a stream seems too deep to ford, turn back. Whatever is on the other side is not worth risking your life.

- **BE CAREFUL AT OVERLOOKS.** Although these areas may provide spectacular views, they are potentially hazardous. Stay back from the edge of outcrops and be absolutely sure of your footing: a misstep can mean a nasty and possibly fatal fall.

- **KNOW THE SYMPTOMS OF HYPOTHERMIA.** Shivering and forgetfulness are the two most common indicators of this insidious killer. Hypothermia can occur at any elevation, even in the summer. Wearing cotton clothing puts you especially at risk because cotton, when wet, wicks heat away from the body. To prevent hypothermia, dress in layers using synthetic clothing for insulation, use a cap and gloves to reduce heat loss, and protect yourself with waterproof, breathable outerwear. If symptoms arise, get the victim to shelter, a fire, hot liquids, and dry clothes or a dry sleeping bag.

- **TAKE ALONG YOUR BRAIN.** A cool, calculating mind is the single most important piece of equipment you'll ever take on the trail. Think before you act. Watch your step. Plan ahead. Avoiding accidents before they happen is the best strategy for a rewarding and relaxing hike.

MAINE

FOREVER WILD"—THOSE ARE THE WORDS of Percival Baxter (1876–1969), a former governor of Maine and a philanthropist and conservationist, who donated Katahdin and the land surrounding it to the state on the condition that it remain "forever wild." Those words perfectly describe Baxter State Park as well. The remoteness, size, and grandeur of the park are profound. Baxter's intent was to keep the park undeveloped. Today, the park is managed as a wildlife preserve first and a recreation resource second.

At more than 200,000 acres, Baxter State Park is a huge place. There are actually ten campgrounds within the park. Truth is, no matter where you end up in Baxter State Park, you're bound to have a remote wilderness experience. Eight of the campgrounds you can reach by driving; the other two are hike-in areas. Camping in these areas requires a bit of additional effort, but the solitude and splendor are well worth it. If you're camping in Baxter State Park, by all means enjoy the convenience of the car-camping areas, but try to spend at least one night at Chimney Pond or Russell Pond, or even at one of the many truly remote wilderness campsites spread throughout the park.

Upon entering the massive park through the Togue Pond Gate along the park's southern border, the first campground you'll come to is Abol Campground. Abol has 9 tent sites and 12 lean-tos; each lean-to can accommodate four people. Abol Campground is situated at the trailhead for the Abol Trail, one of the routes to the summit of Katahdin, so this is one of several popular spots for hikers with designs on summiting the park's centerpiece peak.

Farther up Nesowadnehunk Tote Road that encircles the perimeter of the park is Katahdin Stream Campground. This campground has 9 tent sites, 12 lean-tos that can fit three to five people, and three

> *A night spent camping in Baxter State Park, especially in one of the remote sites, is a true wilderness experience.*

RATINGS

Beauty: ✩ ✩ ✩ ✩ ✩
Privacy: ✩ ✩ ✩ ✩
Spaciousness: ✩ ✩ ✩ ✩
Quiet: ✩ ✩ ✩ ✩ ✩
Security: ✩ ✩ ✩ ✩ ✩
Cleanliness: ✩ ✩ ✩ ✩

group sites that can hold from twelve to twenty-five campers. From here, hikers can head to the summit of Katahdin on the Hunt Trail, which is part of the Appalachian Trail. You can also easily get to the Owl Trail and the Grassy Pond Trail heading east.

Just to the east of Katahdin Stream, you'll find Daicey Pond Campground. You get there by continuing north and west on Tote Road, then heading south just before Foster Field Picnic Area. You could also hike there from Katahdin Stream Campground (or vice versa) on the Grassy Pond Trail. The Daicey Pond Campground doesn't have any tent sites, but it does have ten cabins with two to four beds each. The Appalachian Trail goes right through the campground. There's also a trail that encircles Daicey Pond and leads to the short Lost Pond Trail, which takes you out to the still and secluded waters of Lost Pond.

Continuing north on Nesowadnehunk Tote Road along the western border of the park brings you to Nesowadnehunk Field Campground. Here there are twelve tent sites, eleven three- and four-person lean-tos, and three group sites. This campground is being restructured, so be sure to contact the rangers to make sure what you want is available. From here, you could easily get to the Doubletop Trail, a sturdy hike that takes you up and over Doubletop Mountain and offers some outrageous views of Katahdin.

Taking Roaring Brook Road off to the right from the Togue Pond gatehouse brings you first to Roaring Brook Campground. There are ten tent sites (four of which are walk-in sites), nine lean-tos that accommodate anywhere from two to six people each, three

KEY INFORMATION

ADDRESS:	Baxter State Park 64 Balsam Drive Millinocket, ME 04462
OPERATED BY:	Maine Department of Conservation, Bureau of Parks and Lands
INFORMATION:	Baxter State Park, (207) 723-5140
OPEN:	May 15–October 15 (some campgrounds have variable dates)
SITES:	95 tent sites, 74 lean-tos, 4 bunkhouses, 12 group sites, and 23 cabins in 10 campgrounds
EACH SITE HAS:	Fire ring, picnic table (except hike-in sites)
ASSIGNMENT:	Reservations strongly recommended, accepted Monday–Friday, 8 a.m.–4 p.m.; otherwise first come, first served
REGISTRATION:	At gatehouse and with ranger; check in after 1 p.m., check out by 11 a.m.
FACILITIES:	Pit toilets, water spigots
PARKING:	At sites
FEE:	$12 nonresident vehicle fee to enter park; $9 per person per night for tent spaces and lean-tos ($18 minimum per night); $5 per person per night for group sites ($30 minimum per night); $10 per person, per night for bunkhouses; $25 per person per night for cabins
RESTRICTIONS:	*Pets:* Prohibited *Fires:* Fire rings only *Alcohol:* Prohibited *Vehicles:* Parking at sites only

group sites that hold up to 14, and a bunkhouse with room for ten. From here, you have plenty of hiking options. Follow the Sandy Stream Pond Trail to the Turner Mountain Trail to hike up Turner Mountain. You could also head west on the Helon Taylor Trail to reach Katahdin.

Head west on the Chimney Pond Trail from Roaring Brook Campground, and you'll come to Chimney Pond Campground. This is a remote and supremely beautiful spot. There are no tent sites here, but there are nine lean-tos that can each handle four people, and a bunkhouse that can fit ten. At least your tent is one less thing to carry.

Besides being remarkably scenic, Chimney Pond Campground is a perfect base camp from which to summit Katahdin. You have your choice of the Saddle Trail, Cathedral Trail, or Didley Trail. All of these hikes are steep and strenuous, so plan ahead and be prepared.

Also from the Roaring Brook Campground, follow the Russell Pond Trail to Russell Pond Campground, another incredibly remote and wild camping area. There are three tent sites, four lean-tos that can accommodate anywhere from four to eight people, and a bunkhouse for eight. This campground is also situated within a hub of trails. There are several long hiking trails, including the Russell Pond Trail and the Northwest Basin Trail (which leads to the North Peaks Trail) to the south, the Pogy Notch Trail to the north, and the Wassataquoik Lake Trail to the west. These are all fairly long hikes, so plan and pace yourself carefully, especially if you're doing a round-trip day hike from the campground. If you're looking for a shorter hike from Russell Pond Campground, try the Ledge Falls Trail, Grand Falls Trail, or Lookout Trail.

Entering the park from the northeast at Matagamon Gate Public Landing will get you close to the Trout Brook Farm and South Branch campgrounds. From the gatehouse, follow the road west to Trout Brook Farm Campground. This campground is primarily for tent campers, with fourteen tent sites, four group sites for eight to fourteen people, and just one lean-to. From here, you can also hike in to a number of remote wilderness campsites. To the south, follow Five Ponds Trail to sites spread out along Littlefield Pond, Billfish Pond, and Long Pond. To the north, the lengthy, multiday Freezeout Trail brings you to remote campsites and lean-tos along Second Lake, Webster Brook, and Webster Lake.

From Trout Brook Campground, continue west on the road to The Crossing picnic area. Then head south on South Branch Road to find South Branch Campground, with 21 tent sites, 12 four-person lean-tos, and a bunkhouse for eight. This campground is located at the northern tip of Lower South Branch Pond. From here, you can hike the short and sweet Ledges Trail or the Middle Fowler Trail.

There are also several excellent hikes to nearby peaks, including the North Traveler Trail, which leads up the mountain of the same name; the Howe Brook Trail, which follows its namesake brook past two dramatic waterfalls; and the Center Ridge Trail, which brings you to the summit of the Traveler. To the west of Upper and Lower South Branch ponds, the South Branch Mountain Trail takes you up and over Black Cat Mountain. These hikes aren't very long, but they are very steep. Never underestimate the intensity of the hiking anywhere within Baxter State Park.

MAP

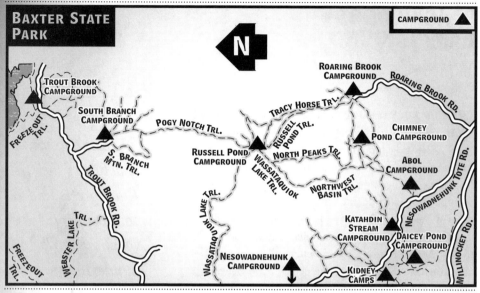

BAXTER STATE PARK

CAMPGROUND ▲

N

ROARING BROOK CAMPGROUND

ROARING BROOK RD.

TROUT BROOK CAMPGROUND

SOUTH BRANCH CAMPGROUND

FREEZEOUT TRL.

POGY NOTCH TRL.

TRACY HORSE TRL.

RUSSELL POND TRL.

CHIMNEY POND CAMPGROUND

S. BRANCH MTN. TRL.

RUSSELL POND CAMPGROUND

NORTH PEAKS TRL.

WASSATAQUOIK LAKE TRL.

ABOL CAMPGROUND

TROUT BROOK RD.

NORTHWEST BASIN TRL.

NESOWADNEHUNK TOTE RD.

WEBSTER LAKE TRL.

FREEZEOUT TRL.

WASSATAQUOIK LAKE TRL.

KATAHDIN STREAM CAMPGROUND

DAICEY POND CAMPGROUND

MILLINOCKET RD.

NESOWADNEHUNK CAMPGROUND

KIDNEY CAMPS

GETTING THERE

To get to the Togue Pond gatehouse, follow Baxter State Park Road northwest from the intersection of ME 11 and ME 157 in Millinocket. To get to the Matagamon Public Landing gatehouse from Patten, take US 1 north to ME 159 north to Grand Lake Road. Follow Grand Lake Road to the gatehouse.

Baxter State Park is a popular destination, and there is a finite number of campsites in and around the park. You could wing it by not making reservations, but you might end up disappointed or driving way out of your way to find an open site. If you do get jammed, there are several private campgrounds just outside the park that provide a backup place to pitch your tent, but do yourself a favor and make a reservation. The peace of mind will be well worth it.

FOR SUCH A HUGE CAMPGROUND, most of the sites at Blackwoods retain a cozy atmosphere. The three-lane paved road (two lanes in, one out) accessing the campground might make you wonder what you're getting into, but rest assured, this is a great place to pitch a tent.

For one thing, Blackwoods Campground is situated just off Park Loop Road, which winds its way around Acadia National Park. Better still, from your campsite it's a short walk to the ocean, Sand Beach, Thunder Hole, Otter Cliff . . . the list goes on. The campground rests on the mostly flat forest floor beneath a loosely spaced forest canopy of mixed pine, balsam, hemlock, and hardwoods. The open forest lets lots of light filter through to the campground floor on sunny days, and there's a near-constant, cool breeze blowing in from the nearby ocean.

Blackwoods is separated into two main loops. Loop A has 160 sites, and Loop B has 154 sites. There are also several group sites available by reservation only. The place is big! Blackwoods accepts reservations from June 15 to September 15. Making a reservation for an in-season trip is not a bad idea, as Acadia National Park receives hordes of visitors during the summer, and Blackwoods is likely to be full on most weekends.

Outside of those dates, it's first come, first served. About 50 campsites on Loop A are open year-round if you've come to Acadia to snowshoe or cross-country ski on the massive network of carriage roads that wind their way in and around the park. Camping during the winter is usually free, unless a ranger at the main station informs you differently. I've frequently visited Blackwoods in the off-season. There has never been a fee, and I've always felt like I had the place to myself.

Looking at the 160 sites within Loop A, there are

> *This campground is set between the still of the forests and mountains of Acadia National Park and the thundering surf of the Atlantic Ocean.*

RATINGS

Beauty: ✿ ✿ ✿ ✿
Privacy: ✿ ✿ ✿
Spaciousness: ✿ ✿ ✿ ✿ ✿
Quiet: ✿ ✿ ✿ ✿
Security: ✿ ✿ ✿
Cleanliness: ✿ ✿ ✿ ✿

ADDRESS:	Blackwoods Campground ME Highway 3 Bar Harbor, ME 04609
OPERATED BY:	National Park Service
INFORMATION:	Acadia National Park P.O. Box 177 Bar Harbor, ME 04609 (207) 288-3338
OPEN:	Year-round; limited facilities December– March
SITES:	306
EACH SITE HAS:	Fire ring with grate, picnic table
ASSIGNMENT:	Reservations required May 1– October 31; otherwise first come, first served
REGISTRATION:	Pay at ranger station at entrance to park; reservations: (800) 365-2267 (camp), www .reservations.nps.gov
FACILITIES:	Flush toilets, water spigots, showers and a camp store 0.5 miles away
PARKING:	1 vehicle per site, additional parking available
FEE:	$20 per site (May 1–October 31); $10 per site April and November; free December 1–March 31, permit required
RESTRICTIONS:	*Pets:* On leash or in cage at all times *Fires:* Fire rings only *Alcohol:* Sites only *Vehicles:* 1 per site *Other:* Quiet hours 10 p.m.–7 a.m.; check out by 10 a.m.

several areas that are especially conducive to quality tent camping. In the first subloop, sites 3, 4, 5, 7, and 10 through 19, are loosely spaced beneath a rich forest canopy. The sites have a welcoming blanket of pine needles, which makes a soft, aromatic bed for your tent and sleeping bag.

The next loop contains sites 2, 6, 8, 9, 22, 27, 29, 32, 33, and 34, which are also loosely spaced.

These two loops are quite close to the path leading down to the cliffs—a bonus. After the day crowds have cleared out, you've had your fireside dinner, and the campfire has died down, grab a flashlight and a mug of tea (or whatever suits your mood) and wander down the path and across Park Loop Road to watch the surf crashing incessantly against the cliffs. That's a sight and sound combination of which I never tire.

Farther up the larger part of Loop A, the sites off to the left of the outer loop offer a nice sense of seclusion. Look for sites 104 through 108, 124 through 131, and 144 through 151. In truth, though, most of the sites within the sweeping expanse of Loop A will offer you a nice spot for your tent.

Over in Loop B, there are several areas where the sites are set apart from each other. The crossroad at the far end of Loop B sets off sites 141, 143, 147, 150, 153, and 154. These are the sites I'd look for first in Loop B.

Taking the second or third left from the main outer loop will bring you to sites numbered in the high 60s and low 70s. Sites 65 through 73 have a good amount of elbow room between them. Site 45 is also stuck onto the far end of this loop. It's right on the main outer loop, but if you set up well within the site, you'll be fine.

There are also several group sites on the left side of Loop B. G4 and G5 offer the most space, although G5 is right across from the restrooms. Each of these reservation-only group sites has room for 15 to 20 campers. There's an amphitheater between Loop A and Loop B where rangers present evening slide shows and interpretive programs. Check the schedule at the campground entrance ranger station.

If you end up pitching your tent at the north end of Loop A, you'll be close to the South Ridge hiking

MAP

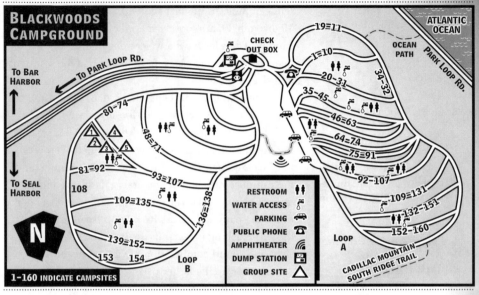

BLACKWOODS CAMPGROUND

ATLANTIC OCEAN

To Bar Harbor

To Park Loop Rd.

CHECK OUT BOX

OCEAN PATH

PARK LOOP RD.

To Seal Harbor

19–11
1–10
20–31
34–32
35–45
80–74
48–71
46–63
64–74
75–91
81–92
93–107
92–107
108
109–135
109–131
132–151
139–152
136–138
152–160
153   154
LOOP B
LOOP A

1   2   3   4   5

N

RESTROOM	♟♟
WATER ACCESS	⚡
PARKING	🚗
PUBLIC PHONE	☎
AMPHITHEATER	📶
DUMP STATION	▣
GROUP SITE	△

CADILLAC MOUNTAIN SOUTH RIDGE TRAIL

1–160 INDICATE CAMPSITES

trail, leading to the summit of Cadillac Mountain. Wherever you land at Blackwoods, or even if you stay elsewhere in or near Acadia National Park, a trip to the summit of Cadillac is one thing you won't want to miss. From the mountain, you'll have a sweeping, panoramic view that defies clichés, platitudes, and expletives! Here's a tip: The sunsets are phenomenal, so much so that one per day may not be enough. Situate yourself along Park Loop Road to watch sunset. The instant it dips below the horizon, hop in your car and boogie up to the summit of Cadillac Mountain to watch it again!

GETTING THERE

From Ellsworth, follow ME 3 onto Mount Desert Island. Follow ME 3 to ME 102/198. Stay on ME 198 when it turns left, and follow this to ME 233. Follow ME 233 to the entrance to Acadia National Park on the left. Enter the park and follow Park Loop Road to Blackwoods Campground on the right.

betw Auburn + Portland

> *The cool breezes and sunlight filtering through the trees add to the peace of Bradbury Mountain State Park.*

DESPITE ITS LOCATION, Bradbury Mountain State Park is an exceptionally quiet campground. There's a bit of sporadic road noise from ME 9, but the fragrant evergreen scent wafting through the loose forest is constant. There's an open, airy character to the forest that lets sunlight brighten the campground floor and lets breezes blow through.

Pick your campsite and the ranger will come by to register you. Sites 3, 5, 6, 14, 15, 25, 28, 34, and 35 are first come, first served. You can reserve any of the other sites. There's a host site on the right as you enter the campground, if you have any questions.

All of the sites have a hard, sandy surface that holds on to tent stakes. Sites 1 and 2 are moderately spacious. There's an old stone wall running along the back of these sites. The open character of the forest here provides lots of light and nice breezes, but consequently not as much privacy as would a densely forested campground. Sites 8 and 9 are very spacious but open to each other and to the road. Sites 14 and 15 are very open to each other; they almost look like one extremely large, sandy spot. They would make a good pair of sites for a larger group or family needing two sites side by side. They're also designated as wheelchair accessible.

The individual sites differ in size, as marked on the campground's map. The sites at Bradbury Mountain, however, are similar when it comes to their level of privacy. There's only a mild sense of seclusion afforded by relatively light undergrowth.

There are three exceptionally secluded sites. Sites 6, 12, and 16 are hike-in sites reserved only for tent campers. The trail leading into 12 is located next to site 11. It's about a 100-foot walk on a flat, sandy path to the site, which gives it a true sense of wilderness and seclusion.

The site itself is set within loosely spaced, mixed

RATINGS

Beauty: ✿ ✿ ✿ ✿
Privacy: ✿ ✿ ✿
Spaciousness: ✿ ✿ ✿ ✿
Quiet: ✿ ✿ ✿
Security: ✿ ✿ ✿ ✿
Cleanliness: ✿ ✿ ✿ ✿

forest with very little undergrowth. There's a very open, breezy character to the forest here as well, but you're so separated from the rest of the campground that the sense of privacy is complete. From this site, you can look around 360 degrees, and all you'll see is the forest. Site 12 at Bradbury Mountain State Park offers a sense of seclusion equal to that of a backpacking site way off in the backcountry. Site 16 is another supremely secluded walk-in site. This site shares all the characteristics and accolades of site 12, but is actually a bit farther into the woods.

You might want to avoid sites 17 and 18, as these are right next to the shelter. Site 19 is huge, but it also has a very open feel. Exposed on two sides to the campground's loop road, site 20 feels too open for me. Site 21 is a bit more secluded. It's set at the corner of the campground road with a decent amount of space between it and site 19. It looks like you could drive right through site 22. It's very open to site 20, as well as being on the inside corner of the campground road.

Sites 29, 31, and 32 are all fairly spacious. The wall of woods behind the sites is also filled in with undergrowth, providing a dense barrier against ME 9. The forest on this side of the campground is denser and has thicker undergrowth.

Even though many of the sites here seem exposed to one another, you still won't feel as if you're piled on top of your neighbors. Although you'll certainly be able to see your fellow campers, the sites are generally spacious and situated far enough apart to offer a modicum of elbow room.

You will have to drive a bit to get to the rest of Bradbury Mountain State Park and the hiking trails, but it's not too far, and it's definitely worth the trip.

KEY INFORMATION

ADDRESS:	Bradbury Mountain State Park 528 Hallowell Road Pownal, ME 04069
OPERATED BY:	Maine Department of Conservation, Bureau of Parks and Lands
INFORMATION:	Bradbury Mountain State Park, (207) 688-4712
OPEN:	Year-round
SITES:	35 sites
EACH SITE HAS:	Fire ring, picnic table
ASSIGNMENT:	First come, first served or by reservation: (800) 332-1501, (207) 287-3824, www.campwithme.com (additional $2 reservation fee per site, per night)
REGISTRATION:	At ranger station as you enter the campground; check in after 1 p.m., check out by 11 a.m.
FACILITIES:	Pit toilets, water spigots, recycling station, playground, ball field
PARKING:	At sites
FEE:	Maine residents, $11; nonresidents, $14
RESTRICTIONS:	*Pets:* On leash only *Fires:* In fire rings *Alcohol:* Prohibited *Vehicles:* Parking at sites only *Other:* No visitors after sunset; quiet hours 10 p.m.– 7 a.m.; 14-day maximum stay

MAP

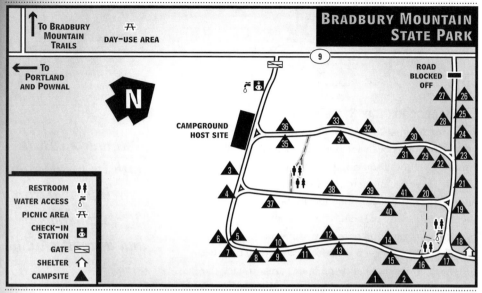

BRADBURY MOUNTAIN STATE PARK

To BRADBURY
MOUNTAIN
TRAILS

DAY-USE AREA

To
PORTLAND
AND POWNAL

9

ROAD
BLOCKED
OFF

N

CAMPGROUND
HOST SITE

RESTROOM	👫
WATER ACCESS	🚰
PICNIC AREA	🍴
CHECK-IN STATION	🏠
GATE	⊠
SHELTER	⬆
CAMPSITE	▲

GETTING THERE

Follow Route 9 North through Pownal. Continue heading north, following signs to the campground. You'll pass the other side of Bradbury Mountain State Park before you come to the campground on the right, if you're heading north.

COBSCOOK BAY STATE PARK

COBSCOOK BAY STATE PARK comes the closest of any park in this book to providing the remote, oceanside, wilderness feeling of island camping without requiring you to actually travel to an island. There are numerous waterfront sites here, and all are spectacular and dramatically beautiful. Since there are so many of them, you have an excellent chance of scoring one of these pristine sites.

When you do get a waterfront site, you'll bear witness to the extreme tidal swing in this area. In fact, the name Cobscook is from the Maliseet and Pasamaquoddy Indian dialect for "boiling tides." The change in tidal depth runs from 24 to 28 feet! Be extremely careful if you venture out onto the mudflats at low tide to dig up some clams (which is perfectly legal, by the way, up to a peck a day). When the tide turns, it comes racing in.

There are several tent-only areas within Cobscook Bay State Park. As you may well imagine, these are the spots you want. Cobscook Point, Broad Cove, and the Harbor Point areas are reserved for our tent-bound brethren. The other areas here are fine, but the tent-only areas are superb.

Cobscook Point includes sites 40 through 74, all carved out of the dense forest of balsam and birch overlooking the waters of Cobscook Bay. These are extremely remote, quiet, and scenic campsites, especially the waterfront sites like 40, 41, 44, and 49. Site 43 is set up on a small hill with a dramatic view of the bay through the trees, and beautiful breezes blow through the site.

There's a short hike into site 48, giving it an amazing sense of seclusion, but not much of a view of the bay. That's not a bad tradeoff—depends on what you're in the mood for. Sites 50 and 52 are also set deep within a dense forest of mostly spruce trees, for a cool, sylvan feeling.

> *A unique treasure, with its picturesque shoreline, waterfront sites, numerous inlets, and dramatic tidal surge*

RATINGS

Beauty: ✪ ✪ ✪ ✪ ✪
Privacy: ✪ ✪ ✪ ✪ ✪
Spaciousness: ✪ ✪ ✪ ✪
Quiet: ✪ ✪ ✪ ✪ ✪
Security: ✪ ✪ ✪ ✪
Cleanliness: ✪ ✪ ✪ ✪ ✪

ADDRESS:	Cobscook Bay State Park RR 1, Box 127 Dennysville, ME 04628
OPERATED BY:	Maine Department of Conservation Bureau of Parks and Lands
INFORMATION:	Cobscook Bay State Park (207) 726-4412
OPEN:	May 15–October 15
SITES:	106 sites
EACH SITE HAS:	Fire ring, picnic table
ASSIGNMENT:	First come, first served or by reservation: (800) 332-1501, (207) 287-3824, www.campwithme .com (additional $2 reservation fee per site, per night)
REGISTRATION:	At ranger station as you enter park
FACILITIES:	Flush toilets, water spigots, pay showers, picnic area, public boat launch
PARKING:	At sites
FEE:	Maine residents, $14; nonresidents, $19
RESTRICTIONS:	*Pets:* On leash only *Fires:* In established fireplaces only *Alcohol:* Prohibited *Vehicles:* Parking at sites only *Other:* Quiet hours 10 p.m.–7 a.m.; 14-day maximum stay; check in after 1 p.m., check out by 11 a.m.; limit of 1 peck of clams per day

At the end of Cobscook Point is a short peninsula with sites 56 through 62 (which actually includes only sites 56, 57, 59, and 62, since a couple of sites must have been taken out of use to allow for regrowth). These are incredibly secluded. This area is reminiscent of the revered (at least by me) Peninsula A at the Mount Desert Campground. There's about a 50-yard hike into site 56, the first site you'll come to. It is a very large site surrounded by dense woods, so this would be perfect for a larger group or family.

The rest of the sites on the end of Cobscook Point—57, 59, and 62—are all set down at the water's edge. They are moderately spacious and extraordinarily secluded from each other. All these sites share a common parking area as you head out onto the peninsula.

Back on the campground loop road, sites 63, 64, and 65 are all set along the water's edge, and are far enough from each other to offer some seclusion. Sites 66 and 67 are spectacularly secluded hike-in sites set on the water's edge about 50 feet from the road. Site 72 is set up on a hill off the inside of the road, so there's a nice sense of seclusion, but you miss the commanding view of the bay afforded by some of the other sites.

Farther along the main campground road heading toward Harbor Point and Whiting Bay, you'll find sites 33, 34, and 35, which are open to the road but next to a small pond that is quite scenic. These sites are also close to the day-use access for the clam flats. You won't find fresher seafood than clams that were deep in the briny mud just a couple of hours ago.

The cozy Harbor Point area is home to sites 29 through 32. Site 29 is at the end of a long, grassy driveway. It is a fairly open site with sweeping views of the bay. Site 30 is on a bluff overlooking the bay. Sites 31 and 32 are nicely private and set along the shore of the bay. All the Harbor Point sites are quite secluded from each other, so there really isn't a bad one here. Site 30 is the best, as it is extraordinarily isolated and affords a priceless view of Cobscook Bay.

The Broad Cove area is another of Cobscook Bay State Park's tent-only areas with a plethora of beautiful hike-in and waterside sites. Sites 75, 77, 78, and 79 are hike-in sites that are spectacularly secluded and give you that feeling of being deep in the woods. Sites 83 and 84 are also nicely isolated hike-in sites that share a parking area. If you can't score a waterfront site, do what you can to land in one of these.

Sites 85 and 86 share a parking area as well, but these hike-in sites are set down on the water from site 89, so they are incredibly private and scenic. It's a short walk down toward the water, but the site itself is not as close to the water as sites 85, 86, and 88. Sites 90, 92, 95, and 96 are also spectacular waterside sites with short walks in to them.

Then we come to Site 101. This is one of those to-die-for campsites. It is a hike-in site, but the hike in is about 200 feet. This makes it a bit more challenging to haul in your gear, but the sense of solitude is worth it. You'll hike up and down the rolling terrain and over a short bridge to reach this profoundly secluded site. It's set within some fairly dense forest, but it's on a bluff overlooking the bay, so you'll get slivers of bay view and fantastic sea breezes.

Heading toward the day-use area, most of the sites include covered picnic tables, which would be nice on a rainy day. Sites 102 and 103 are set off on their own and also have covered picnic tables. Site 111 is another nice hike-in site in this area. Sites 114 and 115 are set off on their own. They are fairly close together but very secluded from the other sites. Site 116 stands alone, offering a deep sense of privacy. Site 119 sits at an inter-section of the campground road and is open to the road, but there are no other sites around; it also overlooks a wildflower meadow that separates the camping area from the day-use area, so it's quite scenic. Sites 124 and 125 are very secluded, with water views.

The Whiting Bay area, home to sites 1 through 27, is designated as the RV zone, but there are still some nice sites with good tent-camping potential. These sites are fairly large and private, so don't panic if you pick one and hear an RV lumbering toward you.

After you pass site 27, you'll come to the loops for sites 1 through 8, and 9 through 26. Site 2 is a medium-size site on an open, grassy spot with an amazing view of the bay through loosely spaced spruce trees. Site 3 is very large and perched on a bluff overlook-ing the bay for gorgeous views and sea breezes.

Most of the sites on the outer edge of the loop have D-shaped driveways to facilitate egress for the land yachts. That also makes them very spacious for tent campers. Site 4 has awesome views, but it's quite open to the road. Site 5 is a pleasant, open spot set down from the road. It's very open to the bay for dramatic views and breezes, but it's also close to the restrooms. Sites 6 through 8 are set in their own little loop. They are slightly open but have fantastic bay views.

There are some other sites here worth exploring. Site 17 is small and open to the road, but it's right next to a trail that leads down to the shore. Site 18 is very spacious and offers a decent sense of privacy because it's secluded from the road and from neighboring sites. Site 22 is large and has that D-shaped driveway, so it's secluded from the road by an "island" of trees and shrubs that form the center of the D.

There's only one thing that bothered me about the Cobscook Bay State Park experi-ence: I can't for the life of me figure out how many clams constitute a peck.

MAP

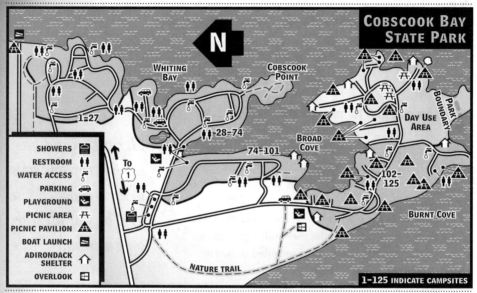

GETTING THERE

Follow US 1 north for what seems like an eternity. Cobscook Bay State Park is on the right in the town of Dennysville.

Bath

near Portland

YOU CAN ADD **HERMIT ISLAND** to your list of favorites right away, even if you've never been here. There are some spectacular oceanfront sites. On its campground-site map, Hermit Island marks sites as Ocean Prime, Prime, Choice, and Value. Generally speaking, you'll be in pretty good shape following those guidelines. They're an honest and accurate assessment of the "wow" factor of the sites, although even the Value sites are nicely wooded and secluded sites. The Ocean Prime sites are absolutely breathtaking. Do yourself a favor and reserve one well in advance.

This is a fairly large campground, with 275 sites. The sites are numbered according to the road upon which they're located, sort of like Wompatuck State Park in Massachusetts. When you're selecting a site or making a reservation, be sure to specify both the road and the site number.

The Joe's Head Way sites are among the top Ocean Prime site. Sites 3 and 4 are a bit open, but they're set against windswept dunes and beach undergrowth. Sites 1 and 2 are nicely secluded right on the beach. Try, try, try to get one of these sites. Once you do, you'll be glad you did, and you'll never want to leave. The sites have a sandy surface and are surrounded by dense beach undergrowth. They're open to the beach as well, so you'll fall asleep to the sound of the crashing surf.

Joe's Head site 10 is nicely secluded right on the beach. You couldn't ask for a more perfect beachfront site. Sites 11 and 12 are higher on a bluff. Joe's Head sites 8 and 9 are set back from the beach and bluff. They're very spacious, yet a bit open to each other. They'd make a great pair of sites for a larger group.

The Ocean Sweep sites are also incredible. As the name implies, these sites are set up on a bluff with amazing views of the ocean, and cool ocean breezes.

> *Hermit Island has it all–beachfront sites, densely wooded sites, and best of all, they're on an island.*

RATINGS

Beauty: ☆ ☆ ☆ ☆ ☆
Privacy: ☆ ☆ ☆ ☆
Spaciousness: ☆ ☆ ☆ ☆
Quiet: ☆ ☆ ☆ ☆
Security: ☆ ☆ ☆ ☆
Cleanliness: ☆ ☆ ☆ ☆

ADDRESS: Hermit Island
42 Front Street
Bath, ME 04530

OPERATED BY: Hermit Island
Campground

INFORMATION: Hermit Island
Campground,
(207) 443-2101

OPEN: Mid-May–
mid-October (full
operation from late
June–Labor Day,
limited facilities
and reduced rates in
off-season)

SITES: 275 sites

EACH SITE HAS: loose rock fireplace,
picnic table

ASSIGNMENT: At check-in at
campground
headquarters

REGISTRATION: By reservation
(make reservations
by mail beginning in
January and by mail
or phone beginning
in February) or first
come, first served
(after Labor Day)

FACILITIES: Flush toilets,
showers, composting
toilets, boat launch

PARKING: At campsites

FEE: $34–$56 per night,
depending on nature
of site

RESTRICTIONS: *Pets:* Not allowed
Fires: In fireplaces
Alcohol: At campsites
Vehicles: 1 car per
campsite (no
visitors)
Other: 2 adults and 2
children or 4 adults
and no children per
site, check in after
2 p.m., check out by
10 a.m.

Site 7 is set back from the edge of the bluff and is more shaded. Sites 5 and 6 are phenomenal, and open up to dramatic ocean views.

Dune Way is home to some Prime sites just off the water. They're still very close to the beach, though. The sites are all quite spacious and nicely secluded from each other, carved out of dense beach undergrowth.

The West Dune Way sites are a bit more open. Set on a sandy surface, site 57 is huge and secluded. Site 59 is a bit more secluded still, while site 58 is fairly open. Site 60 is huge and fairly private. Sites 61, 62, and 63 are set up higher on the bluff for beautiful views and ocean breezes. Site 64 is fabulously secluded, with a dramatic view of the ocean.

West Dune Way sites 66, 66W, and 66N are all set well off the road. These are some top-notch sites—some of the best at Hermit Island, and that's saying something! Site 66W has to be one of the best in terms of seclusion, view, and proximity to the beach. West Dune Way site 69 is also nicely secluded, set in a fairly dense forest. Site 70 is also wonderfully secluded. It's a long, narrow site for a deeper sense of privacy.

On Bayberry, a short crossroad heading off Island Road, sites 14 and 19 are nicely secluded, set in the dense undergrowth. Site 14 is a bit open to site 22, which is also set on a sandy surface—it's truly like camping on the beach. Overall, the closer to the water you are here at Hermit Island, the better off you'll be.

Sites 20 and 21 on Bayberry are both secluded sites tucked down off the road. Site 23 is set a bit farther back. Sites 24 and 25 are also up on a bluff overlooking the water. Site 27 here has sweeping ocean views. The sites here are set on a bluff overlooking the water. Site 32 is fairly secluded; it's near sites 30 and 31, which would also make a nice pair of sites.

Heading back down Island Road, you'll find site 49, which is quite spacious and secluded, with good water views. Sites 50 through 52 are nice on-the-water sites. Sites 51 and 52 are a good pair of sites for a larger group. Site 50 is a spectacular site, very scenic and situated on the water. You can set up your tent beneath a canopy of hemlock.

MAP

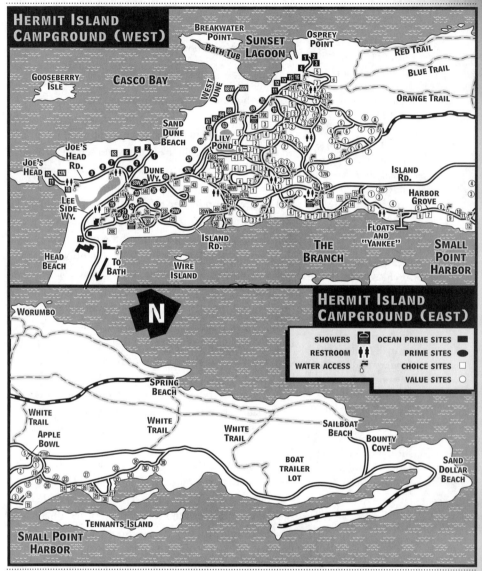

HERMIT ISLAND CAMPGROUND (WEST)

BREAKWATER POINT · SUNSET LAGOON · OSPREY POINT · BATH TUB · RED TRAIL · BLUE TRAIL

GOOSEBERRY ISLE · CASCO BAY · WEST DUNE · ORANGE TRAIL

SAND DUNE BEACH · LILY POND · ISLAND RD.

JOE'S HEAD RD. · JOE'S HEAD · DUNE WY. · HARBOR GROVE

LEE SIDE WY. · FLOATS AND "YANKEE" · SMALL POINT HARBOR

HEAD BEACH · To BATH · WIRE ISLAND · ISLAND RD. · THE BRANCH

HERMIT ISLAND CAMPGROUND (EAST)

N

SHOWERS	OCEAN PRIME SITES ■
RESTROOM	PRIME SITES ●
WATER ACCESS	CHOICE SITES □
	VALUE SITES ○

WORUMBO

SPRING BEACH

WHITE TRAIL · APPLE BOWL · WHITE TRAIL · WHITE TRAIL · SAILBOAT BEACH · BOUNTY COVE · SAND DOLLAR BEACH

BOAT TRAILER LOT

TENNANTS ISLAND

SMALL POINT HARBOR

On Western Reach, sites 11 and higher are somewhat smaller, but they are well secluded and set up on a bluff for sweeping views of the bay and ocean breezes. Sites 12 and 13 have panoramic views of water. Sites 15 and 16 are a bit more open to each other, but still incredibly scenic.

The twisty road called Cross Island is home to more Choice sites and also the trailheads for the Blue, Orange, and Red trails. Site 7 is set in an airy grove of birch and nicely secluded. Site 6 is very secluded. It's also situated within a birch groove but has a dense forest behind it. Site 5 is also fairly well secluded, set at a bend in the road. Cross Island sites 1 through 4 are all set up on a bluff for commanding views and steady ocean breezes—these are also among the finest of Hermit Island's sites.

Back down to the island interior, the Iris Downs sites are wide open to each other. These would make good spots for a huge group or family reunion. Ironically, site 55, which is just next to this area, is nicely secluded by dense undergrowth. On Dune Way heading back to Island Road, sites 45 and 46 are nicely set off in the dense forest and are very well shaded.

Over on East Tack, site 1 is huge and private. It's set right on the water, facing The Branch. It's a bit less breezy and a bit more wooded than the oceanfront sites but beautifully scenic nonetheless. Site 2 is a bit more open but still has a nice sense of privacy. The rest of the East Tack sites are fairly open, but they're also right on the water.

Harbor Grove Road hosts several smaller sites right on the water. They're also tucked into a dense forest of pine and maple. Site 2 is a smallish site, but it's set on the water overlooking The Branch. Sites 4 and 5 are off the water but are still nice sites. Site 6 is set on the water within a loose grove of maple and pine.

On the water and a bit farther down from the road, site 7 is a more secluded site. Site 8 is a large site and also offers a decent sense of seclusion. Site 9 is a private water site that tumbles down to the water's edge. Sites 12, 13, and 15 are fairly open but sin a dramatic waterfront setting.

The Branch water sites are fairly open to each other, but they're right on the water, so that's hard to beat. The inland sites have nice water views with a similar sense of openness. Sites 7 through 9 are under a dense, forest canopy, so they feel a bit more secluded. Site 6 is a bit larger, with sweeping water views. Site 5 on the Branch road is a beautiful site. It's open to the sky and the water. The forest is a bit more dense over Site 4, so that's a nice shady site. Site 3 is on the water side, but set up off the water a bit.

Hermit Island has it all—beachfront sites set on the sand amid hardy, dense beach shrubs; sites overlooking the bay high on a bluff; densely wooded sites encircled by forest—and best of all, they're all on an island. Check this place out and it's sure to become one of your favorites.

GETTING THERE

Follow US Route 1 to Bath. Then follow ME Routes 209 and 216 out to Hermit Island.

06
LAMOINE
STATE PARK

Ellsworth

N. of Bar Harbor

WHAT DO YOU DO WHEN Acadia National Park is packed? Head a bit farther north to Lamoine State Park, which is just far enough away to allow you to escape the swarms of Acadia-area campers and travelers during the summer. There's a very open sense to most of the sites at Lamoine State Park which overlooks the waters of Frenchman Bay toward Bar Harbor.

The view of the ocean and the nearly constant cool breezes, even on the muggiest summer afternoons, give Lamoine State Park an easy combination of pastoral serenity and seaside appeal. The whole gestalt here is that of being on a windswept, coastal bluff—which you are! It's a bit different than the wooded campgrounds to which I usually gravitate, but wild and beautiful nevertheless.

The campground loop road encircles the campground and is intersected by several short roads that run parallel to the seashore. The sites on the outer edge of the loop as you enter the campground, including sites 3, 4, 6, 8, and 9 through 12, are spacious, open sites set on a grassy surface and separated by short stands of trees and shrubs. There's a sunny, breezy, open sense to these sites, but not much privacy.

On the other side of the campground road, the sites are a bit more secluded but still have an open feel. The only trouble here would be if an RV settled in nearby—you would have it right in view. Otherwise, the sites themselves are exposed but comfortable.

Sites 10 through 13 are open, but they are also secluded from each other by short stands of deciduous trees and solid undergrowth. The backs of these sites open to a huge field and the group camping area—a great spot for stargazing on a clear night.

Moving down this side of the campground, there's more of a sense of solitude to sites 13 and 14. These

> *During the thick of summer, when Acadia is mobbed, head north to Lamoine State Park to reclaim the solitude for which Maine is renowned.*

RATINGS

Beauty: ✰ ✰ ✰ ✰
Privacy: ✰ ✰ ✰
Spaciousness: ✰ ✰ ✰
Quiet: ✰ ✰ ✰ ✰
Security: ✰ ✰ ✰ ✰
Cleanliness: ✰ ✰ ✰ ✰

ADDRESS:	Lamoine State Park 23 State Park Road Ellsworth, ME 04605
OPERATED BY:	Maine Department of Conservation, Bureau of Parks and Lands
INFORMATION:	Lamoine State Park, (207) 667-4778
OPEN:	Mid-May–October 15
SITES:	61
EACH SITE HAS:	Fire ring, picnic table
ASSIGNMENT:	First come, first served; by reservation: (800) 332-1501, (207) 287-3824, www.campwithme.com (additional $2 reservation fee per site, per night)
REGISTRATION:	At ranger station as you enter campground
FACILITIES:	Hot showers, flush toilets, water spigots
PARKING:	At sites
FEE:	Maine residents, $15; nonresidents, $20
RESTRICTIONS:	*Pets:* On leash only *Fires:* In fire rings only *Alcohol:* Prohibited *Vehicles:* Parking at sites only *Other:* Quiet hours 10 p.m.–7 a.m.; 14-day maximum stay; check in after 1 p.m., check out by 11 a.m.

sites are set along the outer edge of the campground loop road. Site 14 is encircled by dense, deciduous forest. Situated within a loose grove of spruce and backed into the mixed forest, site 15 open with a delightful wooded-grove feel. It's situated right at a campground-road intersection, but it has a comfortable, charming character.

Heading back toward the campground entrance on one of the intersecting roads brings you to the sites numbered in the high teens and low 20s, which have an exposed feel but are secluded on the sides. Sites 22 through 24 are right at the corner intersection of the campground road.

There are a number of wide-open field sites in the center of the campground at Lamoine State Park, including most of the sites in the 30s. These sites don't provide much privacy, although some are somewhat isolated on the sides. They're also fairly close to (and within view of) the shower building.

Sites 16 and 17 are tiny but cozy and very secluded. This site is carved out of very dense forest of short deciduous trees and dense undergrowth.

Site 41 is wide open to the road but secluded from its neighbors. You're getting closer to the water here, so there are tantalizing views of the bay through the trees. Site 44 is way too exposed and right behind the restroom building. Site 43 opens to site 42 and the restrooms, but it's secluded on the sides and offers views of the bay to balance the view of the restroom.

You're getting closer to the water at sites 55 through 62. These are open to the road and each other, but they're very sunny and breezy. You'll feel what is practically a constant breeze easing in (and sometimes rushing in) off Frenchman Bay.

The sites that open to the water are where you really want to be at Lamoine State Park. Sites 56 through 62 are set along the campground road facing the open view of the ocean. These are views of Frenchman Bay and its islands worthy of the Rockefellers. The view from sites 57 through 60 is through loose crabapple and maple trees growing in the picnic area. From 61 and 62, you view the bay through a majestic stand of spruce. There's also a short path down to the

MAP

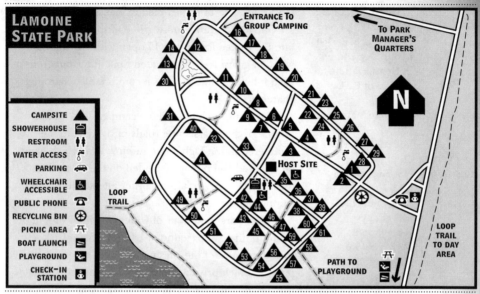

LAMOINE STATE PARK

ENTRANCE TO GROUP CAMPING

To Park Manager's Quarters

N

CAMPSITE ▲
SHOWERHOUSE
RESTROOM
WATER ACCESS
PARKING
WHEELCHAIR ACCESSIBLE
PUBLIC PHONE
RECYCLING BIN
PICNIC AREA
BOAT LAUNCH
PLAYGROUND
CHECK-IN STATION

LOOP TRAIL

HOST SITE

LOOP TRAIL TO DAY AREA

PATH TO PLAYGROUND

water right next to site 62. You can also get to the 1-mile Loop Trail.

All these sites are spacious and open to the road, but they're also open to the view, and they're fairly well secluded from each other. Sites 58 and 59 probably feel the most isolated and farthest from their neighbors. Each is surrounded on three sides by dense undergrowth and shrubs. They open to the bay view through a grove of loosely spaced spruce and pine, trees of hardy stock that stand up to the steady salty breezes.

The scent here is that potent Maine blend of the evergreen forest and the salty tang of the ocean, topped with a bit of wood smoke as the day draws to an end. Take a moment after you've set up your campsite to sit back, draw in a deep breath, and enjoy the sights, sounds, and scents of this oceanside campground.

GETTING THERE

Follow US 1 north through Ellsworth. At the junction of US 1 and ME 184, follow ME 184 south to the park.

> *Lily Bay State Park is just one facet of the north Maine woods jewel that is Moosehead Lake.*

I N NORTHERN MAINE, nestled on the eastern shores of Moosehead Lake, is Lily Bay State Park. There are two separate camping areas at Lily Bay and a large number of sites. On the first business day in January, when the reservation office opens for the season, the world-class lakeside sites start filling up—so make plans early if you want to secure one.

There are several secluded sites in the Dunn Point Area. Drive up a short road to the right, and you'll find Site 245 tucked off on its own. Just past the entrance to the site at the end of its "driveway" is a trailhead for the 1.6-mile hiking trail that leads to Rowell Cove.

The sense of solitude at sites 200 and 201 is priceless. These are moderately spacious and very isolated walk-in tent sites. Each requires a short (20- to 30-foot) hike to the site. They are set on a bluff overlooking the lake, and the views are positively epic.

Farther along this same bluff, site 202 is less exposed to the views and the breeze but still offers sliver views of the lake vista and the hills beyond, through the woods. Site 203 is the last site in this cluster on the bluff. It's very spacious, and the breezes and views filter through a wall of conifers.

There's a trail leading to the lake's beach right before you get to sites 205 and 206. Site 205 is massive. Across the campground road, Site 206 is much smaller but very well secluded in dense forest. Sites 207 through 209 are moderately roomy and private.

At site 210, the forest opens up again to the lake. This site is isolated on one side by a two-level wall of young and old white pines, along with some other coniferous trees. The forest opens dramatically at the opposite side of the site, allowing for sweeping views of the lake through the loosely spaced trees that pepper the site down to the water's edge.

Set within a loose grove of conifers, sites 211 and

RATINGS

Beauty: ✩ ✩ ✩ ✩ ✩
Privacy: ✩ ✩ ✩ ✩ ✩
Spaciousness: ✩ ✩ ✩ ✩
Quiet: ✩ ✩ ✩ ✩ ✩
Security: ✩ ✩ ✩ ✩ ✩
Cleanliness: ✩ ✩ ✩ ✩ ✩

213 are relatively spacious and overlook the lake. Sites 213 through 215 require a short walk and are all on the lake. These sites are jewels, with a perfect mix of forest and lakeshore. It's well worth the short haul. Not that you'll be able to take your eyes off the lake for long, but these sites are also fairly isolated from each other. It's very quiet throughout the campground. All you'll hear is the soft splash of the lake and the cool rush of wind through the trees.

You might want to avoid sites 216 and 220, as they are a bit close to the restroom. Site 219 is spacious and secluded by a wall of conifers at the back but is otherwise open to the road. Site 218 is large and mildly secluded, with a view of the lake.

The next group of walk-in tent sites includes sites 221 through 224. These are completely secluded from the rest of the campground and moderately secluded from each other. They share the same clear view of the lake as the 213 through 215 group.

So, by now, you must think you have to be right on the waters of Moosehead Lake to have one of Lily Bay's primo sites, eh? Well, wait until you see site 231. It is incredibly spacious, set up on a small knoll in the middle of the forest and is absolutely secluded from neighbors on all sides and from the campground road. Its added elevation will help you catch some of the onshore breezes. Just outside the site, there's a trail leading down to the beach.

The forest encircling the site is characteristic of the area's fantastically diverse population of mature spruce, birch, and maple. There's also a small nursery of baby white pine trees to the left of the site as you walk in. Encircled by forest, this spot feels like it's deeper in the Maine wilderness than you might expect.

A shared entryway brings you to sites 235 and 236. This would make a good pair of sites for a larger group or family needing two sites—if you can't score two magical lakeside sites. Another option for families is site 240, which has a U-shaped driveway you could pull right through. Those two openings do leave it fairly exposed to the road, though.

The Rowell Cove Area also has some dramatic

KEY INFORMATION

ADDRESS:	Lily Bay State Park HC 76, Box 425 Greenville, ME 04441
OPERATED BY:	Maine Department of Conservation Bureau of Parks and Lands
INFORMATION:	Lily Bay State Park (207) 695-2700 (207) 941-4014
OPEN:	May 15–October 15
SITES:	91
EACH SITE HAS:	Stone hearth or fire ring, picnic table
ASSIGNMENT:	First come, first served; by reservation: (800) 332-1501, (207) 287-3824, www.campwithme.com (additional $2 reservation fee per site, per night)
REGISTRATION:	At ranger station as you enter campground
FACILITIES:	Pit toilets, water spigots, boat launch, swim area, playground
PARKING:	At sites
FEE:	Maine residents, $14; nonresidents, $19
RESTRICTIONS:	*Pets:* On leash only *Fires:* In fire rings only *Alcohol:* Prohibited *Vehicles:* Parking at sites only *Other:* Quiet hours 10 p.m.–7 a.m.; 14-day maximum stay; check in after 1 p.m., check out by 11 a.m.

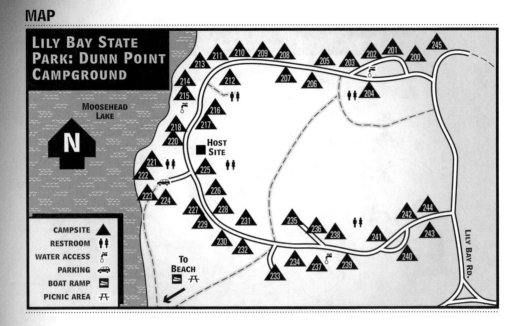

LILY BAY STATE PARK: DUNN POINT CAMPGROUND

MOOSEHEAD LAKE

N

HOST SITE

To BEACH

LILY BAY RD.

CAMPSITE
RESTROOM
WATER ACCESS
PARKING
BOAT RAMP
PICNIC AREA

lakeside walk-in tent sites. Sites 33 through 38 are hike-in tent sites perched along a craggy peninsula that recalls the revered Peninsula A at the eponymous campground on Mount Desert Island. Site 33 is the largest of the group.

There are ample views of the lake through loose trees from sites 20 and 21. They are also nicely secluded by dense spruce just open enough to view the lake. Site 23 is sizable, but a bit open. Sites 25 and 28 each have a nice sense of solitude, plus a slice of the lake view through the forest.

Several massive conifers frame one side of site 26. The inside loop sites in this part of the campground are fairly well secluded from each other, while sites 29 and 30 are both open to the campground loop road. They're also located near the parking for sites 39 through 41.

The cluster of sites that includes 39 through 46 is another majestic spot. These sites are all spacious, set right on the lake within a small cove and beneath a loosely spaced grove of spruce trees. The floor is a soft bed of pine needles over a firm, sandy surface. The sites are open to the lake, with exceptional breezes and views. Walks to the sites range from 50 to 70 feet.

Site 31 opens right to the parking area and feels too open. Site 32 is huge and very secluded. It's surrounded by a thick wall of forest and further isolated because it's a bit farther down the campground road.

The lower-numbered sites here aren't quite as impressive, but they aren't bad. Even though it's set right where the campground loop road rejoins itself, site 8 is spacious and isolated. Site 7 is similar, with glimpses of the lake. Site 5 feels very exposed,

MAP

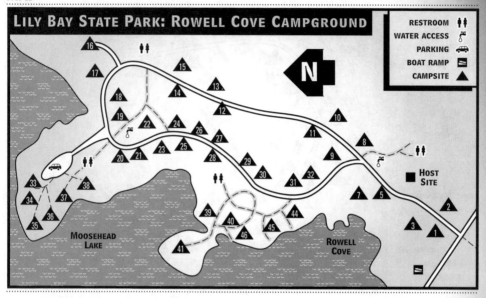

LILY BAY STATE PARK: ROWELL COVE CAMPGROUND

RESTROOM
WATER ACCESS
PARKING
BOAT RAMP
CAMPSITE

N

HOST SITE

MOOSEHEAD LAKE

ROWELL COVE

being open to the road, but it has a fabulous view of the lake.

It may be tiny and exposed to the road, but site 12 is set way off from any neighboring sites. Site 13 has a similar character. It's carved out of fairly dense forest. Site 14 is spacious, secluded, punctuated by three massive spruce trees, and encircled by dense, mixed forest.

There are glimpses and slivers of lake view through the forest here near the sites in the upper teens. Site 15 is open to the road and close to the restrooms. Site 16 is colossal and tucked well off the campground loop road for a deep sense of solitude. Site 17 is large and set off from its neighbors, but it's a bit open to the road. It's also very open to the sky, and the lake is visible from the site.

GETTING THERE

Follow ME 6 north to Greenville. From Greenville, take the Lily Bay Road off to the right and follow it to the park.

N. of Auburn (½ way to Que border)

There's a dense, diverse forest covering the campground at Mount Blue State Park, whose lush quality recalls a rain forest.

MOUNT **B**LUE **S**TATE **P**ARK is actually a pair of parks. There are two sections to the park, one up on Mount Blue itself and the other down alongside Webb Lake. The trails on and around Mount Blue, Tumbledown, Little Jackson, Blueberry, and Bald mountains are suitable for hikers of all abilities. There's also a multiuse trail in the Center Hill section of the park for mountain bikers, hikers, equestrians, and ATVs.

The park's campground is located in the Webb Lake section. All of the 136 sites in the campground are within a fairly short walk of the lake. The sites are set within a dense, diverse forest with thick undergrowth. The woods are a mix of young and old deciduous and coniferous trees, with lots of spruce, birch, and maple.

While the forest varies dramatically, the sites here have a relatively standard shape and layout, though they differ in size. Surprisingly, it's not the quietest place in the world. As I set up camp at Mount Blue, the density of the forest lent me a pleasant sense of seclusion, but I found that sound traveled through the forest quite freely. After dinner, when night settles in, the campground quiets right down, but during the daytime, you'll hear noise from surrounding campsites.

As you enter the camping area, sites 1 through 10 are spread out along the main campground road. The remaining sites are grouped in two loops. The first ten sites are quite spacious but very open to the road. A fair amount of traffic drives by—as everyone going in and out of the campground has to pass these sites. Within this cluster of sites, Site 1 is actually the most secluded, thanks to the forest at the site's edge. It's still quite close to the road, however. Sites 4 and 5 have a pretty solid barrier of trees buffering them from the road, but sites 7 and 8 are exposed.

The forest enshrouding the loop with sites 11

RATINGS

Beauty: ✿ ✿ ✿ ✿
Privacy: ✿ ✿ ✿ ✿
Spaciousness: ✿ ✿ ✿ ✿
Quiet: ✿ ✿ ✿
Security: ✿ ✿ ✿ ✿
Cleanliness: ✿ ✿ ✿ ✿

through 78 is populated primarily by moderately tall spruce and deciduous trees. The trees aren't huge, but they are numerous and crowded with undergrowth. There is an almost primeval feel to the forest that translates into a wonderful sense of seclusion at most of these sites. The sites are very clean and well kept. Some have a bit more forest buffering them from their neighbors, especially sites 5, 7, and 18. Site 19 and the sites in the lower 20s are more tightly packed than those in the rest of this loop, but encircled by thick woods.

There's a trail leading down to the lake between sites 26 and 28. Set a good distance from site 30 at a bend in the road, site 31 is tucked into a dense stand of trees, so it offers an additional measure of privacy.

Site 34 is small, but it feels isolated within a bucolic grove where spruce tower above a thick blanket of ferns. Surrounded by dense deciduous forest with plenty of room between it and the next site, site 35 maintains a marvelously secluded feel.

Sites 38, 40, and 41 are set within a mature forest of tall maples and birch. The loose arrangement of trees in this part of the campground lets more sunlight filter down. Site 44 is colossal. You could land a space shuttle here, if that's how you happened to arrive at the campground.

Though they vary in size, sites 47 through 78 share a similar layout. They are also uniformly spaced. Site 54, in a loose grove of tall spruce, is large and open to the sky. A trail heads off to the beach between sites 57 and 58.

Set along the outside of the loop, sites 58 through 62 are spacious and open. Sites 69 and 71 are particularly secluded, distant from their neighbors, and carved out of a dense, deciduous forest with thick undergrowth. Site 69 is only moderate, but 71 is huge.

Within the loop containing sites 79 through 136, the forest is crowded with trees and underbrush. The sites are uniformly distributed along the inside and outside of the loop. The space between most sites is roughly equal to an average site, affording quite a sense of privacy. Sites 128 and up seem to have slightly more forest between them. There are no hookups in the park, but even if an RV should happen to dock near you, the

KEY INFORMATION

ADDRESS:	Mount Blue State Park 299 Center Hill Road Weld, ME 04285
OPERATED BY:	Maine Department of Conservation Bureau of Parks and Lands
INFORMATION:	Mount Blue State Park (207) 585-2347 (207) 585-2261
OPEN:	May–September
SITES:	136
EACH SITE HAS:	Stone hearth, picnic table
ASSIGNMENT:	First come, first served; by reservation: (800) 332-1501, (207) 287-3824, www.camp withme.com (extra $2 reservation fee per site, per night)
REGISTRATION:	At ranger station
FACILITIES:	Hot showers, flush toilets, pit toilets, water spigots, boat launch, amphitheater, sand beach, nature center, canoe rental, cross- country and snowmobile trails, ice rink
PARKING:	At sites
FEE:	Maine residents, $15; nonresidents, $20
RESTRICTIONS:	*Pets:* On leash only *Fires:* In fire rings *Alcohol:* Prohibited *Vehicles:* Parking at sites only *Other:* Quiet hours 10 p.m.–7 a.m.; 14-day maximum stay; check in 1 p.m., check out 11 a.m.

MAP

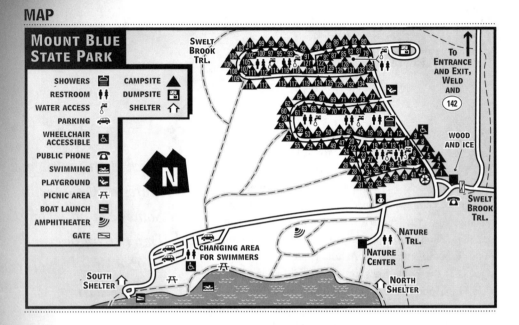

MOUNT BLUE STATE PARK

SHOWERS	🚿	CAMPSITE	▲
RESTROOM	🚹🚺	DUMPSITE	🚮
WATER ACCESS	🜄	SHELTER	⌂
PARKING	🚗		
WHEELCHAIR ACCESSIBLE	♿		
PUBLIC PHONE	☎		
SWIMMING	🏊		
PLAYGROUND	🛝		
PICNIC AREA	🜨		
BOAT LAUNCH	⛵		
AMPHITHEATER	🎵		
GATE	⌦		

SWELT BROOK TRL.

TO ENTRANCE AND EXIT, WELD AND 142

WOOD AND ICE

SWELT BROOK TRL.

NATURE TRL.

CHANGING AREA FOR SWIMMERS

NATURE CENTER

SOUTH SHELTER

NORTH SHELTER

GETTING THERE

From the town of Weld, follow ME 142 to Weld Corner. Follow the signs for the Webb Lake section of Mount Blue State Park.

thick forest in this loop will obscure your view.

A trail to the lake leaves this section between sites 109 and 110. There are trails to the centrally located restrooms spread throughout both site loops. You'll never have to walk very far to find one.

The dense forest at Mount Blue Campground leaves few sites open to the sky. There are a few exceptions to this, sites 44, 54, 93, and 106 among them. If you like to gaze at the night sky, check out one of these sites. Otherwise, once dusk settles, you'll feel enshrouded by the deep woods.

NESTLED NEAR THE APEX of Somes Sound on Mount Desert Island, Mount Desert Campground provides a tent-camping experience as close to perfect as any campground in this book offers. The entire campground is artfully carved out of the rolling woods that reach all the way down to the shoreline. The campground is also conveniently situated near the main entrance to Acadia National Park and right near the Eagle Lake and Witch Hole Pond loops.

The Mount Desert Campground doesn't have any areas set aside specifically for tent camping, but there really isn't a bad site in the place. The A-, B-, and C-area sites are the best, especially the contiguous sites on the A peninsula, A13 through A15 (which accounts for four sites since site A14+ was added). To get to these sites, you have to walk about 50 feet along the peninsula. If those sites are taken, as is often the case, another piece of prime camping real estate is site A5, located on a small bluff overlooking the water.

You're in Maine. You're on an island. Do what you can to get a water site. It's well worth the effort and expense. If you set up somewhere for a night or two, and then a water site opens up, it will be worth the effort to move. Just make sure the site is truly vacant, not reserved, and let the owners know you'd like to relocate.

The waterside sites at Mount Desert follow the undulating terrain as it dives into the headwaters of Somes Sound. The terrain is beautiful, dramatic, and anything but flat. If you saw it from a distance, you'd wonder how you could ever pitch a tent here.

When you check in at the main entrance, they'll ask you if you need some nails. Excuse me, you'll think, did I somehow volunteer for campground maintenance? Say yes; you'll need them. Every site at the water's edge or on any uneven terrain has a solid

> *Perched on the rugged shores at the apex of Somes Sound, Mount Desert Campground is nestled in an absolutely pristine setting.*

RATINGS

Beauty: ✿ ✿ ✿ ✿ ✿
Privacy: ✿ ✿ ✿ ✿
Spaciousness: ✿ ✿ ✿ ✿
Quiet: ✿ ✿ ✿ ✿ ✿
Security: ✿ ✿ ✿ ✿
Cleanliness: ✿ ✿ ✿ ✿ ✿

KEY INFORMATION

ADDRESS: Mount Desert
Campground
516 Sound Drive
Mount Desert, ME
04660

OPERATED BY: Owen and Barbara
Craighead

INFORMATION: (207) 244-3710;
www.mountdesert
campground.com

OPEN: Mid-June–Columbus
Day (weather
depending)

SITES: 148

EACH SITE HAS: Fire pit with grate;
most have wooden
tent platforms

ASSIGNMENT: Reservations
accepted for stays
of 1 week or longer,
otherwise first come,
first served

REGISTRATION: At camp
headquarters at
main entrance

FACILITIES: Restrooms, hot
showers, pay phone,
camp store,
fireplaces, picnic
tables

PARKING: At or near
individual sites

FEE: $30–$45, depending
on site

RESTRICTIONS: *Pets:* On leash only,
before July 1 and
after Labor Day
Fires: In fire pits only
Alcohol: At sites only
Vehicles: 1 per site
Other: Check in after
1 p.m., check out by
11 a.m.; maximum
2 adults per site

wooden deck on which you can set up your tent, using nails in lieu of stakes. If the campground owners had not built these tent platforms, they would be lucky to have one or two sites flat enough on which to pitch a tent.

Each area has its own facilities building with sparkling clean, well-kept restrooms and coin-operated showers. Here's another hint: Even in the summer, the mornings will be cool. Bring more quarters than you think you'll need. Having the water go stone cold over a headful of shampoo may cause itchiness, headaches, and loud cursing.

There's a charming little camp store on the road leading into the campground that sells bundles of firewood; camping-appropriate groceries like cans of soup and Jiffy Pop popcorn; all sorts of items you may have forgotten; such as batteries and toothpaste; and guidebooks to the hiking trails and carriage roads that take you to some of the island's magical spots. It's also handy to pick up a quick cup of coffee and a muffin before you get your own breakfast fire going. You can get some fresh-baked goodies for dessert later that night, or make a special trip down with the kids (of any age) for an afternoon ice cream.

Just outside the campground, there is so much to do on Mount Desert Island and in Acadia National Park that you could write an entire book about it. In fact, people have! You can hike, bike, paddle, or just find a spot to relax and enjoy the view, which alone can restore your soul. This is classic Maine wilderness, with gentle, rolling, forested mountains sloping right down to the craggy coast. The Atlantic obliges to complete the view with an endless supply of crashing surf.

Rent a canoe or kayak and launch out into Somes Sound, the only fjord on the East Coast. Between the rolling mountains, the rocky shoreline, and the water that glistens like a carpet of diamonds, the paddling is perfect. Just off the dock and boat launch at the campground, you'll paddle past a small island as you enter the sound. This is actually a part of Acadia National Park, and atop the tallest pine, in the center of the island, is a bald eagle's nest.

MAP

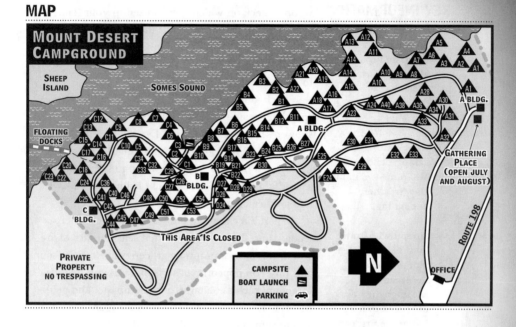

MOUNT DESERT CAMPGROUND

SHEEP ISLAND

SOMES SOUND

FLOATING DOCKS

A BLDG.

B BLDG.

C BLDG.

GATHERING PLACE (OPEN JULY AND AUGUST)

ROUTE 198

THIS AREA IS CLOSED

PRIVATE PROPERTY NO TRESPASSING

CAMPSITE
BOAT LAUNCH
PARKING

N

OFFICE

On one brilliant August afternoon while paddling out into Somes Sound, I was visited by several pods of brown Atlantic dolphins swimming up the sound. I first heard the quick puff of their breath as they surfaced. It didn't take long to determine the source of the noise once I saw the slender, dark shapes rising and disappearing into the water in front of me. One of the dolphins actually dove under my kayak and surfaced behind me. I almost tipped over trying to snap a picture of that bold little guy.

Both inside and outside Mount Desert Campground, you can do as much or as little as you like, but you couldn't ask for a more peaceful setting in which to pitch your tent. One cool foggy evening, while kicking back by the campfire, I heard someone playing the flute. The song was Paul Simon's "Lincoln Duncan." If you know that tune, you know it has a hauntingly beautiful flute melody. Hearing that echoing throughout the trees, smelling the wood fire, and watching its glowing embers through increasingly sleepy eyes is a memory I will always cherish.

GETTING THERE

From Ellsworth, follow ME 3 onto Mount Desert Island. Follow ME 3 to ME 102/198 south. Stay on ME 198 when it turns left. The campground will be on the right, about a mile after ME 198 splits from ME 102.

10
PEAKS-KENNY
STATE PARK

> *The awe-inspiring column of conifers you'll see as you drive into Peaks-Kenny State will put you in the perfect frame of mind for your camping trip.*

DRIVING INTO PEAKS-KENNY STATE PARK will remind you why we seek out natural places. The long, winding road to the park travels through a corridor of tall, statuesque pines. Following this entryway inspires a feeling of reverence. I found myself involuntarily driving much slower and gazing in awe at the magnificent forest through which this road was carved, and wishing I was already out of my car and walking through the woods.

Peaks-Kenny is an exceptionally quiet and remote campground, where all you'll hear is the wind rushing through the treetops. The forest is a dense blend of coniferous and deciduous trees, including numerous birches, lots of dense undergrowth, and large boulders. This area must have been one of the last stops for a southbound glacier a few million years ago.

The sites here have hard, sandy surfaces that hang onto those tent stakes. They're also impeccably clean. The diverse character of the dense forest and the gently rolling topography, peppered with glacial boulders, makes these woodland campsites very scenic and attractive. There are 56 sites located near the shores of Sebec Lake. Most are nicely secluded from the rest, especially on the outer side of the loops. The other sites are a curious blend of solitude and openness.

Site 1 is redolent of the drive in. The site resembles a natural cathedral or amphitheater. Its location at the start of the campground loop road is unfortunate because it is consequently exposed to the road. Two massive white pines frame the site, and a large boulder declares its rear border. Its roadside location aside, this is a spectacular site.

The site has a nice open feel and no neighbors, but it is quite open to the road as well. Site 7 feels particularly secluded. It's a huge site set in open woods. Site 9 shares a similar character. Though sites 7 and 9 are

RATINGS

Beauty: ☆ ☆ ☆ ☆ ☆
Privacy: ☆ ☆ ☆ ☆ ☆
Spaciousness: ☆ ☆ ☆ ☆
Quiet: ☆ ☆ ☆ ☆ ☆
Security: ☆ ☆ ☆ ☆
Cleanliness: ☆ ☆ ☆ ☆ ☆

somewhat close together, the dense forest mutes the sounds of your neighbors.

There's a long entryway leading into site 8, which is set farther off the campground road. The only drawback to this site is that it's close to the restroom. Site 11 is a bit too open and close to the restrooms as well. Site 10, however, is quite spacious and encircled by a brilliant green wall of deciduous forest.

Site 12 is small but secluded. It's also pitched at a bit of angle, so don't use one of those slippery sleeping pads here or you'll end up in a heap at the bottom of your tent by morning. Likewise, there may not be much space in site 14, but it's way off on its own. The surrounding forest is open, but its location gives it a great sense of solitude.

There's a boulder garden at the back of site 13 that provides solid delineation of the site and adds privacy. It's also fun to climb on, for kids of any age. Sites 15 and 16 are right across the campground road from each other, but they're set off from the sites on either side. These might be a good choice for a family requiring two sites.

Site 17 is too open to the road, plus it's fairly small. There's a trail to the lake right across from site 19, which is rather exposed and quite close to the bathroom. Site 20 is spacious but feels very open to the road. Site 21 is very well secluded but backs up against the restroom.

Site 23 is very open and up off the road. It's also quite open to the sky for stargazing. The rest of the sites in the 20s are moderately secluded but also convenient to the trail, the lake, and the bathrooms. The sites on the outside of the loop provide the greatest solitude, particularly site 29, which is on the smaller side, but it's encircled by dense forest and undergrowth.

There's a tall birch marking the entrance to site 30, and a moderately dense forest of hemlock and mixed deciduous trees surrounds the site. Located at the top of a small hill on the campground road, the site feels nicely isolated.

Massive hemlock trees frame site 33. It's good-sized but otherwise feels a bit open, and it's perched right at the intersection of the campground loop road.

KEY INFORMATION

ADDRESS:	Peaks-Kenny State Park Route 1, Box 10 Dover-Foxcroft, ME 04426
OPERATED BY:	Maine Department of Conservation, Bureau of Parks and Lands
INFORMATION:	Peaks-Kenny State Park, (207) 564-2003
OPEN:	Mid-May–October 1
SITES:	56
EACH SITE HAS:	Fire ring, picnic table
ASSIGNMENT:	First come, first served; by reservation. Call (800) 332-1501 or (207) 287-3824 for reservations or online at www.campwithme.com (additional $2 fee per night for reservations)
REGISTRATION:	At ranger station as you enter campground
FACILITIES:	Hot showers, flush toilets, water spigots, canoe rentals
PARKING:	At sites
FEE:	Residents, $15; nonresidents, $20
RESTRICTIONS:	*Pets:* On leash only *Fires:* In fire rings *Alcohol:* Not allowed *Vehicles:* At sites *Other:* Quiet hours 10 p.m.–7 a.m., 14-day maximum stay, 2-day minimum for reservations; check in after 1 p.m., check out by 11 a.m.

Sites 31 and 32 are close to the bathrooms. Site 37 is exposed to the road, but it's otherwise very well secluded, as it's on a small rise and encircled by dense coniferous forest. There's a cool, dark, sylvan atmosphere to this site.

There is a fantastic sense of seclusion to site 38, which is set back from the campground road amid a dense grove of mostly hemlocks, with a few deciduous trees mixed in. You can barely see this site from the campground road, and vice versa. Site 39 is more open, but it's set way down off the road in its own grove of conifers. Several birch trees frame site 40, which is open to both the campground and the sky.

There's a curiously arranged wall of boulders behind site 41. One of those boulders has a white pine growing right on top of it. Site 43 has a boulder ledge behind it and sits in a stately stand of hemlocks. Site 46 is way too open for me. It's set well off the road but still lacks privacy. Site 47 is kind of small but very well isolated from its neighbors within a moderately dense grove of smaller mixed deciduous and coniferous trees. Sites 48 through 51, especially 49 and 51, are too exposed to the rest of the campground.

Being set off the road gives site 52 a nice sense of privacy and seclusion. There's a long entryway leading into the site with just enough of an opening to the sky to allow shafts of sunlight to filter down to this spot. There's a trail to the lake right near the entrance to site 52 as well.

Site 53 is close to the restrooms. Site 55 is large and well secluded, encircled within a moderately dense, mostly deciduous forest. There's not much undergrowth in this part of the campground, so there's an open feel on the forest floor.

Several massive boulders block site 56 from view of the road. The site itself is set down off the road as well and is framed on one side by a stand of hemlock and beech trees that further blocks views of the road. The forest opens up toward the back of the site, giving it a combined sense of solitude and openness.

Most of the activities in which you'll participate while camping here will be on Sebec Lake—the showcase of Peaks-Kenny State Park. Bring your canoe, kayak, and fishing gear, and you won't have any reason to leave the lake or the campground. There are several hiking trails that run through the campground as well, including the Brown's Point Trail and the Birch Mt. Ledge Trail. Neither of these trails is particularly steep or challenging, so they make for a nice, relaxing hike.

MAP

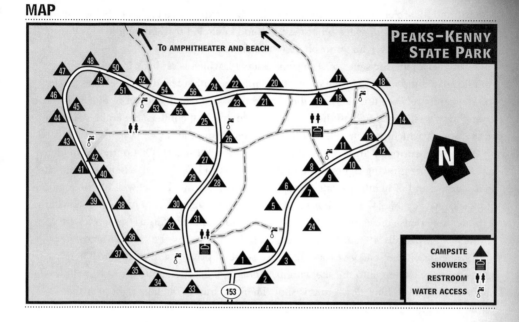

Follow Route 153 north from
Dover-Foxcroft for about
6 miles until you see signs
for the park.

11
RANGELEY LAKE STATE PARK

> *Rangeley Lake is the perfect spot if you just want to unplug for a while in the sylvan solitude of northwestern Maine.*

THE CAMPGROUND AT Rangeley Lake State Park is exceptionally quiet. You'll occasionally hear the sound of a motorboat cruising by on the lake, but other than that, it's just you, the wind through the trees, and the birds. The loons out on the lake are an essential part of the soundtrack on an evening at Rangeley Lake State Park.

There are 50 sites here spread out around a single large loop. Sites 3, 6, 10, 14, 17, 21, 27, 33, 42, and 48 are first come, first served. The rest can be reserved. The campsites here are set beneath a dense, truly mixed forest of young and old, deciduous and coniferous trees. A nice amount of forest and space between sites provides a solid sense of seclusion in almost all of them. This is a very remote campground with relatively few sites, so there is lots of privacy and silence.

There is a delightfully secluded atmosphere at site 9. It's surrounded by a dense forest of birch and spruce trees. Just past site 9, there's a footpath leading down to the beach on Rangeley Lake. Just past the footpath is a small open field with a playground area and a volleyball net. The playground is quite scenic itself, overlooking the lake through the trees.

Site 11 is also extraordinarily secluded. This moderately spacious site is carved out of a dense grove of conifers. All the sites numbered in the teens are actually very well screened from each other. Site 13 is a bit more open, but you can catch brief glimpses of the lake through the woods. Site 17 is very secluded, carved out of the coniferous forest.

A thick wall of forest encircles site 19, but privacy isn't the best aspect of this site. There's a 50-foot path leading from the site to your own little slice of the lake. This artfully composed lakeside cove has several birch trees growing out over the lake and a short rock jetty leading out from shore. (I suspect some of the other

RATINGS

Beauty: ✿ ✿ ✿ ✿
Privacy: ✿ ✿ ✿ ✿
Spaciousness: ✿ ✿ ✿ ✿
Quiet: ✿ ✿ ✿ ✿ ✿
Security: ✿ ✿ ✿ ✿
Cleanliness: ✿ ✿ ✿ ✿ ✿

sites on the lake side of the loop also have these little escape routes to the water, but I couldn't intrude on my neighbors' sites to find out.)

There is also a path leading to the lake from site 23. There's a more airy feel here because it's open to the sky and set within a loose grove of young trees. As you come to site 25, the campground road starts to head slightly uphill. Site 26 has a very open, sunny feel and is encircled by a grove of mostly young deciduous trees that form a solid green wall. Site 30 is similarly bright and green. Sites 27 and 29 are quite close to the restrooms, so I'd stay away from these.

Sites 30 and up seem to have a bit more forest between them generally. Though site 33 is small, it's tucked into dense forest and relatively distant from its neighbors—even site 34, which is across the road. Site 34 is back at an angle, and screened by a dense stand of trees. The site has a dark, cool feel.

There's a solid sense of seclusion to site 35, but it's also open to the sky, allowing sunlight to make its way to the site floor. Site 36, like site 34, is nestled in the trees. There's a large hemlock tree growing on the right of the site as you enter. Site 38 is secluded but very spacious and open to the sky.

The sites on the outside of the loop, including sites 40 and up, have plenty of forest between them for privacy. Most of these sites are also open to the sky, so stargazers take note. Site 42 has a long entryway, which adds to the considerable sense of seclusion.

Site 44 is open to the road, and thus has less privacy than most of the other sites at Rangeley Lake. Site 47 is right across from the restroom, but it's set back and up from the road in thick mixed forest. Sites 49 and 50 are spacious, but they're situated right where the campground road splits off and consequently receive more traffic noise.

Rangeley Lake is pristine. Its remote location in northwestern Maine means it receives a lot less traffic than Sebago Lake farther south in Maine or Lake Winnipesaukee in New Hampshire. The lake is perfect for whatever draws you to water: canoeing, kayaking, swimming, or fishing. If you're fond of the latter, you'll appreciate that Rangeley is renowned amongst anglers

KEY INFORMATION

ADDRESS: Rangeley Lake State Park HC 32, Box 5000 Rangeley, ME 04970-5000

OPERATED BY: Maine Department of Conservation, Bureau of Parks and Lands

INFORMATION: Rangeley Lake State Park, (207) 864-3858

OPEN: Mid-May– October 1

SITES: 50

EACH SITE HAS: Fire ring, picnic table

ASSIGNMENT: First come, first served; by reservation. Call (800) 332-1501 or (207) 287-3824 for reservations or online at www .campwithme.com (additional $2 fee per site per night for reservations)

REGISTRATION: At ranger station as you enter campground

FACILITIES: Hot showers, flush toilets, playground, boat launch

PARKING: At sites

FEE: Maine residents, $15; nonresidents, $20

RESTRICTIONS: *Pets:* On leash only
Fires: In established fire rings only
Alcohol: Not allowed
Vehicles: Parking at sites only
Other: Quiet hours 10 p.m.–7 a.m.; 14-day maximum stay; check in after 1 p.m., check out by 11 a.m.

MAP

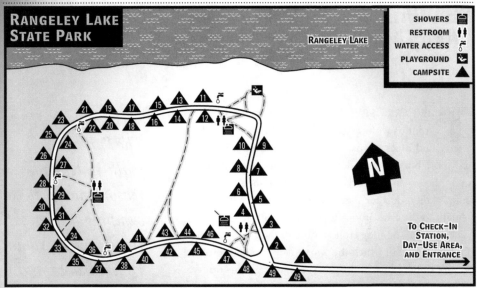

RANGELEY LAKE STATE PARK

RANGELEY LAKE

SHOWERS
RESTROOM
WATER ACCESS
PLAYGROUND
CAMPSITE

N

TO CHECK-IN STATION, DAY-USE AREA, AND ENTRANCE →

GETTING THERE

Follow Route 4 North from Farmington to Rangeley, and follow the signs to the state park.

for its population of landlocked trout and salmon.

There's plenty to do on land here as well. Hiking trails for all abilities abound. Try the nearby 3-mile trail up Bald Mountain, a 2,443-foot peak with commanding views of the lake and the surrounding forests and hills. Within the park, the Moose Country Corridor Trail is a good choice for a short hike with the little ones. As always, when in this remote, densely forested part of Maine, the birding and wildlife viewing are unparalleled. When passing any wet marshy spots in your travels, keep an eye out for moose.

THE PARK SERVICE MANAGES two campgrounds within Acadia National Park: Seawall and Blackwoods. The latter is more popular, and more often crowded, by virtue of its location right along the oceanside Park Loop Road. In fact, I've often camped there just for that reason. It is extremely convenient to the Park Loop Road's prime attractions, Sand Beach, Thunder Hole (a hole in the rocks carved out by the surf in which the waves cause a thunderous boom), Otter Cliffs, and some great hiking trails up and over the short, steep cliff known as The Beehive.

So I was pleasantly surprised, if not completely converted, the first time I pulled into Seawall Campground. There are three areas to check out at Seawall, the drive-in tent sites in areas A and B and the walk-in tent sites in area D. There are no tents allowed in area C, but that's the RV section, so why would I want to be there anyway?

The A loop is set beneath a dense coniferous forest. The character of the forest and the fact that most of the sites are set well off the road gives a complete sense of solitude. The campground road runs along two sides and rejoins itself after making a large loop right at site 1, which is a bit open but quite spacious. Site 2 is also a spacious site, and it's set farther from the road in a dense grove of mixed conifers. Site 3 is tucked into a grove of slender, young conifers and is open to the sky. Site 6 is way back from the road and offers isolation. Sites 7 and 8 share an entryway. Site 8 is completely separated from the road and site 7 is partially private. Site 10 is buffered on the sides, but it's a bit close to the road.

Dense undergrowth surrounds sites 11 and 13, giving them an air of being in deep woods. Sites 14 and 15 are airy and abut a clearing. They are open to each other, which may appeal to groups and large families,

> The "village" of walk-in tent sites is reason enough to come camping at Seawall. Its setting on Mount Desert Island and near all of Acadia National Park makes it just that much better.

RATINGS

Beauty: ✪ ✪ ✪ ✪
Privacy: ✪ ✪ ✪ ✪
Spaciousness: ✪ ✪ ✪ ✪
Quiet: ✪ ✪ ✪ ✪
Security: ✪ ✪ ✪ ✪
Cleanliness: ✪ ✪ ✪ ✪ ✪

ADDRESS: Seawall
Campground
Route 102A
Southwest Harbor,
ME 04679

OPERATED BY: National Park
Service

INFORMATION: Acadia
National Park
P.O. Box 177
Bar Harbor, ME
04609
(207) 288-3338

OPEN: Late May–
September 30

SITES: 170 tent sites (plus 5
group sites and 43
sites in the RV loop)

EACH SITE HAS: Fire ring, picnic
table

ASSIGNMENT: First come, first
served
(get there early in
the summer!)

REGISTRATION: At ranger station
as you enter the
campground

FACILITIES: Flush toilets, water
spigots

PARKING: At sites and central
area within D loop

FEE: $14–$20 (depending
on site location)

RESTRICTIONS: *Pets:* On leash only
Fires: In established
fire rings only
Alcohol: At sites only
Vehicles: Parking at
sites only, or
parking areas near
D sites
Other: Quiet hours
10 p.m.–7 a.m.;
6 people per site
maximum

but fairly secluded from the campground road. Site 16 is set far back in this clearing, farther from the road but open to the field shared by 14 and 15. A wall of foliage surrounds the field, clearly defining its borders.

Perched at a campground-road intersection as it is, site 20 feels too open to the road. Sites 19 and 22 are set within the woods and way off the road for absolute solitude. Sites 23 through 25 also have moderately long entryways. They are screened by greenery but open to the sky. There's a long entryway into site 31, which is very well secluded but a bit close to the restrooms. Site 33 also has a fairly long "driveway."

Even the sites that feel open here are thoughtfully spaced within the ample, thick forest. The ingenuity of the layout joins the beauty of the setting to complete your experience of sylvan solitude. Another positive element of this campground's design is that site 27 is intended for wheelchair access.

Site 35 is a prime example of the smart layout at Seawall, placed so as to be unseen from the road. This site is fantastically secluded and set within dense hemlocks. Sites 36 and 38, however, are a bit open to the road.

A more loosely spaced forest is predominant along the B loop, at least at the forest-floor level. There's much less undergrowth, and the forest is populated with older spruce and hemlock that are bare halfway up the trunks, so there's an airy feeling on the ground with a soothing, evergreen canopy overhead. The predominantly coniferous forest here imparts a heady perfume—a lingering spicy, tangy scent.

Site 3 is tucked into the trees off the road. Site 5 is a bit small and open, and sites 6 and 7 are very exposed to the road. Sites 8 through 11 are moderately secluded from each other. These sites are all quite spacious and set within a stately hemlock grove.

Sites 12 and 13 are very open to each other and somewhat open to the road. However, these sites are huge, so they're perfect for a group needing two contiguous sites. Sites 15 and 16 are another good pair of sites, although they're a bit smaller. The large sites 21 and 22 share an entryway and are fairly open to each other.

Site 19 enjoys solitude being well off the road. Site 26 is very spacious and fairly distant from the campground road. Note, however, that sites 23 and 24 are very open to the road and the dumpster, of all things. I don't know of anyone who would want a dump lurking just outside their campsite. Also, site 27 is oddly positioned just outside the B loop and sees passing traffic.

Generally, the spaciousness of the forest in the B loop doesn't mean a lack of privacy, though you will see your neighbors. It's more like you're nestled within the deep woods. There's a comforting openness to the forest floor, with moss and fern ground cover that lends a rain-forest feel to the woods. The dense, deep, rich greens of the trees contrast dramatically with the lighter greens of the ferns. It's also very quiet here, except for the sounds of the woodland birds and critters. The caws of seagulls remind you that you're not only in the forest, but also right near the ocean.

The D area has the walk-in tent sites. This is the stuff. This "village" of tent sites scattered throughout the forest is sublime. You park along a central loop, then walk into your site. The sites are anywhere from 20 feet to more than 100 feet from the parking area. There are signs along the parking loop that tell you which sites you're parking near.

These tent sites are all relatively uniform in size and character, and they are liberally sprinkled throughout the fairly thick forest of slender coniferous trees. The sites are all moderately spacious. You'll be able to see a few of your neighbors, but there's not an obnoxious lack of privacy so much as a quiet sense of being covered by the forest canopy. There's an airy quality to the sub-canopy here similar to that of the B loop. At night, the forest seems to close in around you and your campsite. It is very quiet here. All you'll hear are muffled conversations punctuated by the occasional snap of a campfire.

This community of tent sites is unlike anything I've seen at any other campground. The sense of solitude here is deep and complete. There's a network of walking paths just inside the woods that leads you to all the sites, and little signposts at the intersections that guide you to specific sites. It could get a bit confusing back here, so you'll definitely want to make sure you have one of the campground-site maps handy.

The whole D area is phenomenal. There are a few sites spread farther out than the others, but overall the character of the forest, the site spaciousness, and the solitude are relatively similar throughout. Anywhere within the D area is a great place to spend a few nights in a tent.

You can tell the veteran D-area campers (like the veteran campers at Grout Pond in Vermont), because they arrive with some sort of wheeled cart or wagon to haul in their gear. Whether you have wheels or not, it is well worth the extra effort to get yourself to one of these sites within the D-area tent village in the woods. You will be rewarded with refreshing of wilderness solitude.

MAP

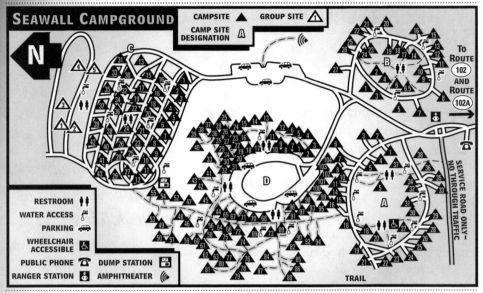

GETTING THERE

Follow Route 3 onto Mount Desert Island. Bear right onto Route 102/198 toward Southwest Harbor. Stay on Route 102. Follow Route 102 to Route 102A. Stay on Route 102A and follow the signs to the campground.

13 WARREN ISLAND STATE PARK

WHEN YOU JOURNEY TO WARREN ISLAND, you'll see the truth in the statement "half the fun is getting there." After all, Warren Island is an island! You can't drive there, you can't hike there, and you certainly can't park an RV there. You can get there by kayak or canoe, one placid paddle stroke at a time. You can also get there by motorboat or sailboat, but most of the people you'll see camped out on Warren Island arrive by sea kayak.

Most of the island's ten campsites (and arguably the nicest sites) are spread along the shore; the rest are located toward the center of the island. There are eight primitive tent sites and two Appalachian Mountain Club–style lean-tos. The day-use picnic sites and the overnight camping sites are available by reservation or,else on a first come, first served basis. The only sites you can't reserve are 4, 5, and 6.

The island is covered in a verdant, dense spruce forest. Island camping in general, and certainly a night spent on Warren Island, is an olfactory experience. At any moment, in any breath, you can smell the crisp aroma of the spruce forest and the rich, heady scents of the sea.

It's funny to look down as you're walking along the Island Trail and see bits of shell mixed in with the pine needles and fallen leaves on the forest floor. The Island Trail is a walking trail that essentially circumnavigates the 70-acre island and brings you past most of the sites.

As you start to set up your camping gear, you'll notice a five-gallon white bucket next to every fireplace and grill. It should be full of water. If it's not, be a good citizen and fill it up at the shore. This is Warren Island's volunteer fire department, and you're the firefighter. If your fire gets out of control, there's no calling 911. There's no truck on the island waiting to come

> *Warren Island is a slice of paradise. After an adventurous day of paddling on the ocean, you can relax by your campfire and enjoy the pristine view and the magnificent scent of both sea and forest.*

RATINGS

Beauty: ☆ ☆ ☆ ☆ ☆
Privacy: ☆ ☆ ☆ ☆ ☆
Spaciousness: ☆ ☆ ☆ ☆ ☆
Quiet: ☆ ☆ ☆ ☆ ☆
Security: ☆ ☆ ☆ ☆ ☆
Cleanliness: ☆ ☆ ☆ ☆ ☆

douse the flames. An out-of-control campfire could be lethal, and that scenario is a major concern for island dwellers and Warren Island State Park's ranger. Be extra cautious with your fire, and make sure that bucket is full and next to the hearth.

There's no camp store on Warren Island, and it is strictly forbidden to cut down or otherwise damage trees. The rangers leave small caches of firewood here and there for campers. Be frugal and conserve wood. Only build a fire as large as you need to cook, stay warm, and keep the fireside ambience in your site. You'll save wood, minimize the risk to Warren Island, and still have a fantastically peaceful evening. OK, end of sermon— I promise!

After reaching the island from whichever direction you approach, you can access it via the pier on the east side, facing the Islesboro ferry terminal. Just off the end of the pier is the ranger station and the day-use area with grills and picnic tables. If you're just pulling in for the day, the fee is $1, which you pay at the Iron Ranger posted at the head of the pier.

Head out on the Island Trail to the north (or to the right as you look onto the island from the end of the pier) and you'll find the campsites. Site 1 is situated on a grassy area, close to the restrooms and the pier, on the island's eastern shore. This site is on the inland side of the Island Trail.

KEY INFORMATION

ADDRESS:	Warren Island State Park P.O. Box 105 Lincolnville, ME 04849
OPERATED BY:	Maine Department of Conservation, Bureau of Parks and Lands
INFORMATION:	Contact Camden Hills State Park (207) 236-3109 or (207) 941-4014 (off-season)
OPEN:	Mid-May–mid-September
SITES:	8 tent sites, 2 lean-tos
EACH SITE HAS:	Picnic table, stone hearth, fire bucket
ASSIGNMENT:	First come, first served; by reservation. Call (800) 332-1501 (out of state) or (207) 287-3824 (in state) for reservations or online at www.campwithme.com (additional $2 fee per site per night for reservations)
REGISTRATION:	At ranger station as you enter campground; check in after 1 p.m., check out by 11 a.m.
FACILITIES:	Pit toilets, water spigots, pier and moorings
PARKING:	Pull your kayak up on the beach!
FEE:	Maine residents, $14; nonresidents, $19; day-use fee, $1
RESTRICTIONS:	*Pets:* On leash only *Fires:* In established fire rings only *Alcohol:* Not allowed *Vehicles:* No vehicles on the island *Other:* Cutting or damaging trees is prohibited; campers must carry out all trash; no dishwashing at water spigots; quiet hours 10 p.m.–7 a.m., 14-day maximum stay

Site 2 is the first of the sites situated right on the water. This site is marvelously spacious and well secluded. You can see the narrow bay that separates Warren Island and Islesboro through the loosely spaced trees that define the site. This site has two picnic tables and a stone hearth.

Deep in the woods on the forest side of the trail, site 3 is secluded and private. The inland sites at Warren Island are indeed lovely campsites. But this is an island, so you'll probably be tempted to try to secure a waterfront site. It's well worth a little extra effort or wait.

The next oceanfront site is site 3A, which is spacious and open, with cool breezes blowing off the ocean. It has dramatic views of the bay. You can pull your kayaks right up to the edge of the site. If you arrive by a larger boat, or don't paddle right up to the campsite, there are wheeled carts available for hauling your gear from the pier.

Keep heading up the trail past sites 3 and 3A and you'll come to the North Shelter, one of the island's lean-tos. The North Shelter is set in an open grove of birch and spruce trees, and it looks out over Penobscot Bay to the north. Its location perfectly blends a woodland setting and proximity to the island's shoreline.

The remaining inland sites are 4, 5, and 6. These are set in a grassy field and among grove of mixed forest in the center of the island. To reach them, take the short hiking trail that leads straight from the pier (heading west) and past the ranger station on the left. There are remnants from the foundation of a historic mansion out here. A water pump lies between sites 4 and 5, within the stone piles that suggest that a mansion stood here more than 80 years ago.

This mansion must have been quite a sight. Once the property of William Folwell, a wool manufacturer from Philadelphia who purchased the land in 1899. At $75,000 (in turn-of-the-century dollars), it was believed to be one of the most expensive log cabins ever built in New England. The elegantly appointed "cabin" had 22 rooms, including a massive living room, dining room, and kitchen. Sadly, the cabin burned to the ground in 1919.

Beyond sites 4 and 5 and the remnants of the Folwell mansion, site 6 is set off in its own little field. The trio of inland sites is quite open and extraordinarily spacious. They offer less privacy than do the shoreline sites, and lack ocean views, but they are still beautiful. The breezes, the scent of the ocean, and the melancholy cry of the seagulls will remind you you're on an island.

The West Shelter is set way down on the Penobscot Bay (west) side of the island. Follow a short hiking trail from the open area near sites 4 and 5 and you'll find the shelter, which faces an absolutely priceless bay view.

Site 7 is down toward the southern end of the island. You can pull up to the pier on the east side and cart your gear down, or spot the site from the water and paddle right up to it. Not surprisingly, I prefer the second option.

This site has the most complete and deep sense of seclusion of any campsite in New England. You're at least 100 feet from your nearest neighbor, and all you can see are the woods and the bay. There are two picnic tables and makeshift log benches by the fireplace at site 7. Set within a moderately spaced grove of spruce and other deciduous trees, it is quite open from above, so plenty of sunlight and moonlight filter in.

More often than not, there's a nice breeze on the island, but on those still days, or during the morning and evening lull, the bugs can be ferocious. There is simply no escape. Think ahead, and be prepared. Bring a head net and some of your favorite bug repellent.

Despite my earlier reverie about peaceful paddle strokes, the crossing from Camden or Lincolnville to Warren Island is wide open across more than 3 miles of Penobscot Bay. I've crossed the bay when it was still as glass. I've also crossed it with clenched teeth, white knuckles, and the bow of my kayak slicing into the oncoming swells like a broadsword. Penobscot Bay is big water. Exercise all sorts of caution. Don't paddle to Warren Island on your first kayak camping trip, or your second for that matter. Plan your trip carefully with respect to the winds, the tides, and the weather. If you're at all hesitant, wait for better weather or hire one of the area's registered guides.

If you do go over by yourself and get in a jam so you don't feel comfortable paddling back, paddle over to the ferry terminal on nearby Islesboro and see if you can hop on the ferry, which leaves Islesboro every hour on the half hour. A one-way adult ticket runs $3.25. Bikes are $2 and vehicles less than 20 feet are $10.50. A kayak would be somewhere in between, I'd imagine.

A trip to Warren Island is one you'll remember for a long time to come. The combination of paddling or boating there, exploring the island, falling asleep to the delightful rustling of sea breeze in the pines, and waking up to the panorama of Penobscot Bay completes a mystical experience.

MAP

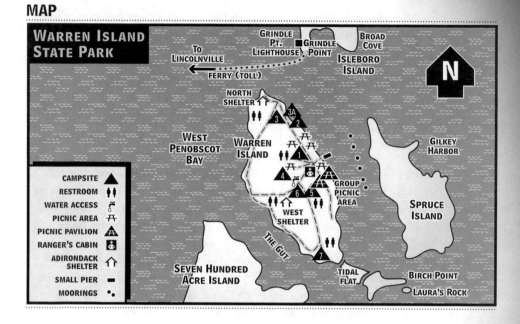

WARREN ISLAND STATE PARK

To LINCOLNVILLE
FERRY (TOLL)

GRINDLE PT. LIGHTHOUSE — GRINDLE POINT

BROAD COVE

ISLEBORO ISLAND

NORTH SHELTER 1

WEST PENOBSCOT BAY

WARREN ISLAND

3 3A 2

1

4

6 5

GROUP PICNIC AREA

WEST SHELTER

GILKEY HARBOR

SPRUCE ISLAND

THE GUT

7

TIDAL FLAT

SEVEN HUNDRED ACRE ISLAND

BIRCH POINT

LAURA'S ROCK

CAMPSITE	▲
RESTROOM	♦♦
WATER ACCESS	
PICNIC AREA	⊼
PICNIC PAVILION	
RANGER'S CABIN	
ADIRONDACK SHELTER	⇧
SMALL PIER	—
MOORINGS	•.

GETTING THERE

Drop your kayak in at
Camden Harbor,
Lincolnville Beach, or
Ducktrap Harbor, and
paddle east toward
Islesboro. Warren Island is
just southwest of the
Islesboro ferry terminal.

NEW HAMPSHIRE

BEAR BROOK STATE PARK IS ENORMOUS—it's the largest state park in New Hampshire. Its size (the entire park spans 8,008 acres) and the myriad outdoor activities available here make this as much a destination as a place to set up camp. On the long road leading through the park and to the campground, I was convinced I had missed it. If you get this sensation, keep on going because you're almost there. You'll come to another Bear Brook State Park sign that points the way into the campground. The last stretch is a beautiful ride through a stately forest of pine and spruce trees that are at least 100 feet tall.

Bear Brook State Park has a massive network of trails, some of which pass right through the campground. You'll see trailheads for the Broken Boulder Trail and the Pitch Pine Trail on the last section of the campground road. Both of these trails eventually lead to Smith Pond.

The first loop within the campground (with sites 1 and up) is set beneath an open forest with very little undergrowth. These sites don't offer a lot of privacy, but they are spacious and centrally located within the campground. They're also covered by a blanket of pine needles. This loop is near an open field with a baseball diamond. There is even a small playground with a slide and swings—nice if you're camping with kids. If you want to be near these parts of the campground, check out sites 35 and 36, which are close to the baseball field.

Past the field, there are sites tucked into the woods on the stretch of the campground road leading down to the small beach area on Beaver Pond. Sites 22 through 24 are nicely secluded and close to the pond. Of the other sites near the pond, site 31A is nice, as it's set on the end of a short road jutting off the main campground road.

> *Bear Brook State Park has some great spots to camp while you explore the rest of the park on foot, on a bike, or in a canoe.*

RATINGS

Beauty: ✪ ✪ ✪ ✪
Privacy: ✪ ✪ ✪ ✪
Spaciousness: ✪ ✪ ✪ ✪
Quiet: ✪ ✪ ✪
Security: ✪ ✪ ✪ ✪
Cleanliness: ✪ ✪ ✪ ✪

ADDRESS:	**Bear Brook State Park 157 Deerfield Road Allenstown, NH 03275**
OPERATED BY:	**New Hampshire Division of Parks and Recreation**
INFORMATION:	**Bear Brook State Park, (603) 485-9869 (campground office) or (603) 485-9874 (park office)**
OPEN:	**Early May– mid-October**
SITES:	**96**
EACH SITE HAS:	**Fire ring, picnic table**
ASSIGNMENT:	**First come, first served; by reservation: (603) 271-3628, www.nhstateparks .org, or through reserveamerica.com**
REGISTRATION:	**At campground headquarters**
FACILITIES:	**Flush toilets, showers, laundry, camp store, boat and canoe rentals**
PARKING:	**At sites**
FEE:	**$23**
RESTRICTIONS:	*Pets:* **Dogs on leash only** *Fires:* **In fire rings only** *Alcohol:* **At sites only** *Vehicles:* **Parking at campsites only, maximum 2 vehicles per site** *Other:* **Reservations require 2-night minimum stay; check in 1–8 p.m., check out by noon; quiet hours 10 p.m.–7 a.m.**

The beach at Beaver Pond is a great spot to spend an afternoon. You can paddle, fish, or just sit in the sand. Being out in the deep woods and far from the ocean, this beach has no seashells—only pine cones! You don't have to worry about finding anything else in the sand either: as there are no glass bottles, pets, or horses allowed on the beach. The Beaver Pond trailhead is at the far end of the beach. This trail circumnavigates the pond, coming back in through the campground. There's also a small dock toward the end of the beach to launch kayak or canoe adventures.

Heading back toward the main part of the campground, sites 40 and 41 are quite spacious, although they're close to the headquarters and set within the open forest that covers most of the central campground loop. Like the lower-numbered sites, these are also blanketed with pine needles.

Site 55 is excellent; it's one of the more secluded at Bear Brook. A short perimeter of pines stands around the border as if guarding the site. Its neighbor, site 56, is also nicely isolated.

If you set up camp at site 64, you'll be able to pick up the Beaver Pond Trail right next to your campsite. Site 65 is off on its own, with a view of the pond through the loosely spaced forest that divides the campsites from the shores of the pond in this section of the campground.

Farther back on the campground loop road and away from the campground headquarters, you'll find site 94, another of Bear Brook's better choices. It is a spacious site set off on a small loop heading away from the pond. There is open forest both on the far side and overhead, so a lot of sunlight reaches it—you'll have a nice view of the night sky too. There's also a self-guided nature trail adjacent.

Site 95 is truly secluded, set at the end of a short spur leading off the main campground road. It has its own little cul-de-sac right in front of the site, so it's extremely spacious. It's set up against a small embankment and nestled within a grove of mixed hardwoods and conifers. Just outside the site to the left, there's a break in the forest that gives you access to the pond. There's no beach, but there's plenty of room to launch

MAP

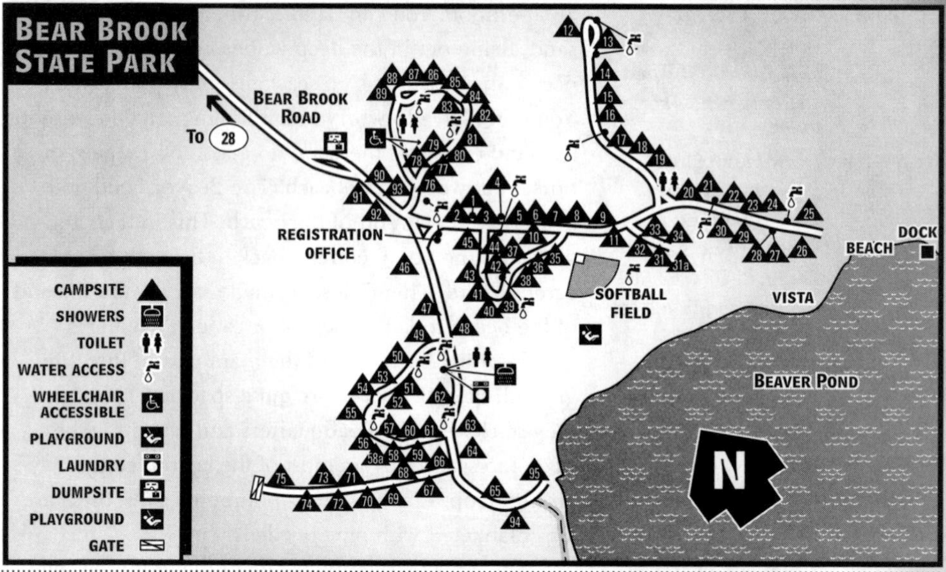
BEAR BROOK STATE PARK
BEAR BROOK ROAD
To 28
REGISTRATION OFFICE
SOFTBALL FIELD
VISTA
BEACH
DOCK
BEAVER POND
N
CAMPSITE
SHOWERS
TOILET
WATER ACCESS
WHEELCHAIR ACCESSIBLE
PLAYGROUND
LAUNDRY
DUMPSITE
PLAYGROUND
GATE

a canoe or kayak. This site is also near a trailhead that leads out of the campground.

Site 75 is another secluded spot, at another end of the campground loop road and right on a dirt road leading out of the campground proper. Overall, sites 46 through 75 are more secluded than those in the rest of the campground. Some are much more spacious, and a few are positively perfect. The shower and laundry facilities are also located within this group.

There's a special pond just for fly-fishing near the beginning of the road winding in toward the campground. The season runs from the fourth Saturday in April through October 15, and there's a limit of two brook trout per day. There are also two archery ranges within the park (apparently the only ones within the New Hampshire state park system). For information on fishing licenses, see Appendix C, page 232.

If hiking, mountain biking, and paddling are more your speed, there's plenty of room for those as well. Many trails wind through Bear Brook State Park—more than 40 miles' worth—so you will have to spend a lot of time here before you cross the same trail twice.

GETTING THERE

Take Interstate 93 north through Manchester to the exit for NH 28 and NH 3 north. In Suncook, take NH 28 toward Allenstown. Turn right on Bear Brook Road.

> *You'll know how this campground got its name as soon as you pull in.*

THE MOMENT YOU PULL INTO Big Rock Campground, you'll see the unique geological feature for which the campground was named— a huge rock. Besides being a namesake and a curiosity, this massive chunk of granite (a phrase that proved far too cumbersome for a campground name) gives climbers a good spot for a little spontaneous bouldering. It's a nice way to warm up for or cool down from a day spent climbing the massive walls of Cathedral Ledge in nearby North Conway.

Big Rock is actually quite a small campground, which makes it an excellent place to set up camp. There are only 28 sites, many of which have a decent amount of space and some privacy. If you've come camping with a group or need several sites, try to secure something in the range of sites 24 through 29. There's a small central parking area, so you'll have to haul in your gear, but not too far. These sites sit atop the small hill around which the campground is situated, isolating them from the rest of the campground, if not from each other. There's also a restroom right down the access road.

Other prime tent spots within Big Rock are sites 7 through 10, and 13 through 18. All are on the same loop (the main loop of the campground). The forest here is a bit thicker than the open woods of nearby Hancock Campground (see page 82). It's a mixed forest of coniferous and deciduous trees, so at the height of summer, the dense woods separate the sites as well.

I especially like the fact that this is such a small campground. Yes, it fills up quickly as a result, but if you get here early enough and secure a spot, you can rest assured that you'll have peaceful, quiet nights in the woods. Big Rock is only the second campground you'll come across as you travel east on Kancamagus Highway (or the "Kanc," as this delightful stretch of

RATINGS

Beauty: ✩ ✩ ✩ ✩
Privacy: ✩ ✩ ✩ ✩
Spaciousness: ✩ ✩ ✩ ✩
Quiet: ✩ ✩ ✩ ✩ ✩
Security: ✩ ✩ ✩ ✩
Cleanliness: ✩ ✩ ✩ ✩

road is known to the locals and regulars), so it's still fairly close to Lincoln.

Big Rock is a great spot from which to launch your outdoor adventures, being a short drive or walk from some prime hikes and sights along the Kanc. Right across the road runs the Hancock Branch of the Pemigewasset. Stroll over there with a fishing rod or a towel, depending on your preference (for information on fishing licenses, see Appendix C, page 232).

Several hiking trails are just a stone's throw down the Kanc. Turn left out of the campground, heading toward Conway, and you'll soon come to trailheads for the East Pond Trail and the Hancock Notch Trail. This trail follows the North Fork of the Pemigewasset for a while, then bears east toward Mount Huntington, Hancock Notch, and the Sawyer Pond Scenic Area. It would be a fairly sturdy hike from the Hancock Notch trailhead all the way to Sawyer Pond, so bring plenty of food and water if you're coming this way.

Across the Kanc from these trailheads is the Greeley Ponds Trail, which leads to the Greeley Ponds Scenic Area. If you hike in this far and still want to explore, the Mount Osceola Trail leads you up to East Peak, West Peak, and Mount Osceola. You'll also be able to sneak occasional views of Mount Kancamagus to the east.

It can sometimes be a challenge to secure one of the prime tent spots at Big Rock because it is one of the first campgrounds to fill during the busy summer weekends. Even if you've come to the Kanc at the height of the season, it's well worth your time to take a swing through Big Rock just in case there's an open spot.

Who knows what the campground might have been called had a careless glacier not casually dropped that massive boulder near the entrance several million years ago? On the other hand, who cares? Big Rock is small and cozy, and that makes it a perfect-sized campground and a great spot to pitch a tent.

KEY INFORMATION

ADDRESS: Big Rock Campground Kancamagus Highway Lincoln, NH 03818

OPERATED BY: U.S. Forest Service

INFORMATION: Saco Ranger Station 33 Kancamagus Highway RFD 1, Box 94 Conway, NH 03818 (603) 447-5448

OPEN: Year-round, but not plowed in winter

SITES: 28

EACH SITE HAS: Fire ring, picnic table

ASSIGNMENT: First come, first served

REGISTRATION: Select site, then pay at self-service fee station

FACILITIES: Vault toilets

PARKING: At sites

FEE: $18 for 1 vehicle, $5 for extra vehicle

RESTRICTIONS: *Pets:* Dogs on leash only
Fires: In fire rings only
Alcohol: At sites only
Vehicles: Maximum 2 per site
Other: Maximum 8 people per site; 14-day maximum stay

MAP

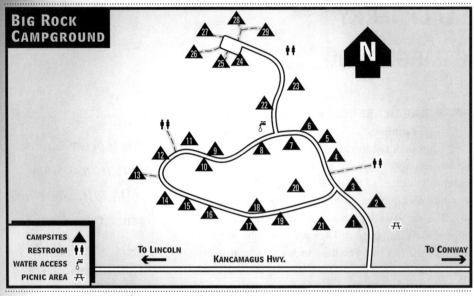

BIG ROCK CAMPGROUND

N

CAMPSITES ▲
RESTROOM ♀♂
WATER ACCESS
PICNIC AREA 🛆

TO LINCOLN ←
KANCAMAGUS HWY.
TO CONWAY →

GETTING THERE

From Lincoln, follow Kanca-
magus Highway to Big Rock
Campground on the left.
From Conway, follow Kanca-
magus Highway to Big Rock
Campground on the right.

16 BLACKBERRY CROSSING CAMPGROUND

THERE MAY BE JUST SIX SITES set aside for tent camping at Blackberry Crossing Campground, but its character, history, and location on Kancamagus Highway make a trip here time well spent. It's another of the area's fairly small campgrounds, about the same size as Big Rock.

The six tent sites are in a small field on the eastern edge of the campground. They are tent-only sites by virtue of the fact that you have to lug your gear in a short distance from the parking area for this loop. Sites 21 through 26 are at the woods' edge around a central clearing about one-quarter the size of a football field. The open space between these tent sites adds a community flavor to this part of the campground. On those crystal-clear, jet-black New England nights, you'll be thankful that you're far from any light pollution that might interfere with stargazing. The break in the trees over the field affords magnificent views of the skies. Keep an eye to the sky if you're there in mid-August, and you could catch the Perseid meteor showers.

During the daylight hours, the field is a great spot for a quick game of Frisbee or a group picnic. It's also a great space to let the kids run around in and blow off steam while you kick back in the sun—or in the shade of the birch, pine, and mixed deciduous forest. Either way, you'll still have a full view of your gang. It's also just 6 miles west of Conway if you need anything, from groceries to a hot pizza.

If you've come to pitch your tent at Blackberry Crossing during the winter, the clearing in the middle of the tent loop is especially nice because you'll get the full benefit of the sun (when it's out). The campground isn't plowed in the winter, so you'll have to ski or snowshoe in with your gear. Of course, during the winter, you might not need to hike your gear over to the tent loop. Hancock tends to get most of the winter

> *Blackberry Crossing is rich in history, with tall, stone hearths remaining from its days as a Civilian Conservation Corps camp.*

RATINGS

Beauty: ✩ ✩ ✩ ✩
Privacy: ✩ ✩ ✩
Spaciousness: ✩ ✩ ✩ ✩
Quiet: ✩ ✩ ✩
Security: ✩ ✩ ✩ ✩
Cleanliness: ✩ ✩ ✩ ✩

KEY INFORMATION

campers, so you might have Blackberry Crossing all to yourself.

Blackberry Crossing looks quite different than it did 60 years ago. Nearly 200 men lived and worked here between 1935 and 1941 as part of President Roosevelt's "Tree Army." Blackberry Crossing was home to Company 1177 of the Civilian Conservation Corps, which cut most of the trails in and around the White Mountains that we still enjoy today.

Besides preserving and providing access to wilderness, the CCC employed men during the depths of the Great Depression. There are still a few remnants from Blackberry Crossing's days as a CCC encampment, most notably two large stone hearths—one right by site 20 and the other between sites 8 and 9. These are all that remain of the camp's original headquarters and recreation hall.

The sites in the tent loop are obviously the best for tent camping, but if you've come with a large group or several families and that loop is already occupied, you could also look into sites 7 through 10. These are located around the central loop, off to the left as you enter the campground. You'll be close to one of the beautiful old stone hearths and a historic marker with photos of the camp in its heyday. These sites are wide open, but they're set amid a lovely grove of birch trees. Sites 14 and 15, roughly between the central loop and the tent-only loop, are also off on their own.

Whether you've come to Blackberry Crossing to camp for one night or for a whole week, don't miss Rocky Gorge. Visit it by heading out of the campground and taking a left. A series of natural pools and rock baths leads to a fairly steep and wild waterfall. The Swift River gets narrow and speeds through Rocky Gorge here. There's a footbridge right over the waterfall, so you can get a spectacular view of the show beneath.

Follow the footbridge to the trail on the opposite side of the river, and a short hike will lead you to the placid, quiet Falls Pond. There's a hiking trail that leads all the way around the pond as well.

Blackberry Crossing Campground is directly opposite the Covered Bridge Campground, which is

MAP

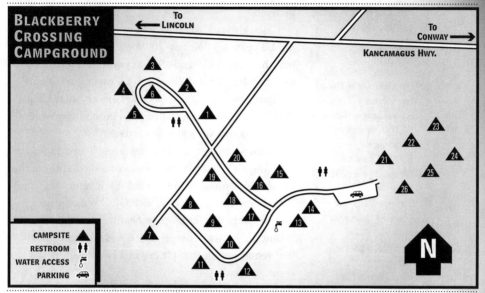

BLACKBERRY CROSSING CAMPGROUND

To LINCOLN ←

To CONWAY →

KANCAMAGUS HWY.

CAMPSITE
RESTROOM
WATER ACCESS
PARKING

N

GETTING THERE

From Lincoln, follow Kancamagus Highway to Blackberry Crossing Campground on your right. From Conway, follow Kancamagus Highway to Blackberry Crossing Campground on your left, right across the street from Covered Bridge Campground.

kind of amusing. It's your choice. If you're camping with a large group or have a particular affinity for historic sites, Blackberry Crossing is definitely worth a look. If it's just you and a friend, you might want to head across the road to Covered Bridge.

COVERED BRIDGE CAMPGROUND

> *The campground's proximity to massive rock garden and two trailheads make Covered Bridge a great spot for hikers.*

WHAT DO BIG ROCK AND COVERED BRIDGE campgrounds have in common (besides the fact that they're both located on Kancamagus Highway)? As soon as you pull in to either, you'll see the campground's namesake. In the case of Covered Bridge Campground, it's a classic New England covered bridge that spans the Swift River. The original bridge was built in the late 1800s by the townsfolk of Albany; it was rebuilt in the 1970s.

On either side of the road leading to the bridge, there are huge timbers spanning the road at an eight-foot height to ensure that "adventurous" RV or camper owners don't try to drive through the bridge. Effective in preserving this historic covered bridge, the timbers also help keep the larger RVs out of Covered Bridge Campground. (You can get into the campground from the Dugway Road, 6 miles west of Conway, but don't tell anyone in an RV!)

Coming into the campground from the Kancamagus, you'll pass under the RV trap with ease, traverse the covered bridge (keep an eye out for pedestrians—covered bridges throughout New England always draw camera-toting crowds), and bear right on Dugway Road. The campground is on the left, about half a mile down the road. As soon as you cross the bridge and bear right, you'll see the parking area and trailhead for the Boulder Loop Trail on the right. Make a mental note to walk back later for a quick hike.

Covered Bridge Campground is moderate in size, with 49 sites. There aren't any sites designated tent-only, but there are some practical landscape considerations that make this a great campground for a night in the nylon. As soon as you pull into the campground, keep bearing left. This will bring you to the small, dead-end loop with sites 25 through 27. These are great sites, set off on their own amid the fairly dense, mostly

RATINGS

Beauty: ☆ ☆ ☆ ☆ ☆
Privacy: ☆ ☆ ☆ ☆
Spaciousness: ☆ ☆ ☆ ☆
Quiet: ☆ ☆ ☆ ☆ ☆
Security: ☆ ☆ ☆ ☆
Cleanliness: ☆ ☆ ☆ ☆ ☆

coniferous forest. Just outside this loop is site 24, which is set against a garden of massive boulders—no doubt spilled over from the aptly named Boulder Loop Trail.

Generally speaking, the outer-loop sites are the best. If you're fortunate enough, you'll be able to score one of the northernmost sites set off on their own platforms, which means you have to lug your tent and other gear up a short incline. If you're on the southern end of the loop, you might be somewhere near an RV, but the sites are spacious and distant enough to provide solitude.

The northern-loop sites that make up the prime tent spots at Covered Bridge are 17, 19, 41, 43, 45, 47, and 49. These sites back up to a massive cliff that rises just behind the campground. During the summer, the forest may be too dense for you to fully appreciate this grand formation, which is part of the granite pile left by the glaciers that scraped through here thousands of years ago.

One other way to appreciate the geologic uniqueness of this area is to head down Dugway Road back toward the covered bridge and take a spin around the Boulder Loop Trail. The trail will take you up and around the side of this cliff and through a delightful garden of huge boulders. The beginning of this trail resembles a massive stone staircase. You almost expect it to lead to a giant's castle. The glaciers inadvertently created a hiker's playground here, but watch your step: It's quite easy to twist an ankle when hiking and bounding through the boulders.

Another nice trailhead right near the campground is the Lower Nanamocomuck Ski Trail, which is just past the covered bridge coming from the campground. This makes a fairly level hike during the spring, summer, and fall, and a dramatic backcountry ski or snowshoe trek in the winter. While Covered Bridge Campground isn't open during the winter, Blackberry Crossing, just opposite, is open for camping at half the regular rates because it isn't plowed out like Hancock, the other Kancamagus campground that is open year-round.

There's one historical aspect to Covered Bridge that can add a bit of spice to your ghost stories around the campfire. As soon as you enter the campground,

KEY INFORMATION

ADDRESS:	Covered Bridge Campground Kancamagus Highway Albany, NH 03818
OPERATED BY:	U.S. Forest Service
INFORMATION:	Saco Ranger Station 33 Kancamagus Highway RFD 1, Box 94 Conway, NH 03818 (603) 447-5448
OPEN:	Mid-May– mid-October
SITES:	49
EACH SITE HAS:	Fire ring, picnic table
ASSIGNMENT:	First come, first served; sites 29–49 by reservation: (877) 4446777, www .reserveusa.com
REGISTRATION:	Select a site, then pay at self-service fee station
FACILITIES:	Vault toilets near fishing pier on Swift River
PARKING:	At sites
FEE:	$18 for 1 vehicle, $5 for extra vehicle
RESTRICTIONS:	*Pets:* Dogs on leash only *Fires:* In fire rings only *Alcohol:* At sites only *Vehicles:* Maximum 2 per site *Other:* Maximum 8 people per site; 14-day maximum stay

MAP

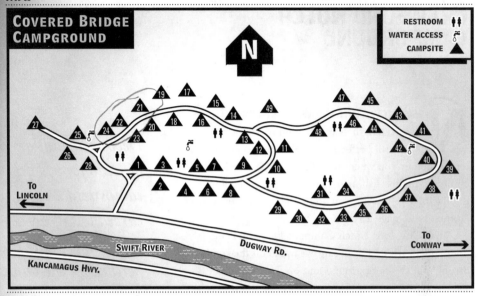

COVERED BRIDGE CAMPGROUND

RESTROOM
WATER ACCESS
CAMPSITE

N

To LINCOLN ←

To CONWAY →

SWIFT RIVER   DUGWAY RD.

KANCAMAGUS HWY.

GETTING THERE

From Lincoln, follow Kanca-magus Highway to Covered Bridge Campground on your left. From Conway, follow Kancamagus Highway to Covered Bridge Camp-ground on your right, oppo-site the Blackberry Crossing Campground.

there's a small, fenced-off burial plot. After dinner, take a stroll down to the burial site, make sure no one from the Lane family (the name on the headstone) is up and about, then go whip up a couple of ghoulish ghost stories with a local connection!

18
CRAWFORD NOTCH CAMPGROUND

NESTLED WITHIN THE WILDERNESS of Crawford Notch, the campground of the same name is a perfectly peaceful spot to pitch your tent—whether you've come to Crawford Notch for the climbing, hiking, fishing, or just sitting and watching the Saco River (for information on fishing licenses, see Appendix C, page 232).

The Crawford Notch Campground is meticulously maintained, with a clean, sandy surface on the roads throughout the campground and on the individual sites. A dense forest, mostly young maples and beech, covers the campground. The deciduous forest imparts a brilliant, shimmering green character to the forest, especially when all the leaves are backlit by the sun. The dense forest also gives most of the sites a marvelous sense of seclusion. There are many sites here located on or near the shores of the Saco River, and these are by far the most spectacular.

Close to the campground entrance is the S loop. These sites are all encircled with short stone walls built within the forest of young birch trees. This makes for a peaceful and scenic setting. The sites are all moderate in size and fairly well secluded by the birch forest. There's a bright, open character to the forest here, as it is populated primarily by deciduous trees and fewer conifers. Sites 5 through 9 are set back a bit farther from the road and closer to the river, making them preferable.

The rest of the first sites as you drive into the campground are the RV sites with hookups. These sites are also close to the road and are fairly open to each other. Considering the magical quality of some of the riverside hike-in spots here, you should keep driving to find the primo sites.

A bit deeper into the campground, sites 38 and 39 are hike-in sites carved out of the beech forest. As

> *Deep in the wilderness of Crawford Notch, campsites here are carved out of dense forest, and many are perched on the banks of the Saco River.*

RATINGS

Beauty: ✪ ✪ ✪ ✪ ✪
Privacy: ✪ ✪ ✪ ✪
Spaciousness: ✪ ✪ ✪ ✪
Quiet: ✪ ✪ ✪ ✪
Security: ✪ ✪ ✪ ✪
Cleanliness: ✪ ✪ ✪ ✪ ✪

ADDRESS:	**Crawford Notch Campground US 302 Harts Location, NH 03812**
OPERATED BY:	**Crawford Notch General Store and Campground**
INFORMATION:	**Crawford Notch Campground (603) 374-2779**
OPEN:	**Mid-May– mid-October**
SITES:	**74**
EACH SITE HAS:	**Fire ring or stone hearth, picnic table**
ASSIGNMENT:	**First come, first served; by reservation (recommended in July and August or during foliage season, late September–early October)**
REGISTRATION:	**At campground office and store located on US 302**
FACILITIES:	**Portable toilets, shower building, water spigots**
PARKING:	**At campsites or in shared parking areas**
FEE:	**$20–$30 (depending on location of site)**
RESTRICTIONS:	*Pets:* **Dogs on leash only** *Fires:* **At fire rings only** *Alcohol:* **At sites** *Vehicles:* **Maximum 1 vehicle per site** *Other:* **Check in 1–9 p.m., check out by 11 a.m.**

such, they are very private. Site 42 requires about a 50-foot hike. It's nicely secluded on all sides and not far from the portable toilets. It's also close to the river. Site 43 is also secluded by a hike. Continuing on the path that leads to this site will bring you to site 45—more on that in a minute.

Site 43 is near a cul-de-sac with parking for sites 44, 45, 46, and 46A. All of these sites are set near the Saco, all share open views into Crawford Notch, and breezes sweeping through all—site 46A a bit less so, as it's open to the cul-de-sac but set deeper in the woods.

Sites 47 and 48 are hike-in sites with shared parking. This area also includes Site 47A, which is located at the end of a 30-foot hike to a modest-sized and delightfully secluded site. Sites 47 and 48 are set a bit deeper into the woods, but still near the riverbanks. These two sites are carved out of a grove of older beech trees and their saplings and are perfectly secluded and absolutely beautiful.

The trail that leads you to these two sites continues on to sites 45 and 44. Site 45 is the site at Crawford Notch Campground. It is absolutely perfect, pristine, intensely secluded, and very spacious; has a stone hearth; is set on the shore of the Saco River at a picturesque bend; and is open to the sky for stargazing and a commanding view up into the cliffs of Crawford Notch. Need I say more? There are some dramatically beautiful hike-in sites along the Saco River here at the Crawford Notch Campground. Site 45 is the granddaddy of them all.

The drive-in sites are easier to get into to unload your gear, but the hike-in sites offer a sense of wilderness and seclusion that astounds me. I always prefer these types of sites, even if it means a little extra effort hauling gear.

Located near the intersection of the campground road, sites 49 and 50 are open to that road. Still, at night when everyone is snug in their sites, sitting around the campfires cooking dinner and telling stories, this won't be a big deal. Even when the moon is full, once night falls at the Crawford Notch Campground, the dense forest ensures a dark night.

These hike-in sites in the lower 50s—53, 54, 55,

55A, 55B, and 55C—are the crown jewels of the Crawford Notch Campground. Incredibly remote-feeling, yet easily accessible, they are all perched along or near the shores of the Saco River, so you'll fall asleep to the soft rushing of water. Of these, site 53 is the most private, set at the end of a 75-foot hike. Sites 54 and 55 are closest to the river, so they are off the charts in seclusion and beauty.

The end of the campground road has sites 56 through 64. Site 56 also has a short hike in. It's a secluded but somewhat smaller site. There's also a short hike to site 62, but it's huge and very private. This would be an excellent site for a larger group. There's a short hike into site 61. Although this site is much smaller, it's isolated from the road and from neighboring sites.

Site 63 is very spacious. It also has its own tent platform, so you're guaranteed a level, dry space upon which to pitch your tent. Sites 63A and 64 are both secluded and set against the stream leading off the Saco River.

Sites 65 through 71 are all drive-in sites situated on a short spur off the primary campground road. Sites 65 and 66 are both moderate in size, and they are very secluded from each other and from the other sites on this part of the loop. The locations are staggered on either side of the road, so your site here won't be open to the neighboring one across the way. Plus, these sites are all carved from a dense forest.

Site 68 is large, and it's peppered with slightly older beech and birch trees that provide a beautiful canopy of leaves. Site 69 is set well off the road and somewhat private, even though it is also close to the toilets. Sites 70 and 71 share a parking area, but there is enough forest separating the two sites that they also share a deep-woods seclusion. Site 70 is framed by a bed of ferns that give it an almost primeval feeling. This site is a bit smaller than the others in this loop, but the scenic seclusion is well worth it. Site 71 is much larger.

The rest of the sites in this loop, 72 through 75, are along a cul-de-sac at the end of the road. Sites 74 and 75 are especially close to the water, which makes them preferable.

Crawford Notch is home to renowned climbing routes at Frankenstein Cliffs, hiking trails that wind past numerous waterfalls, and of course the Saco River. Whatever brings you to the area, the Crawford Notch Campground is a scenic and secluded spot to set up base camp.

MAP

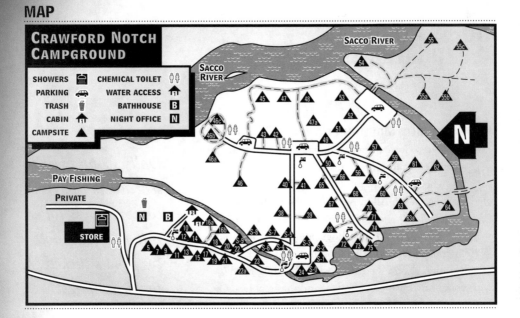

GETTING THERE

From North Conway, follow US 302 north into Crawford Notch and the White Mountain National Forest. The campground will be on your right, 13.5 miles past the intersection where NH 16 splits from US 302.

19
DOLLY COPP CAMPGROUND

THE **WHITE MOUNTAIN NATIONAL FOREST** is a paradise for camping, hiking, biking, fly-fishing, canoeing, and nearly every other outdoor pursuit: It's "The Land of Many Uses," as the Forest Service signs proclaim. All those sound like pretty good uses to me, and I'm certainly not alone. During all four seasons, a steady flow of fun-hogs pours into the Mount Washington Valley. Don't be too dismayed if it seems like everyone else in the free world is heading north with you. Many also come for the indoor activities, like outlet shopping in North Conway.

You can escape some of the crowds that may not head any farther north than the outlets by heading farther north yourself, to Dolly Copp Campground. The campground is just north of Mount Washington and right off NH 16. Don't make the mistake of pulling in to the Dolly Copp picnic area. The campground is another mile up the road.

Dolly Copp is a good-sized campground, and it's not crowded with sites. There are 176 sites in four separate areas within the campground, and there is plenty of room between those areas. There aren't any tent-specific areas within Dolly Copp, but there are a few areas where trailers aren't allowed. These loops are more secluded, densely forested, and perfect for pitching a tent. The only area that you would definitely want to avoid is the Big Meadow area, which includes sites 1 through 50. This area has most of the open sites where the land yachts come to drop their anchors.

A respectful distance farther up the campground access road is where you'll find the prime tent sites. Brook Loop is a great spot for tent campers. No trailers are allowed here. This loop includes sites 75 through 91. Within Brook Loop, sites 80 through 84 are in their own little mini-loop—perfect if you're camping with a large group. Even if some other folks are already

> *Dolly Copp is like several small campgrounds rolled into one, with lots of cozy spots tucked into the dense forest.*

RATINGS

Beauty: ✿ ✿ ✿ ✿
Privacy: ✿ ✿ ✿ ✿
Spaciousness: ✿ ✿ ✿
Quiet: ✿ ✿ ✿ ✿
Security: ✿ ✿ ✿ ✿
Cleanliness: ✿ ✿ ✿ ✿

ADDRESS:	Dolly Copp Campground NH 16 Gorham, NH 03581
OPERATED BY:	U.S. Forest Service
INFORMATION:	Androscoggin Ranger Station 300 Glen Road Gorham, NH 03581 (603) 466-2713
OPEN:	Mid-May– mid-October
SITES:	176
EACH SITE HAS:	Fire pit
ASSIGNMENT:	First come, first served; sites 29–49 by reservation: (877) 444-6777, www.reserveusa.com
REGISTRATION:	At campground headquarters
FACILITIES:	Flush toilets, water
PARKING:	At sites
FEE:	$20 for 1 vehicle, $5 for extra vehicle
RESTRICTIONS:	*Pets:* Dogs on leash only *Fires:* In fire pits only; no unattended fires *Alcohol:* At sites only *Vehicles:* Maximum 1 per site; trailers prohibited in Spruce Woods and Brook Loop

camped out in the 80-through-84 loop, you'll still be able to experience solitude. From where you park your vehicle, you have to walk up to tent platforms for two of the sites within the loop, and down to a platform for another, so they are a bit more set off.

Spruce Woods is another great spot for tents. No trailers are allowed here, and the road is narrow and winding, so you're not likely to see any large, self-contained campers. The Spruce Woods Loop includes sites 51 through 72. As soon as you turn in to this loop, you'll feel as if you're driving deeper into the forest. The whole area is densely wooded with fir, pine, and spruce trees, so there's a nice sylvan atmosphere. The forest floor remains cool even on the sultriest summer day, and the sunlight filters down through the trees in fractured columns, adding a mystical air to the woods. Even if you have neighbors on both sides, you may not be able to see them. This is my favorite section of Dolly Copp.

The only drawback to the dense forest is that you won't have a very good view of the night sky for stargazing. On a clear night, you can always take a short walk to an open area or even down to the banks of the Peabody River, which flows by just outside the campground.

There are several campground hosts who stay at the same well-marked sites throughout the season. The hosts are a good source of information on campground regulations, what to do in the area, and Rockwellian local lore, if you have a moment to chat. The rangers at Dolly Copp also run various visitor programs and interpretive walks during the season. If you've come to the White Mountains for some fly-fishing, you'll be able to find quite a few secluded fishing spots on either the Peabody River or the Moose River, which is just a bit farther north (for information on fishing licenses, see Appendix C, page 232).

Then, there's the hiking. It's everywhere. Dolly Copp is a great place to set up your base camp if you have come to the White Mountains to hike Mount Washington, the rest of the Presidential Range, or anywhere within the White Mountain National Forest.

Along Kancamagus Highway and up NH 16, are

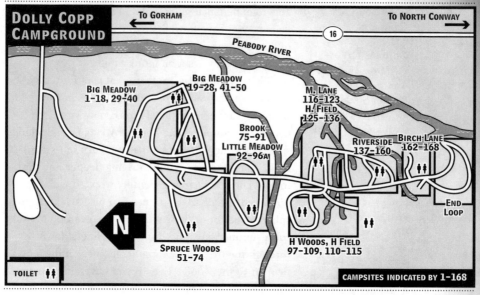

DOLLY COPP CAMPGROUND

TO GORHAM

TO NORTH CONWAY

PEABODY RIVER

16

BIG MEADOW
19-28, 41-50

BIG MEADOW
1-18, 29-40

M. LANE
116-123
H. FIELD
125-136

BROOK
75-91
LITTLE MEADOW
92-96A

RIVERSIDE
137-160

BIRCH LANE
162-168

N

END LOOP

SPRUCE WOODS
51-74

H WOODS, H FIELD
97-109, 110-115

TOILET

CAMPSITES INDICATED BY 1-168

numerous trailheads. You can find a hike that is long, short, steep, gradual—whatever suits your mood, energy level, or the amount of time you have before heading back to the real world.

As someone who skis Tuckerman Ravine every spring, I always find myself questioning my sanity when I get a good view of the Left Gully and the rest of the ravine without snow. It's almost unthinkable that people hike up there, much less ski down.

If you come to the Mount Washington area for winter activities such as mountaineering or ice-climbing and you want to camp, you won't be able to camp in Dolly Copp, which closes in mid-October. However, Barnes Field, which is off the access road leading into Dolly Copp, is open year-round for individual camping, or for group camping in season by reservation only.

GETTING THERE

From North Conway, follow NH 16 north past the AMC Pinkham Notch Base Camp and the Mount Washington Auto Road. The campground will be on the left. From Gorham, follow NH 16 south to the campground on your right. If you come to the Mount Washington Auto Road, you've gone too far.

> *Dry River Campground is quiet and intimate. It's one of those campgrounds where there's really not a bad site in the whole place.*

DON'T GET CONFUSED as you drive up through Crawford Notch State Park. The park campground is called the Dry River Campground. There is a Crawford Notch Campground as well. That's a private campground located across US 302. Both are excellent spots and situated near some fantastic hiking and climbing routes.

Dry River is one of those campgrounds where there's not a bad site in the place. It's a small campground set within a moderately dense forest of mixed deciduous trees. There are lots of maple, birch, and ash trees in the forest. All of the campsites are very clean and spacious. The setting in Crawford Notch doesn't hurt one bit either. From your campsite, you are minutes from dramatically beautiful and challenging trails, world-class rock-climbing at Frankenstein Cliffs, and towering waterfalls. You won't run out of things to do or places to explore when staying here.

Most of the campsites are spread out along a short loop that shoots off to the left as you enter the campground. There are several sites down a short road running straight off to the right, but we'll get to those later.

There is a deep wilderness atmosphere at this campground. The trees open above most of the sites, which allows lots of light to filter down. Overall, Dry River's sites are laid out thoughtfully, both individually and in relation to one another. The sites aren't too densely packed together, and they fit in well with the forest's character.

The campsites situated on the outside of the campground loop road provide the greatest seclusion and are also a bit larger. In fact, site 12 is huge! This would be a great site if you have no more than five adults in your camping group. You'll have plenty of room to spread out your tents and the rest of your gear, and still have room to let the kids run around

RATINGS

Beauty: ☆ ☆ ☆ ☆ ☆
Privacy: ☆ ☆ ☆ ☆
Spaciousness: ☆ ☆ ☆ ☆
Quiet: ☆ ☆ ☆ ☆
Security: ☆ ☆ ☆ ☆ ☆
Cleanliness: ☆ ☆ ☆ ☆

and tire themselves out.

There is simply more room to spread out on the outer side of campground loops, and there's typically more forestation between sites, which deepens the feeling of solitude. Sites 9, 11, and 16 through 21 are located on the outside of the campground loop road, and all provide pleasant isolation and lots of space. Just past site 9, there's a trailhead for a short path down to Dry River.

One of the prettiest sites here is site 16. It's set off the campground loop road, with lots of room between it and neighboring sites. It's also the site closest to Dry River. Between sites 18 and 19, there are trails to the Dry River Connection. From the campground, it's 0.2 miles to Dry River, 2 miles to the Webster Cliff Trail, and 3 miles to the historic Willey House site.

Way off on its own, site 20 is another epic spot. It's incredibly spacious and surrounded by colossal deciduous trees with a few conifers mixed in, which gives the forest a diverse and interesting character.

There is still a decent sense of solitude to site 8, even though it's probably the most open site at Dry River. It's situated right where the campground loop reconnects with itself. Sites 4 through 7, and 22 through 24 are set up along the campground road leading to the loop, but they are all well off the road.

Sites 27 through 31 are closer to US 302, but they are among the nicest sites I've seen. Situated along a short spur off the road, just off to the right as you enter the campground (even before the ranger station), these sites are spacious and spread out.

The only site to which I wouldn't immediately gravitate is site 31, which is set at the very end of this short road and opens directly to it, so anyone driving down the road would look like they're going to drive right into your site. Still, it's very spacious and otherwise isolated, so it's not that bad. The only other drawback—and this is very minor—is that these sites are closer to US 302. This can make for a bit of daytime road noise, but at night, it's as silent as the rest of the White Mountains.

The character of Dry River Campground mirrors that of its setting within Crawford Notch. There's a

KEY INFORMATION

ADDRESS: Dry River Campground Crawford Notch State Park P.O. Box 177 US 302 Twin Mountain, NH 03595

OPERATED BY: New Hampshire Division of Parks and Recreation

INFORMATION: Crawford Notch State Park, (603) 374-2272

OPEN: Early May– early December

SITES: 36

EACH SITE HAS: Fire ring, picnic table

ASSIGNMENT: First come, first served; by reservation: (603) 271-3628, www.nhstateparks .org

REGISTRATION: At campground headquarters

FACILITIES: Hot showers, pit toilets

PARKING: At sites

FEE: $23

RESTRICTIONS: *Pets:* On leash only *Fires:* In fire rings only *Alcohol:* At sites only *Vehicles:* Parking at campsites only *Other:* Reservations require 2-night minimum stay; check in 1–8 p.m., check out by noon; quiet hours 10 p.m.–7 a.m.

MAP

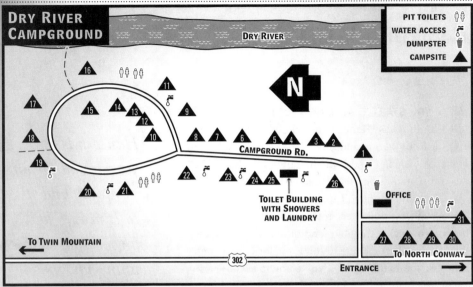

DRY RIVER CAMPGROUND

DRY RIVER

PIT TOILETS
WATER ACCESS
DUMPSTER
CAMPSITE

N

CAMPGROUND RD.

TOILET BUILDING
WITH SHOWERS
AND LAUNDRY

OFFICE

TO TWIN MOUNTAIN

302

ENTRANCE

TO NORTH CONWAY

GETTING THERE

From North Conway and Bartlett, continue north on US 302 and look for signs for the campground on the right.

pleasant feel to the diverse forest and campground, and no matter where you end up, you'll be in an excellent spot.

21
HANCOCK
CAMPGROUND

IF YOU START TRAVELING ALONG New Hampshire's fabled Kancamagus Highway heading east, or from the Lincoln side to the Conway side, Hancock Campground is the first of the six Kancamagus campgrounds you'll encounter.

It's also one of two campgrounds along the Kancamagus that is open year-round. The other is Blackberry Crossing, at the other end of the "Kanc," as the locals call it. If you come to the Kanc for cross-country skiing or snowshoeing, or if you come to ski at nearby Loon Mountain and you want to do it on the cheap and with a dash of added adventure, pitching your tent at Hancock is the way to go.

Sites 1 through 21 are Hancock's tent-only sites. Within this tent zone, the sites that seem the most off on their own are 1, 2, 10, 12, 14, and 15. Check out these sites first to see if they're available and if they fulfill your need for solitude.

There's a central parking area situated near the two loosely spaced loops along which all the tent sites are located. You don't park right at the site in many campgrounds, so be prepared to lug in your gear a short distance. There are several areas within the Kancamagus campgrounds that have these types of sites, which are perfect for tent camping.

The tent-only sites at Hancock are moderate in size and reasonably spaced. This area also has its own restroom, located right across from the sites, in the parking area, so you don't have far to walk when nature calls in the middle of the night.

The rest of the campground's 56 sites are a respectable distance from the tent-only area. You shouldn't discount these sites (22 through 56), even though you might find an RV or two. The sites are fairly spacious, and since the forest is pretty dense

> *Hancock is open year-round for winter camping, and it's close to Lincoln—so it's a good spot to camp with kids.*

RATINGS

Beauty: ✩ ✩ ✩ ✩
Privacy: ✩ ✩ ✩
Spaciousness: ✩ ✩ ✩
Quiet: ✩ ✩ ✩ ✩
Security: ✩ ✩ ✩ ✩
Cleanliness: ✩ ✩ ✩ ✩

KEY INFORMATION

here, they're nicely buffered from each other, especially those on the outer end of the loop (sites 35 through 40).

These sites are also set within a beautiful birch grove. The first time I visited Hancock Campground was on a classic New England fall day. There wasn't a cloud in the sky, and the air was cool and dry. The sky took on a crystalline azure color. With the combination of the brilliance of the sun and the reflection of the light off the green and yellow leaves of the birch trees, the forest seemed to sparkle.

Also within this loop is where you'll find the trailhead for the short path to the East Branch of the Pemigewasset River, which is a perfect spot to drop a hook in the water (the trail departs between sites 43 and 45 on the outer side of the loop). There are also a few spots where you can drop yourself in the water, but be careful. Even late in the summer, that water can be mighty chilly. When you're looking for the path, just look beyond the trees for the looming presence of Black Mountain to the south of Hancock Campground, and you'll know you're heading in the right direction.

All of the Kancamagus campgrounds are a stone's throw from a pristine river or any number of fabulous hiking trails. It would take you most of the summer to hike them all. Hancock is certainly no different. Right across the street, there's a trail that takes you up and over Potash Knob and Big Coolidge Mountain (and all the way to Mount Flume and Mount Liberty, if you want to go). For a mellower hike, you can walk along the course of the Pemigewasset River.

Hancock is also the campground on the Kancamagus that is closest to civilization. At 5 miles east of Lincoln, it's close enough to run over and pick up bread, milk, batteries, or anything else you may have forgotten or run out of. You could also have dinner or see a movie if you've been sleeping in a tent for several nights on end and need a little diversion.

The proximity to Lincoln makes Hancock one of the better Kancamagus campgrounds for families with small children. Kids love camping, but sometimes their tastes for dinner might include a pizza or hamburger,

MAP

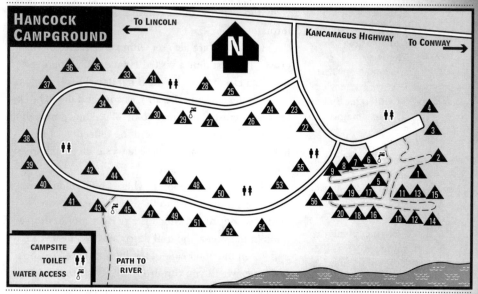

HANCOCK CAMPGROUND

To LINCOLN

N

KANCAMAGUS HIGHWAY   To CONWAY

CAMPSITE
TOILET
WATER ACCESS

PATH TO
RIVER

and if the weather hasn't been cooperative, an afternoon matinee can be just the antidote for a case of crankiness.

GETTING THERE

From Lincoln, follow Kancamagus Highway to Hancock Campground on your right. It's the first campground you'll come to. From Conway, follow Kancamagus Highway to Hancock Campground on your left. From this side, it will be the last campground you come to.

JIGGER JOHNSON CAMPGROUND

Jigger Johnson is the biggest campground on the Kancamagus, but it still has a cozy feel.

JIGGER **JOHNSON IS THE LARGEST** campground on the Kancamagus, but with its well-spaced loops, there's plenty of room for some high-quality tent camping beneath the statuesque conifers. There's one tent-only loop, which has nine sites reserved for our nylon-bound brethren, but the rest of the campground has plenty of sites where you can experience woodland solitude.

The tent loop is the first loop on the left, containing sites 1 through 9—spacious and set amid the forest's rolling contours. There is also a water spigot and a restroom just for this loop, so you won't have to go far for those essentials. Sites 6, 7, and 8, located at the far end of the loop, are the most spread out within the tent-only area. Whether you're occupying only one site or have come with several sites' worth of campers, head to the end of the loop first to see what's available.

If the tent loop is full, don't despair. There are plenty of other great sites throughout Jigger Johnson. Most of the sites along the northeastern end of the campground near the banks of the Swift River are spacious and set within a fairly dense forest. I especially like sites 47, 48, 50, 51, 53, 54, and 57. These feel most insular, plus they're close to the water spigots and the Swift River.

The sites on the loop to the right as you enter the campground, while a bit more out in the open, are also excellent spots. True, you run the risk of an RV lumbering up next to you, but if there are already a number of tents in the area and on either side, which is often the case, you know you'll be in for a nice night. Most of the RVs seem to gravitate toward the sites on the main road heading through the campground.

Over on the right-side loop, the shorter trees and lower brush are somewhat sparse. This does open up the whole area at the ground level, but that effect

RATINGS

Beauty: ✩ ✩ ✩ ✩
Privacy: ✩ ✩ ✩
Spaciousness: ✩ ✩ ✩ ✩
Quiet: ✩ ✩ ✩ ✩
Security: ✩ ✩ ✩ ✩
Cleanliness: ✩ ✩ ✩ ✩

combines with the towering pines that form the tall forest canopy to engender the forest with a surreal, almost mystical quality. This is particularly noticeable as dusk draws near. The sky overhead is still light, and the smoke from the campfires wafts through the trees and up to the forest canopy as darkness sneaks in beneath the pines. There's a cathedral-like atmosphere in this part of the campground in the quiet hours after dinner. The stillness is broken only by the occasional crack of a campfire.

Jigger Johnson, like the other campgrounds along the Kancamagus, is a self-serve kind of place. Enter the campground and find your perfect spot, then return to that odd-looking green cylinder, the "Iron Ranger," in Forest Service vernacular. Here's where you fill in your registration envelope, pay your fee, and slip it through the Iron Ranger's drop slot. If you need to speak with a real ranger or buy some firewood, you'll find the rangers down the road that leads off to the right just past the Iron Ranger.

This is also where you'll find the showers. Jigger Johnson is the only campground along the Kanc that has coin-operated hot showers, so don't be surprised if there are a few people waiting to clean up. There's even a little parking loop (off to the left as you enter the campground) for shower-seekers from the other Kanc campgrounds.

A series of interpretive programs on Saturday evenings throughout the summer focuses on a particular aspect of the local flora and fauna and can be quite informative and entertaining. The rangers who present these programs truly know their stuff, and they love to share their knowledge. The programs are usually held in the small, open area off to the left as you're heading down the short road to the showers.

Jigger Johnson is located near the intersection of Bear Notch Road and the Kanc, so you could get here easily from Bartlett or from either side of the Kanc. If you run out of something, it's 9 miles to Bartlett and 13 miles to Conway.

The campground is also very close to some classic White Mountain hiking. Turn left out of the campground to get to trailheads for the Champney Falls

KEY INFORMATION

ADDRESS:	Jigger Johnson Campground 33 Kancamagus Highway Albany, NH 03818
OPERATED BY:	U.S. Forest Service
INFORMATION:	Saco Ranger Station 33 Kancamagus Highway RFD 1, Box 94 Conway, NH 03818 (603) 447-5448
OPEN:	Mid May– mid-October
SITES:	74
EACH SITE HAS:	Fire ring, picnic table
ASSIGNMENT:	First come, first served
REGISTRATION:	Select site, then pay at self-service fee station
FACILITIES:	Pay showers, flush toilets, water spigots
PARKING:	At sites
FEE:	$20 for 1 vehicle, $5 for extra vehicle
RESTRICTIONS:	*Pets:* Dogs on leash only *Fires:* In fire rings only *Alcohol:* At sites only *Vehicles:* Maximum 2 per site *Other:* Maximum 8 people per site; 14-day maximum stay

MAP

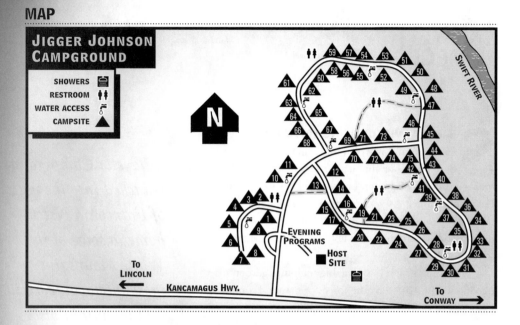

JIGGER JOHNSON
CAMPGROUND

SHOWERS
RESTROOM
WATER ACCESS
CAMPSITE

N

SWIFT RIVER

EVENING
PROGRAMS

HOST
SITE

TO
LINCOLN

KANCAMAGUS HWY.

TO
CONWAY

GETTING THERE

From Lincoln, follow Kancamagus Highway to Jigger
Johnson Campground on
your left. From Conway, follow Kancamagus Highway to
Jigger Johnson Campground
on your right, shortly after
Bear Notch Road, also on the
right.

Trail (which leads to the Three Sisters and the Middle
Sister trails) or the Bolles Trail. Turn right on the Kanc
out of Jigger Johnson to get to the Oliverian Brook,
Downes Brook, Sabbaday Brook, or Sawyer Pond
trails. Pack a few extra energy bars and plenty of water
if you embark on a hike up the Champney Falls or
Middle Sister trails. These lead to Mount Chocourua
and the Three Sisters, a beautiful but intense hike.

You can enjoy some great hikes leaving right out
of the campground as well—no driving required! The
trail that leads down to the banks of the Swift River
intersects a trail that runs along the backside of the
campground. This mellow path follows the Swift both
upstream and downstream for a distance, passing by
some beautiful bends in the river and through delightfully aromatic groves of birch and pine. It's a great
hike to take with kids because it's relatively flat and
there are all sorts of wonderful things to see and experience. Kids can spend hours poking around the banks
of the Swift River, and despite its name, this segment
of the river is usually fairly tame.

SIMPLY BY VIRTUE OF ITS LOCATION, Lafayette Campground is worth including in this guidebook. The fact that it's a super campground makes it that much better. Lafayette is nestled in the Franconia Valley. As you drive up the Franconia Notch Parkway toward the campground, your view is framed by Cannon Mountain to the left and Mount Lafayette to the right.

Franconia Notch is a veritable sculpture garden displaying works shaped by the forces of nature. From the glaciers that carved the landscape millions of years ago to the tenacious and incessant wind and water, the lay of the land here is as dramatic as anywhere else in New Hampshire. From the waterfalls of the Flume Gorge and the swirling pools of the Basin to the Old Man of the Mountain and Indian Head formations presiding over the eastern flanks of the Presidential range, you could spend weeks here before retracing your steps.

The notch is also headquarters for just about every outdoor activity. There's fly-fishing at nearby Echo Lake (for information on fishing licenses, see Appendix C, page 232); a bike path that winds along the base of the notch; and some fantastic treks for hikers of any ability. Right from the campground, the Lonesome Lake Trail takes you 1,000 feet above the floor of the notch to Lonesome Lake. The trailhead for the 1.5-mile hike is near the entrance to the campground.

There's also a trailhead between sites 67 and 68 that leads to the Basin. From the Basin, you could hike up to Kinsman Falls on Cascade Brook. Follow the half-mile Basin Cascades Trail from the Basin to reach this beautiful and secluded spot.

Lafayette Campground is set beneath a fairly dense forest of conifers and hardwoods. Sites 1 through 51 are available only by reservation, so if you haven't made one, start your search at site 52 and work your way up.

> *Lafayette Campground is tucked into the valley of Franconia Notch, home to some of the White Mountains' most spectacular hiking and mountain vistas.*

RATINGS

Beauty: ✩ ✩ ✩ ✩
Privacy: ✩ ✩ ✩
Spaciousness: ✩ ✩ ✩ ✩ ✩
Quiet: ✩ ✩ ✩
Security: ✩ ✩ ✩
Cleanliness: ✩ ✩ ✩ ✩

ADDRESS: Lafayette
Campground
Franconia Notch
State Park
Franconia Notch
Parkway
Franconia, NH 03580

OPERATED BY: New Hampshire
Division of Parks
and Recreation

INFORMATION: Lafayette
Campground,
(603) 823-9513

OPEN: Mid-May–
Columbus Day

SITES: 97 sites

EACH SITE HAS: Fire ring, picnic
table

ASSIGNMENT: First come,
first served; by
reservation (88 sites
by reservation only):
(603) 271-3628,
www.nhstateparks
.org

REGISTRATION: At campground
headquarters

FACILITIES: Hot showers, flush
toilets, water

PARKING: At sites

FEE: $24

RESTRICTIONS: *Pets:* Prohibited
Fires: In fire rings
only
Alcohol: At sites only
Vehicles: Parking at
sites only
Other: Reservations
require 2-night
minimum stay;
check in 1–8 p.m.,
check out by noon;
quiet hours
10 p.m.–7 a.m.

The sites numbered in the upper 40s are very spacious. The forest overhead is open to the sky, which lets a lot of sunlight filter down to the floor of the campsites. Sites 47 and 49 are too open. These sites are also situated right along the campground road. Site 50 is open and set right on the road, but it also has the Pemigewasset River running along behind it. Site 51, across the campground road from 50, is also very exposed to the road.

Farther down the campground road on this side, site 52 is a secluded site. It's set off the road and also has the Pemigewasset running behind it. The platform where you'd set up your tent and a picnic table are a bit lower than the road, which adds a degree of seclusion.

The Lonesome Lake Trail runs between sites 53 and 54. Sites 54, 56, and 57 are open to one another and to the neighboring sites. Sites 56 and 58 would be good pair of sites for a larger group needing two contiguous sites. There is a bit of road noise in the background in this part of the campground from the Franconia Notch Parkway. This decreases as you get farther from the road and deeper into the woods.

Sites 61 and 63 are secluded from one another and the neighboring sites. These two sites are also quite spacious. Sites 64 and 66 make another good pair of sites well suited for a large group. They are right along the banks of the Pemigewasset, which defines the eastern border of the campground.

Both the ground cover and the forest canopy are less dense in this corner of the campground, so sites 58 through 70 are spacious and sunlit. Lots of breeze flows through here.

A huge maple tree grows up through the center of site 88. This spacious site is on the outside of the campground loop. It's fairly well isolated from the sites on either side, but it's a bit open to the road.

Set off the campground road on a small rise and surrounded by a fairly dense grove of young deciduous trees, site 97 is nicely secluded. However, it's right across the road from the restrooms. Sites 92 and 94 are too open, and 94 is also next to the restroom building on the same side of the road. The Lonesome Lake Trail runs through the campground between sites 93 and 95 on one side of the road and sites 92 and 94 on the other, so these would be good sites to choose if you wanted to be right on the trail; but expect passersby.

The area with sites 73 through 78 is pleasant. These sites feel a bit more privately than some of the sites on the outside of the campground loop. Site 73 is very spacious, open, and sunny. Site 76 is a bit more shaded. Site 75 is also bright, airy, and framed by a wall of maple trees. Alas, site 79 is too close to the restrooms.

Now, back to the reservation-only sites. Perched at an odd little intersection of the campground loop roads, site 43 has lots of woods surrounding it, with no neighbors on either side. Sites 40 and 29 are also at odd angles in this three-way intersection, but consequently they offer decent privacy. Site 29 is very open and sunny, with large granite boulders framing the back border of the site.

Sites 36 and 37 are set up for wheelchair access. These are large sites set within a grove of fairly dense, mixed forest. Site 27 is very spacious, but it's a bit too open and is on the campground loop road.

Set in the woods around a small grassy field, sites 22 through 26 are open and pastoral. They are not quite as private as the more densely wooded sites, but scenic nonetheless. It almost feels as if they were an afterthought.

Site 17 is open but secluded and set on a small rise overlooking the field through a loosely spaced grove of young deciduous trees. Sites 15 and 16 are group sites. Right on the grassy field, is wide-open prairie camping. There's no privacy, but you'd have plenty of room for a group, and a clear shot at the sky for stargazing. Sites 18 and 19 are close to the restrooms but tucked into the woods a bit deeper for privacy. Within this group, sites 11 and 12 are also a bit too close to the restrooms.

The small loop with sites 1 through 10 also surrounds a small grassy field. These areas make great spots to let kids run around, throw a Frisbee, or otherwise burn off some steam while you're relaxing. Sites 7 through 10 are quite nice; spacious, open, and fairly well isolated from neighbors. Sites 5 and 6 and sites 1 and 3 would make good pairs of sites for larger groups, as they are open to each other. If you didn't know your neighbors before setting up camp here, you would shortly thereafter.

There's a small amphitheater and rows of benches at the entrance to the 1-through-10 loop, where the rangers run nature programs. Check with them as you register to find out what's on the schedule.

MAP

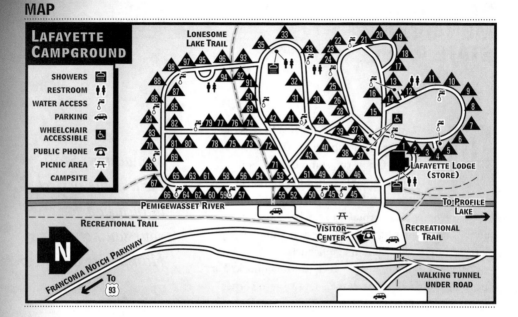

GETTING THERE

Follow Interstate 93 north to
Franconia Notch Parkway.
This is a divided highway, so
you'll actually drive past the
campground and take the
next exit off the parkway,
then head south. From there,
follow the signs for the
campground on the right as
you head south.

24
MONADNOCK
STATE PARK

MOUNT MONADNOCK IS RENOWNED as one of the most frequently climbed mountains in the world. On warm, summer weekend days, there is often a veritable conga line of hikers making their way up the fabulous White Dot Trail, or any of the other classic routes, to the bald, treeless summit. Its popularity, however, does nothing to detract from its allure and magnificence.

Why do so many people flock to Monadnock? For one thing, perched as it is in the southwestern corner of New Hampshire, it's fairly accessible from most of southern New Hampshire, northern Massachusetts, and eastern Vermont. It's a moderate hike, certainly when compared to some of the longer or steeper hikes you'll find farther north in New Hampshire's White Mountains or Vermont's Green Mountains. The predominant attraction has to be the view from Monadnock's summit. It is absolutely huge. It's expansive. It's a sweeping, panoramic view that extends in every direction as far as you can see, which is pretty far when the air is clear and the sun is brilliant.

From there you see nearby Dublin Lake and the gently rolling and densely forested topography of southern New England. Small towns here and there punctuate the undulating coniferous carpet. The unfettered views from Monadnock's summit are a product of Monadnock's history. It appears to poke above the tree line, but at 3,165 feet, it's really not quite tall enough. The mountain owes its treeless summit to massive fires of the early 1800s. They resulted in Mount Monadnock going prematurely bald.

While the day crowds at the mountain may seem a bit overwhelming, once they've returned home for the night, you and a small group of campers will have the park and the campground at the mountain's base to yourselves. The campground is fairly small, with 21

> *Monadnock State Park is the perfect launch pad for your southern New Hampshire adventures.*

RATINGS

Beauty: ✪ ✪ ✪ ✪
Privacy: ✪ ✪ ✪
Spaciousness: ✪ ✪ ✪ ✪ ✪
Quiet: ✪ ✪ ✪ ✪
Security: ✪ ✪ ✪ ✪
Cleanliness: ✪ ✪ ✪ ✪ ✪

ADDRESS: Monadnock
State Park
P.O. Box 181, NH 124
Jaffrey, NH
03452-0181

OPERATED BY: New Hampshire
Division of Parks
and Recreation

INFORMATION: Monadnock
State Park,
(603) 532-8862

OPEN: Year-round;
campground not
plowed in winter;
reservations
taken mid-May–
Columbus Day for
family sites; group
sites reservable
year-round

SITES: 21 individual sites,
7 group sites

EACH SITE HAS: Fire ring, picnic
table

ASSIGNMENT: First come, first
served; by
reservation:
(603) 271-3628, www
.nhstateparks.org or
(877) NHPARKS

REGISTRATION: At campground
headquarters

FACILITIES: Coin-operated
showers, flush
toilets, vault toilets,
camp store, water
spigots

PARKING: At sites; additional
parking available

FEE: $23

RESTRICTIONS: *Pets:* Prohibited
Fires: In fire rings
only
Alcohol: At sites only
Vehicles: At sites only
Other: Reservations
require 2-night
minimum stay

individual and 7 group sites. A new family site is opening in 2009 in the Gilson Pond area. As you enter the park, you pass the ranger's toll station. Here, you instantly discover the park's primary restriction if you happen to have a four-legged member of the family in your car. There are no dogs allowed at the campground or anywhere within Monadnock State Park. Assuming you're not breaking that most sacred of rules, continue into the park. The campground is just up the road off to the right.

Most of the sites within this campground are available by reservation only. The letter-designated sites, A through G, are the group sites. These are available exclusively by reservation. This poses an interesting predicament, as some of the nicer sites, in my view, are the non-reservable sites. You could wing it and try your luck getting one of them. If fortune smiles, you'll have a grand camping experience. However, you could also find the campground full to capacity, which is a very real possibility considering the traffic this state park gets during the summer.

Even though the campground is right off the road leading into the park (near the day parking for hikers, the camp store, and the primary trailhead for getting onto the mountain), you'll still feel as if you've left all that behind when you turn into the campground. Heading right on the campground loop road brings you to sites 6 through 8. These are tucked off on their own. The forest of mixed conifers, birch, and other hardwoods is fairly dense here, so you still feel as if the woods are surrounding you and your campsite. Site 14 is another of the non-reservable sites that's tucked into its own grove of trees. All of these sites on the outer side of the campground seem to have a bit more space in between.

Monadnock State Park is a great spot to come with a group for some weekend hiking. The sites designated for group camping are quite nice, and I'd be thrilled to spend a few nights in one of these group sites with a band of hiking compadres. Site C is one of the nicer group sites. It's set against a gently sloping hill within a grove of loosely spaced, very homogenous pine trees. Site D is another beautiful site that is also set within its own pine grove. There's a stand of young white pines lining the perimeter like vigilant sentries. All of the group sites have two picnic tables (the individual sites have one), which is a thoughtful setup since you'll certainly have more people in these sites needing a place to sit.

There are numerous vault toilet facilities spread throughout the campground, so you'll never have to amble too far when nature calls. If you prefer, there are also flush toilets located just outside the campground. There are several water fountains, but when you need to fill your drinking-water bottles, there's a spring up on the mountain about 0.75 miles from the campground. Assemble the troops and take a short hike up the White Dot Trail to the spring off to the left, just below the junction where the Spruce Link Trail veers off to the left. Treat yourself to some cold, crystal-clear, mountain spring water. It's well worth the effort.

Ah yes, the hiking. There is a plethora of hiking trails wending its way throughout Monadnock State Park, all leading up, over, and around the mountain. The White Dot Trail is the most popular route up to the summit. The White Cross Trail, which forks off the White Dot Trail just past the Spruce Link Trail, is another good option. Both have a few spots where you're doing a little hand-over-hand scrambling up and over the rocks. Both also pass across a couple of open ledges on the way up, where you'll get your first taste of the sweeping vistas.

From the summit, and from several other trails leading off the mountain in all directions, you could hike as far as Mount Sunapee if you're so inclined. That brings up a point about directions. If you're coming into the park from Dublin on Dublin Road, you'll see two places marked as Monadnock State Park. The first is the trailhead for the Birchtoft Trail. Don't turn in here, keep going another half mile or so to the main part of the state park, where you'll find the campground. Keep the location of that trailhead in mind though. If you want to try a longer route to the summit of Monadnock, the Birchtoft Trail is a fantastic hike.

Mount Monadnock does get a lot of hikers, but there's always a bit of the mountain with a good view that you can have all to yourself, just for the moment.

MAP

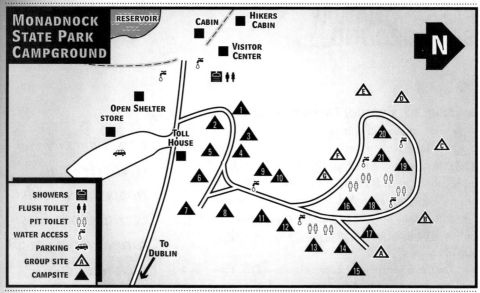

GETTING THERE

Follow Route 101 to Dublin. If heading west on 101, take Jaffrey Center Road on the left after going through town. There's a sign for Monadnock State Park. Heading east on 101, take Jaffrey Center Road on the right, after Dublin Lake and before downtown Dublin. Follow this road for several miles to the campground on the right.

25
PASSACONAWAY CAMPGROUND

THE SITES WITHIN **PASSACONAWAY** Campground are all quite spacious. This can be both a blessing and a curse. Of all the campgrounds along the Kancamagus, Passaconaway is probably most conducive to RVs. They are neither catered to (no hookups) nor excluded, but many of the smaller campsites at the other Kancamagus campgrounds naturally keep out the land yachts just by virtue of their size or shape.

On the other hand, the spaciousness of the Passaconaway sites makes them well suited to larger groups or families that need a little extra breathing room. The relatively central location along Kancamagus Highway also puts you in a good spot if you're not sure what part of the Kanc you want to explore. You'll be close to Rocky Gorge, Sabbaday Falls, the Swift River picnic area, and the myriad trailheads spread along the length of this superlative stretch of road.

The forest separating the individual sites at Passaconaway is fairly dense, so even if an RV or a larger group plunks down next to you, you won't see all that much of them. There is lots of undergrowth, which provides seclusion and adds to the silence of the woods. Besides spacious sites, quiet is a prevailing attribute of Passaconaway. All you'll hear is an occasional vehicle zipping past on the Kanc and the soft rush of the wind in the evergreens, punctuated by the chatter of the forest birds and animals.

There are two loops. Sites 1 through 11 are in the loop off to the right as you enter the campground. Sites 12 through 33 are in the loop off to the left. The campsites are carved out of a dense forest of mostly coniferous trees, so there's a cool, dark, shaded feeling to the campground.

At the beginning of the 1-to-11 loop, sites 2, 3, and 11 are too open and close to the restrooms for my

> *Passaconaway is a relatively small campground with very spacious sites carved out of a dense evergreen forest.*

RATINGS

Beauty: ✪ ✪ ✪ ✪
Privacy: ✪ ✪ ✪ ✪
Spaciousness: ✪ ✪ ✪ ✪
Quiet: ✪ ✪ ✪ ✪ ✪
Security: ✪ ✪ ✪ ✪
Cleanliness: ✪ ✪ ✪ ✪

ADDRESS:	Passaconaway Campground Kancamagus Highway Bartlett, NH 03812
OPERATED BY:	U.S. Forest Service
INFORMATION:	Saco Ranger Station 33 Kancamagus Highway RFD 1, Box 94 Conway, NH 03818 (603) 447-5448
OPEN:	Mid-May– mid-October
SITES:	33
EACH SITE HAS:	Fire ring, picnic table
ASSIGNMENT:	First come, first served
REGISTRATION:	Select site then pay at self-service fee station
FACILITIES:	Vault toilets, hand pumps for water
PARKING:	At sites
FEE:	$18 for 1 vehicle, $5 for extra vehicle
RESTRICTIONS:	*Pets:* Dogs on leash only *Fires:* In fire rings only *Alcohol:* At campsites only *Vehicles:* 2 per site maximum *Other:* 8 people per site maximum, 14-day maximum stay

taste. Sites 5 to 10 are set along the outer edge of the loop off to the right. These sites, mostly by virtue of their location on the outside of the loop road, provide the most solitude. There's simply more room between the sites.

My favorite site on this loop, and one of the best in the campground, is site 10. This site is set well off on its own, with plenty of space between the neighboring sites on either side. It's also farther off the campground loop road, for an enhanced sense of isolation.

In the 12-to-33 loop, the forest is even denser than in the 1-to-11 loop. On this side of the campground, the forest is composed primarily of pines and maples, many towering around 80 feet. A moderately dense understory fills in the forest picture and adds to the sense of seclusion between the individual campsites. In this loop, sites 13, 14, and 15 are close to the restroom.

The sites on this loop are located both along the inside and outside of the campground road. There's a small picnic area near site 13. There are pros and cons to this. It's a nice place to have the kids running around close to the campsite, but it could also be a bit noisier during the day. Like most of life's major decisions, whether or not you choose this site will probably be dictated by the presence of little ones.

There's a trailhead right next to site 18. From the Passaconaway Campground, you are near several hiking trails suitable for all ability levels. There is the long, but not too steep, Sawyer Pond Trail and the shorter but steeper Downes Brook, Sabbaday Brook, and Oliverian Brook trails across the Kanc.

The campground host is at site 19. This is a good place to stop if you need a suggestion for daytime activities, or just to catch a bit of local lore.

The sites numbered in the lower 20s are generally a bit smaller than the rest of Passaconaway's sites and are packed in more tightly. In this group, you're closer to your neighbors and sacrifice a modicum of privacy and quiet, but you're also less likely to have an RV drop anchor nearby. Still, there is a decent amount of forest buffering these sites.

Huge maples frame sites 22 and 23. There are also massive maples growing up within the sites themselves.

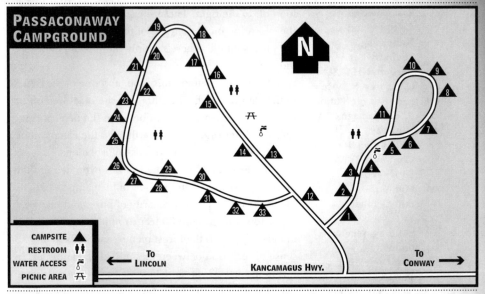

PASSACONAWAY
CAMPGROUND

N

CAMPSITE ▲
RESTROOM ♀♂
WATER ACCESS
PICNIC AREA ⛱

To
← LINCOLN

KANCAMAGUS HWY.

To
CONWAY →

You feel as if you're camping among magnificent trees, and you truly are.

There's a short hike in to site 24 from where you park. This is the key site here at Passaconaway. The distance from the campground loop road lends it a deep sense of seclusion.

Considering Passaconaway's central location on the Kanc, it's a fine spot to set up camp, especially if you are able to secure site 10 or site 24.

GETTING THERE

Passaconaway Campground is almost in the center of Kancamagus Highway. From Lincoln, follow Kancamagus Highway 16 miles to Passaconaway Campground on the left. From Conway, follow Kancamagus Highway 15 miles to Passaconaway campground on the right.

> *The campground at Pawtuckaway State Park has a lot of sites, but they're split into three different areas so it has a more intimate feel than you might expect. There are also many sites right on the shores of Lake Pawtuckaway.*

THERE ARE CAMPSITES AT Pawtuckaway State Park that give you the atmosphere of island camping with the ease of car camping. It's a big place, with 193 sites, but the three separate camping areas feel like individual campgrounds.

Horse Island has many of the best sites within the campground—that is to say the most sites right on the shores of Pawtuckaway Lake. Big Island has some pristine water view sites, but most of the sites in this area are inland. Neal's Cove is near the store, the beach, and the group camping area. These sites, because of their proximity to the beach and playground, are great for families with kids.

Horse Island is home to sites 1 through 80. The island is covered in a fairly dense forest, which lends a nice woodland feel and sense of privacy to most of these sites. The forest is composed of mixed hardwoods and conifers, although it's a bit heavier on the conifers, which fill in the forest and provide cool, dark stillness and seclusion. The sites themselves are clean and spacious, and most have a firm, sandy surface on which to pitch your tent.

I was camped on Horse Island once and had just finished cleaning up from breakfast when a gray heron walked right through my site as if he owned the place. He may well have, but I was too flustered and spellbound to ask him. At Pawtuckaway State Park, Horse Island is where you want to be. The sites that aren't right on the water at least have a water view.

The top-notch Horse Island waterfront sites include 38, 42, 43, 44, 45, 46, and 47. Swimming is not permitted from campsites because there is a considerable amount of boat traffic on the lake, especially on the weekends. But, you could easily launch a canoe or kayak right from your site. Swimming is allowed in the beach and boat-launch areas.

RATINGS

Beauty: ✿ ✿ ✿ ✿
Privacy: ✿ ✿ ✿ ✿
Spaciousness: ✿ ✿ ✿ ✿
Quiet: ✿ ✿ ✿
Security: ✿ ✿ ✿ ✿
Cleanliness: ✿ ✿ ✿ ✿

While site 48 is situated near an intersection of the campground road, its lakeside setting more than compensates for any traffic might pass. Sites 74, 75, and 77 also have nice lakeside settings.

The cluster of sites 65 through 70 is grouped at one end of Horse Island. These sites have dramatic, lakeside settings. Sites 67 through 69 are perched on their own peninsula jutting out from the southeastern end of the island. If your group is large enough to need three sites and you secure these, you will indeed be set.

There is a boat launch and lake access right near sites 58, 60, 62, and 63. These are perfect sites if you like to begin or end your day with a blissful paddle on the still waters of the sleepy lake. Sites 53, 54, and 55 are also primo lakeside spots. These sites are set within loosely spaced forest right on the shores of Pawtuckaway Lake, which allows for dramatic views, cool breezes, and shafts of sunlight. I have no scientific evidence to support this, but these lakeside sites seemed less buggy than the inland sites to me.

Sites 1, 2, and 25 are right off the campground road leading onto Horse Island, but they offer seclusion, being tucked down off the road amid a dense grove of spruce. Sites 4 and 7 are nicely isolated and set down off the campground loop road facing a small cove. These sites are in a dense spruce grove, where the forest floor gently rolls down to the lakeside. The main body of the lake is around the corner, so it's quieter here as you're removed from the primary thoroughfare through Pawtuckaway Lake. The lake can get pretty heavily populated with ski boats, jet skis, and other vessels making more noise than the rhythmic splash of a kayak or canoe paddle.

KEY INFORMATION

ADDRESS:	Pawtuckaway State Park
	128 Mountain Road
	Nottingham, NH 03290
OPERATED BY:	New Hampshire Division of Parks and Recreation
INFORMATION:	Pawtuckaway State Park, (603) 895-3031
OPEN:	Early May–early October (although Neals Cove and Big Island close after Labor Day weekend)
SITES:	195
EACH SITE HAS:	Fire ring, picnic table
ASSIGNMENT:	First come, first served; by reservation at www.nhstateparks.org or New Hampshire Division of Parks and Recreation office at (603) 271-3628
REGISTRATION:	At campground headquarters
FACILITIES:	Flush toilets, hot showers, water spigots, boat launch, canoe and paddle-boat rentals
PARKING:	At sites
FEE:	$24–$32, depending on location of site
RESTRICTIONS:	*Pets:* On leash only
	Fires: In established fire rings only
	Alcohol: At sites only
	Vehicles: Parking at campsites only, 2 vehicles per site maximum
	Other: Reservations require a 2-night minimum stay, check in between 1 p.m. and 8 p.m., check out by noon, quiet hours from 10 p.m.–7 a.m.

MAP

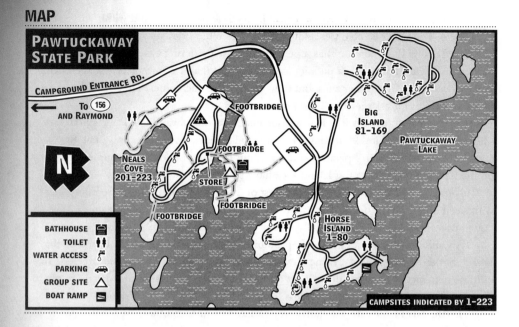

PAWTUCKAWAY STATE PARK

CAMPGROUND ENTRANCE RD.

To 156 AND RAYMOND

FOOTBRIDGE

FOOTBRIDGE

BIG ISLAND 81-169

PAWTUCKAWAY LAKE

NEALS COVE 201-223

STORE

FOOTBRIDGE

FOOTBRIDGE

HORSE ISLAND 1-80

BATHHOUSE	
TOILET	
WATER ACCESS	
PARKING	
GROUP SITE	
BOAT RAMP	

CAMPSITES INDICATED BY 1-223

MAP

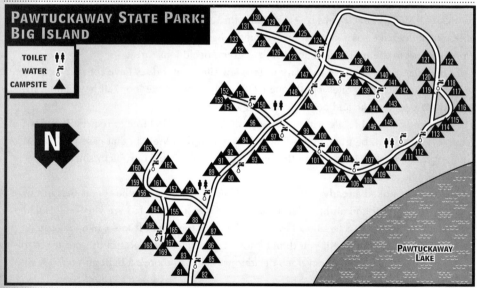

PAWTUCKAWAY STATE PARK: BIG ISLAND

TOILET	
WATER	
CAMPSITE	

PAWTUCKAWAY LAKE

The sites numbered in the teens are set beneath a loose forest and within view of a small cove. The water is often peaceful and quiet here but does get stirred up during the day. Site 21 is on the water and has a perfectly flat area, offering easy access for launching a canoe or kayak. This site is a paddler's dream. Sites 26 and 27 are nicely isolated from both the road and from other sites, but they are close to each other. They would make a nice pair of sites for a larger family or group.

The Big Island (sounds like Hawaii) section of Pawtuckaway State Park is home to sites 81 through 169. Sites 96 through 169 are available by reservation only. The first come, first served sites are spacious and set within fairly dense forest. A couple of the sites on the left as you enter the Big Island area have steep driveways.

Overall, Big Island is hillier than the rest of the campground. There are many sites with steep entries up or down from the road. Just keep that in mind as you select a site so you're not surprised. This is especially true of sites 164 through 169.

RVs and trailers are not expressly prohibited from the sites on Horse Island or Big Island, but those steep, twisty, or narrow entries leading into the sites would preclude one of these behemoths plunking down next to you. There are some sites that are more open than others, but for the most part, access (or lack thereof) is your best friend.

The Big Island sites are also fairly well isolated from each other, especially sites 162 and 163. These two are situated at the end of a short spur off the campground road and are set within a dense forest of mixed hardwoods and evergreens.

Sites 90 through 93 are set within a deep, dark spruce forest. After Site 93, the forest population shifts to deciduous trees. Walking through the campground road past these sites, it can feel like someone just turned on the lights. You move from the dense, dark spruce forest to the more open and brilliant green deciduous forest.

Big Island doesn't have as many water-view sites, but it does have some. Site 108 gets you back on the water. Sites 113 through 118, in their own little loop, all have an unimpeded view of the lake and access to launch a canoe or kayak.

The most desirable site within this section is site 122. Feel free to request it, unless, of course, I happen to be traveling to Pawtuckaway that day. Well, in that case you can still request it. We'll just have to share the site, which shouldn't be a problem since site 122 is absolutely huge.

Site 122 booked already? Not to worry. There are plenty of other great sites in this part of the campground and the 123-to-133 loop. Sites 130 and 133 are very well isolated at the end of this loop. Site 131, on the other hand, is too open. It looks like you could drive right through the site if you didn't know it was there. The sites in this corner of the campground are set beneath an open deciduous forest, so there's a light and open feel to them.

At the end of the 134-to-146 loop, sites 141 to 143 are quite secluded in their own little cluster. Sites 141 and 142 are actually quite close together but very well situated for a group needing two contiguous sites. Sites 150 through 152 are up off the road for a solid sense of seclusion. Site 96 is perched down off an intersection of the road where the 150-to-154 road heads off, but the site is well isolated by the dense forest and quite large.

MAP

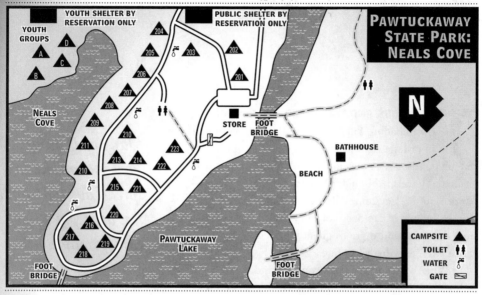

YOUTH SHELTER BY
RESERVATION ONLY

YOUTH
GROUPS

204

A D

205 203 202

C 206 201

B

207

208 STORE FOOT
BRIDGE

NEALS
COVE 209 210

BATHHOUSE

211 223

213 214 222 BEACH

210

215 221

220

216

217 219

218

PAWTUCKAWAY
LAKE

FOOT
BRIDGE

FOOT
BRIDGE

PUBLIC SHELTER BY
RESERVATION ONLY

PAWTUCKAWAY
STATE PARK:
NEALS COVE

N

CAMPSITE ▲
TOILET 👫
WATER 🚰
GATE

GETTING THERE

Follow Route 101 to 156 in Raymond. Follow Route 156 to Mountain Road, and then follow the signs for the park.

Neals Cove is actually the first camping area you come to on the 2-mile access road leading into Pawtuckaway State Park. Most of these sites are smaller but carved out of dense forest, so what they lack in spaciousness they make up for in seclusion. There's a dense, inland feel as you enter this part of the campground, even though you're still quite close to the lake. The beach, camp store, reservation-only group camping areas, picnic area, playground, and baseball field are also near Neals Cove.

Within this part of the campground, sites 206 and up are set along the water within a loosely spaced forest for dramatic water views and some nice breezes to cool down your campsite. Site 221 is somewhat open to the road but set beneath a dense and statuesque spruce grove. The towering spruce trees populating the forest at Neals Cove give the woods a majestic feel. There's a footbridge right next to site 218 leading onto another small island. This island doesn't have any campsites, but it's a perfect spot to hike out with a lunch or to just sit and watch the lake in the early morning or at dusk.

THE WOODS AND THE WATER are a powerful combination. Pillsbury State Park has both and in just the right proportions—a series of crystalline ponds cast against a dense blanket of forest like scattered jewels. Although it's part of the New Hampshire State Park system, Pillsbury is a little-known gem. It rests quietly in the deep forest just south of the far more popular and more frequently visited Sunapee State Park, and that's just fine.

When I first entered this campground, I was immediately struck with a moral and ethical dilemma. "Do I really want to tell anyone else about this place?" I honestly didn't ruminate on this for long, though. After considering the proclivities and desires of the sort of reader who would buy this book and would naturally seek out magical spots like this, I had to include Pillsbury State Park. There is not a bad site in the whole place, and many of the sites are elevated to paradise status, especially those at the water's edge.

As soon as you pull into the lengthy access road, which winds along the shores of Butterfield Pond and then May Pond, you'll know you've found someplace special. If you've come to fully immerse yourself in the solitude of the deep wilderness, you have most definitely come to the right place. The campsites are spread out along this road, either alone or in clusters. Most are right on or very close to the shores of May Pond. Several are inland, tucked into the dense forest that surrounds the ponds and marshy areas in the park.

The first sites you'll come to are 1 and 1A, off the main access road to the left at the end of a short drive. You can park at site 1, but 1A is a walk-in site. These are the only two sites on the shores of Vickery Pond, one of the smaller ponds in the park. Want to be off by yourself? Bring a small group, even just two couples; you'll have this pond to yourself.

> *Many of Pillsbury State Park's campsites are so spread out that you'll feel as if you have the campground to yourself.*

RATINGS

Beauty: ✩ ✩ ✩ ✩ ✩
Privacy: ✩ ✩ ✩ ✩ ✩
Spaciousness: ✩ ✩ ✩ ✩ ✩
Quiet: ✩ ✩ ✩ ✩ ✩
Security: ✩ ✩ ✩ ✩ ✩
Cleanliness: ✩ ✩ ✩ ✩ ✩

ADDRESS: Pillsbury State Park
Route 31
Washington, NH
03280

OPERATED BY: New Hampshire
Division of Parks
and Recreation

INFORMATION: Pillsbury State Park
(603) 863-2860

OPEN: Early May–
late October

SITES: 41 sites, including
2 canoe sites

EACH SITE HAS: Fire ring

ASSIGNMENT: All but 7 sites are by
reservation only; the
rest are first come,
first served. Make
reservations at
www.nhstateparks
.org or New
Hampshire Division
of Parks and
Recreation office at
(603) 271-3628.

REGISTRATION: At campground
headquarters

FACILITIES: Pit toilet, water
spigots, playground,
canoe rentals

PARKING: At sites or in small
parking areas for
hike-in or canoe sites

FEE: $21

RESTRICTIONS: *Pets:* Dog on leash
only
Fires: In fire rings
only
Alcohol: At sites only
Vehicles: Parking at or
near campsites, only
2 vehicles per site
Other: Reservations
require a 2-night
minimum stay; check
in between 1 p.m.
and 8 p.m., check out
by noon; quiet hours
from 10 p.m.–7 a.m.

Next along the main road is site 2. Although this site is right off the access road, it, too, is completely on its own. This is a great spot if you want to enjoy water-front camping in relative solitude because it is perched on the shore of Butterfield Pond. The only other site on this pond is site 39, on the other side of the pond—accessible only by canoe or kayak.

Sites 3 through 7 are grouped together in a small cluster farther up the road on the right. These are set on a small peninsula that helps define the border between Butterfield Pond and May Pond. There is also a pair of pit toilets here. Farther along the road, also waterside, is the small loop with sites 9 through 19. These sites are within the largest and most densely packed cluster of sites in the park, but even these are quite nice. Within this loop, go for sites 11, 12, and 14, as they are right on the shores of May Pond. Site 15 is pretty darn close to the pond as well.

Toward the end of the campground road are sites 23, 24, 26, and 40. At site 40, you park across from a footbridge over a small stream. Cross the bridge and turn right on the footpath that leads down to site 40, nestled right on the shoreline of the pond. It is well worth every trip to the car. You'll have your own slice of forest right on your own corner of the pond.

If you're a paddler, do what you can to reserve either site 38 or 39. These are the canoe- or kayak-accessible sites. It's just a short paddle across May Pond to site 38 or Butterfield Pond to site 39. Then you'll feel as if you're camping on an island, and you'll have your canoe or kayak right there to explore both of the interconnected Butterfield and May ponds. Some of the same considerations of island camping apply here, such as the pack-in, pack-out ethic. Be sure you have brought everything you need. A trip back to your vehicle will take some effort.

Besides the paddling, wildlife viewing, and relaxing by the shores of the pond, there is a massive network of hiking trails winding through Pillsbury State Park. This park and its trails form part of the Monadnock–Sunapee Greenway, a 51-mile route that connects the two peaks. It's sort of like a mini (very mini) Appalachian Trail.

The Monadnock–Sunapee Trail is the main trail

MAP

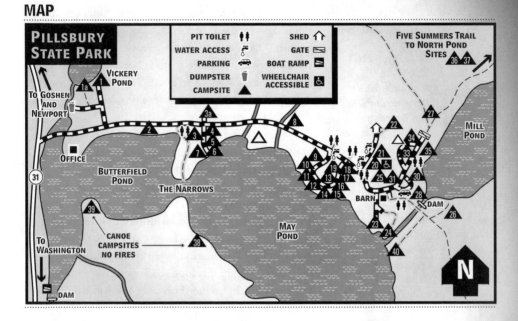

here. You could get quite far along the trail, so set a predetermined turnaround time to leave yourself enough light to make it back to camp. The peaks of Kittredge Mountain and Lovewell Mountain, both within Pillsbury State Park, are good day hikes from the campground on this trail. The Ayers Pond Trail is a nice, long route that ultimately leads out to Ayers Pond.

Back at camp, the mirror-like surface of a pond will reflect the last light of the day. You may be treated to the sight of a great blue heron swooping down for a final landing, or you might spot a moose wandering about the wetlands. Pillsbury State Park is a true wilderness getaway.

GETTING THERE

Follow Route 31 from Hillsborough and Washington. The park is on the right, about 15 miles past the center of Washington.

28
WHITE LAKE
STATE PARK

White Lake may not offer as much seclusion, but you can't beat being right near the lake.

WHITE LAKE STATE PARK is divided into three separate camping areas, none of which are too far from the day-use area and the park's main attraction and namesake—the lake. Being close to the lake is nice, but it also means it could be a bit noisy and there will be a lot of foot traffic. At night, though, when the day crowds have left, you and your camping brethren have the lake and the forest to yourselves.

Area 1 is closest to the day-use beach area, which is often fairly crowded, especially on nice hot summer days. The campsites are far enough away to be fairly quiet, yet close enough to be an easy walk. All sites have picnic tables and fire rings.

As you come into Area 1, there's a cluster of sites situated around where the roads forks off in two directions. Site 1D is very open to the road there. Sites 2 and 3 are moderate in size, but also fairly open to the road. They're nicely shaded, but some sunlight filters through.

Farther into the campground, site 4 is a good-sized site and is more open to the sky. Sites 5 and 6 are very open to each other, so they'd be a good pair of sites for a larger group that wanted two contiguous sites. The same could be said of sites 7 through 10. These are set farther back but are very open to each other.

Generally speaking, the forest in Area 1 is older growth, so it has a high canopy. Consequently, there's less ground cover and less forest defining and secluding the sites from each other. Most of the sites feel fairly open at forest floor, yet they're still shaded from above.

If you're looking for space, sites 11 and 12 are quite large but less private. Sites 13 through 16 are set in a fairly open forest. These sites are very scenic, yet they don't afford much of a sense of privacy. Site 19 is huge but, again, fairly open. Site 20 is smaller but a bit

RATINGS

Beauty: ✪ ✪ ✪ ✪
Privacy: ✪ ✪ ✪
Spaciousness: ✪ ✪ ✪
Quiet: ✪ ✪ ✪
Security: ✪ ✪ ✪
Cleanliness: ✪ ✪ ✪ ✪

more secluded. Site 32A is up off the road, so it's a bit more secluded on either side.

Overall, the sites on the outer loop of the campground road are preferable, as they're more private. Sites 40A and 39A on the outside of the road are more secluded sites, certainly when compared to the rest of the A sites. They're a bit open to each other, though. Site 39 is on the inside of the road, fairly protected on the sides yet open to 40A and 39A. Site 38A is definitely more private.

These outside-edge sites are also a bit larger, so there is the risk that a trailer will plop down next to you, but they're very scenic and private.

Sites 35, 36, and 37 are situated at the campground road intersection, so they're a bit more open to the road. Sites 34B and 34C at the end of the campground road are set well off the road. These sites are a good bet.

Site 34 is a nice-sized site but somewhat open. Site 33 is also open to the road, while 33A is a bit more secluded. Site 27A is somewhat private, certainly at the back of the site, but site 26A is right next door. Site 26 is of decent size, but it's fairly open.

Site 24A is fairly private, as it's situated in a loosely spaced forest of maple,pine, and birch. Site 23A is blocked from the road by more deciduous trees, so it's a bit more secluded. Site 22 is way too open for my tastes. It's a decent size, but set beneath the high forest canopy, so there's no ground cover sheltering you from your neighbors.

Closer to the entrance to Area 1, site 1C is set back a bit more so it isn't bad. Site 1B is fairly open to the road. Site 1A is also somewhat open to the road and to site 1B, but it's fairly secluded at the back and right side of the site looking in.

Site 51 is one of the better sites in this area. It's secluded at the back and sides of the site, even though it's closer to the playground. Site 60 is similar. It's private, but across the road from the playground. Most people are going to be spending their days down by the water, so I wouldn't worry too much about that. What I would do is wait until nightfall, grab a blanket, and lie on my back out in the open area of the playground to look at the stars.

KEY INFORMATION

ADDRESS:	White Lake State Park Route 16 Tamworth, NH 03886
OPERATED BY:	New Hampshire Division of Parks and Recreation
INFORMATION:	White Lake State Park office (603) 323-7350
OPEN:	Mid-May– mid-October
SITES:	204
EACH SITE HAS:	Fire ring, picnic table
ASSIGNMENT:	25 sites first come, first served, the rest by reservation only. Call (603) 271-3628 or www.reserve america.com.
REGISTRATION:	At campground office
FACILITIES:	Toilets, hot showers
PARKING:	At campsites
FEE:	$24–$32, depending on site
RESTRICTIONS:	*Pets:* On leash *Fires:* In established fire rings *Alcohol:* At campsites *Vehicles:* Park at campsites *Other:* Quiet hours 10 p.m.–7 a.m.; 2-week maximum stay

THE BEST
IN TENT
CAMPING
NEW ENGLAND

Sites 75 and 76 are good-sized yet veiled only by a thin wall of forest from the interior sites. Site 76 is also a bit more open to the road. Power lines run alongside the site and it's closer to a side road, so you will hear occasional traffic.

Sites 77 and 78 are a bit more secluded but open to each other. Site 79 is a good choice, as it's off on its own a little more. There is more road noise on this side of the campground, however. Site 80 is set back in a loosely spaced forest, so it's fairly open to the interior sites. Sites 80A and 74A are moderately secluded, but you will be able to see into the interior sites. Definitely try to stick to those on the outer side of the campground road in this area. They'll be more secluded, and generally larger.

There's a noticeable temperature difference as you walk from the coolness of the woods toward to the sunny warmth of the beach area. If you want to be near the lake, consider the Area 2 sites, especially the primo water-view sites. The sites near the path to the beach are convenient because they're near the beach. They're also wide open to each other, and this is a fairly high-traffic area, certainly during the day. Proximity to the beach versus open sites and high foot traffic—that's the tradeoff you make.

At night, though, as the campground settles down, you also have a view of the lake, so there's something to be said for that. This situation applies to water-view sites 1 through 13, which are all grouped down close to the beach. Generally speaking, there's a bit more undergrowth on this side of the campground, so even sites that are open to the road or to each other will have more growth setting them off from each other.

Sites 5, 6, and 7 are nice, moderately secluded water sites, yet they're still slightly open to each other. Sites 8 and 9 are huge and fairly well secluded but also right across from the playground on this side of the campground. Sites 10 through 12 are very open to each other but do have that soothing view of the lake.

Site 35 is open, yet spacious. Sites 38 through 43 are packed in a bit tightly. They're sheltered at the back, but open to each other. Site 44 is open to the road and the somewhat small and cozy site 45 yet nicely secluded on the sides.

As with Area 1, you should go for the outer rim sites in Area 2. Site 46 has a decent sense of privacy. Site 47 is open to the road but is also nicely shaded by the forest. Sites 48 and 49 are open to the road and to each other but fairly well secluded on the sides.

Sites 23 and 24 are quite open. Site 25 is open to a footpath but fairly secluded on the sides. Site 26 is a huge and private. It's a bit open to site 27, which is smaller, a bit sunnier, and moderately secluded.

Most of the sites in this area feel a bit more open to the road. Sites 28, 29, 30, and 11A are all also fairly open. Sites 13 to 16 a relatively open, but they're nicely secluded from behind by the dense forest. Sites 1 through 5 are very open—these are different from the similar sites indicated with a W, which means a water-view site.

Moving into Area 3, which is the smallest of the three areas here, sites 24 and 25 are quite open to the road. Sites 21 through 23 are open to the road and also to each other. The other outer-rim sites in Area 3 are the keepers. Sites 15 through 20 are quite open to the road and to each other.

Site 14 starts getting rather more secluded, with more undergrowth alongside. There is certainly more undergrowth to the forest here, which adds to their privacy, but the

MAP

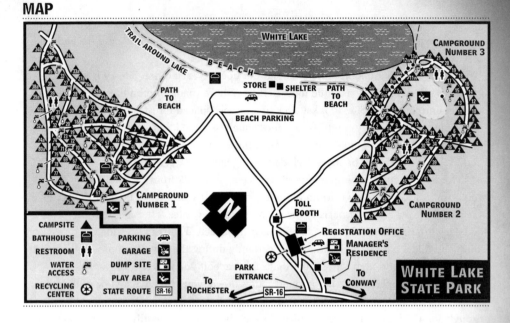

outer sites are still preferable. The inner-loop sites are fairly open to each other. Site 12 is set a bit farther back, so it has more privacy. Sites 8 and 11 are very open. Sites 7, 9, and 10 are moderately secluded yet somewhat open to each other. Sites 1 and 2 are wide open to the road and to neighboring sites.

You won't come to White Lake State Park for that deep-woods sense of seclusion. What you will come here for is beautifully scenic camping and proximity to the clear and cool waters of White Lake—and proximity to the myriad outdoor adventures in the White Mountains, just a quick hop north from the campground.

GETTING THERE

Follow Route 16 north heading toward North Conway. White Lake State Park will be on the left in Tamworth, shortly after the New Hampshire State Police station. If you're coming from the north, it will be on the right.

VERMONT

29
ALLIS STATE PARK

ALLIS STATE PARK IS ONE PLACE you won't find by accident, but it's definitely worth the trip. It's not too far from Interstate 89, which cuts through the middle of Vermont, but it's a circuitous route to the park from the highway. You'll turn down a state road that starts out looking like someone's driveway and then promptly turns into a dirt road. At that point, you're almost there! When you do arrive, you'll be glad you found it, as it is a phenomenally peaceful campground. Its isolation is part of its charm.

While there are a few sites along the edge of an open field in the center of the campground, most are fantastically nestled into the dense forest. Allis State Park has 18 tent sites. Sites 15 through 18 are set along the border of the forest and the field. This pleasant pastoral setting is not quite as private. You'll also get some delightful breezes blowing across the field and through your site, and you will be in a perfect spot to relax in the sun or spend time stargazing at night.

There's a combined sense of isolation and pastoral openness to site 13. It's carved out of the dense forest and set down from the edge of the field. Although sites 17 and 18 are visible across the field, site 13 is still quite isolated from the rest of the campground.

The next site along the campground loop road is one of the most profoundly secluded sites in Vermont. Site 14 is set along a road leading off the main campground loop to the right. This road eventually rejoins the main road leading into Allis State Park, but site 14 is the only campsite on this road—it's completely on its own. You couldn't ask for a deeper sense of solitude and wilderness isolation.

The moderately spacious site is set within a fairly dense forest, and the undergrowth is thick with lush ferns. The road leading up to and past the site becomes increasingly less maintained, and it would

> *If silence and solitude are what you seek, Allis State Park is a fantastic choice.*

RATINGS

Beauty: ☆ ☆ ☆ ☆ ☆
Privacy: ☆ ☆ ☆ ☆
Spaciousness: ☆ ☆ ☆ ☆ ☆
Quiet: ☆ ☆ ☆ ☆ ☆
Security: ☆ ☆ ☆
Cleanliness: ☆ ☆ ☆ ☆

make a perfect short hike or mountain-bike ride, as its connection with the entrance road allows for a loop route. The beautiful, diverse character of the surrounding forest and its absolute isolation make site 14 at Allis State Park one of the top sites you'll find anywhere in New England.

There's a solid sense of seclusion to site 12 as well, even when compared to the magical solitude of site 14. For site 12, park right on the campground loop road and hike in about 50 feet. You can see through the forest to neighboring site 13, but it's still very quiet and secluded, set beneath a moderately dense grove of mixed spruce and maple trees.

Site 11 bears off to the left, which adds to the privacy from the road. There's also a lot of woodland between this site and its neighbors. The site is open to the sky, moderately spacious, and set within a grove of mixed birch and maple trees.

The juxtaposition of sites 9 and 10, and the fact that they are mirror images of each other, makes for an unusual situation. Site 10 is set off the road at an angle to the left within a dense grove of spruce. Site 9 mirrors its shape and character to the right. Despite their proximity, each site provides decent privacy, but this would also make a good pair of sites for a larger group needing two.

Site 8 is long and narrow. It's a very open and spacious site but quite exposed to the road, which makes it a bit less appealing than some of Allis State Park's other sites; however, if you need or want a lot of room, this is a great spot. Set beneath a dense grove of spruce, maple, and birch trees, the spacious site 7 bends back to the left, so the trees surrounding it provide further isolation from the road. The only other site you'll probably be able to see from here is the Elm lean-to (more on the lean-tos momentarily).

There's a charmingly diverse character to site 6. This one is set off the road on a hill with separate levels for parking your car and setting up your tent. It's mostly covered with grass punctuated by baby and adult spruce and maple trees. An extraordinarily varied forest of young and old deciduous and coniferous trees frames the site. It faces the road, but it's otherwise secluded.

The drive into site 5 is actually a short loop. This spacious and secluded site is set beneath a varied forest of young and old birch and spruce trees. From site 5, you can see site 4, but no others. Site 4 is moderately spacious and set in a spruce grove. It has a moss- and grass-covered surface. Between sites 4 and 5 is a trailhead for the Tower Trail. These two sites would be great for a large group.

To get to site 3, you have to drive down off the campground loop road. Once you're down in the site, you can't even see the road. The towering spruce as you enter the short driveway separates the site from view of the road, but the back of the site opens to the grassy field in the center of the park, so it feels both open and secluded. The site itself is also dotted with several birch trees.

Even though it's tucked back off the road, site 2 is still very exposed. It is spacious, narrow, long, and grassy, so it would make a comfortable surface for your tent. Site 1 is huge and grassy, but it's wide open to the road. The water spigot is also near site 1, so you'll have thirsty campers tramping by.

The lean-tos at Allis State Park are grouped together in a small neighborhood at the far end of the campground loop road. They look like true wilderness cabins with their own yards and lawns.

The Elm, Oak, Hemlock, and Spruce lean-tos are all set on grassy lawns buffered from one another by dense forest. The Apple lean-to is set up for wheelchair access, so it's also close to the restroom. The Pine lean-to is on the outside of the campground loop road.

The Poplar lean-to is set way off on its own, mixed in with a grove of spruce and birch. This is the one to go for if you want seclusion.

The Bear Hill Nature Trail, the nearest and most prominent hiking attraction within Allis State Park, is a self-guided nature trail that highlights the varied stages of forest growth; it features a stand of red spruce, butternut trees, and a view to north and south ponds that just opened following the great ice storm of 1998. Eventually though, this view will be reclaimed by the steady and undeniable persistence of the forest.

MAP

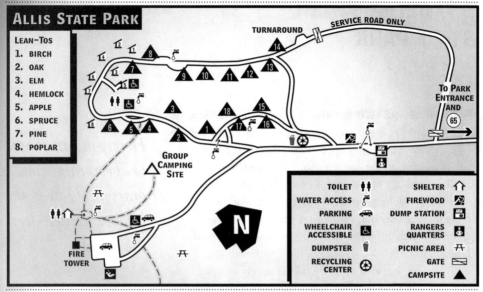

GETTING THERE

From Interstate 89, take Exit 4. Head west on VT 66 to the intersection with VT 12. Turn right on VT 12 north. Follow this 12 miles to VT 65. Turn right here and follow the road to the park entrance on the right.

30 BRANBURY STATE PARK

THERE ARE TWO SEPARATE CAMPING AREAS at Branbury State Park. One is pretty nice, but the other is positively spectacular. Branbury State Park is located on the eastern shore of Lake Dunmore, and there's plenty to do on this beautiful central Vermont lake: paddling, fishing, sailing, swimming, or just sitting on a beach chair burrowing your feet into the sand (for information on fishing licenses, see Appendix C, page 232).

> *Here you can choose between campsites on a grassy field near the lake or nestled deep in the woods.*

The camping area near the lake is set on an open field back from the beach. For the Lake Dunmore side of the campground, the privacy rating is one star, since it's an open field. There are a few trees spread out within the field, but for the most part, the only thing between you and the neighboring sites is air. The campsites across the street rate a four on the privacy scale, and some a solid five.

Sites 1 through 17 are the open sites near the lake. These are pleasant, as they're close to the lake and you'll get some cool breezes, but they are all quite similar and all very open. If you prefer seclusion, the campsites across the street (sites 18 through 41) are where you want to be. This portion of the campground is set within a beautiful mixed forest of old and young trees. This loop has some scenic and secluded sites, as well as a few lean-tos. In Vermont State Park style, the lean-tos are all named for tree varieties: Elm, Spruce, Oak, and so on. These are unobtrusively mixed in with the tent sites.

Site 25 isn't bad. It's slightly elevated from the road, but it's right at the entrance to this side of the campground where campers drive in, so it lacks privacy and quiet. Sites 27 and 28 are probably the least private of the sites on this side, as they have the main road (VT 53) on one side and the campground loop road on the other. Travel just a bit farther up this loop,

RATINGS

Beauty: ✩ ✩ ✩ ✩
Privacy (west): ✩
Privacy (east): ✩ ✩ ✩ ✩
Spaciousness: ✩ ✩ ✩ ✩
Quiet: ✩ ✩ ✩ ✩
Security: ✩ ✩ ✩ ✩
Cleanliness: ✩ ✩ ✩ ✩

ADDRESS: Branbury State Park
3570 Lake Dunmore
Road, VT 53
Salisbury, VT 05733

OPERATED BY: Vermont Agency of
Natural Resources
Department of
Forests, Parks, and
Recreation

INFORMATION: Branbury State Park
(802) 247-5925
(summer)
(888) 409-7579
(October–May)

OPEN: Mid-May–Columbus
Day

SITES: 41 tent sites, 6 lean-
to sites

EACH SITE HAS: Fire ring, picnic
table

ASSIGNMENT: First come, first
served; by reserva-
tion: (888) 409-7579

REGISTRATION: At ranger station

FACILITIES: Flush toilets, water,
coin-operated hot
showers, sandy
beach on Lake Dun-
more, boat rentals

PARKING: At sites

FEE: $16–$18 for tent sites,
$23–$25 for lean-tos

RESTRICTIONS: *Pets:* Dogs on leash
only
Fires: In fire rings
only
Alcohol: At sites only
Vehicles: At sites only
Other: Reservations
require 4-night mini-
mum stay; check in
after 2 p.m., check
out by 11 a.m.; quiet
hours 10 p.m.–
7 a.m.; maximum
8 people per site

though, and the sites become increasingly gorgeous.

Site 32 is nicely isolated, situated on the inside of the campground loop near the Birch lean-to. Sites 29 and 31 are even farther up on the spectacular scale. These well-isolated sites are set up on a small rise from the campground road and are surrounded by thick forest. Site 30 sits in the middle of these two sites, so it's more open, but it's still a fine site. Sites 29 and 31 on either side are set far back enough in the woods that you won't be too close to your neighbors.

Farther up the loop, there are several sites against small, granite cliff walls. Sites 36 and 37 are tucked right against these ledges. The whole side of the loop here is quite dramatic in its scenery, thanks to the cliffs, forest, and gently rolling terrain.

There are three sites on this side of the Branbury State Park campground that are set at the end of cul-de-sacs within the campground: sites 34, 41, and 21. Site 34 is perfectly situated for deep wilderness isolation. It's nestled in a dense grove of conifers, so it feels like a campsite from some deep mystical woods out of Tolkien's Middle Earth.

Site 41 might as well be the companion to site 34, set off on its own in a pine grove up against the cliffs. This site is next to the Spruce lean-to. Sites 39 through 41 are interspersed with the shelters against and among the cliffs. Site 39 is an isolated site, even though it sits right next to the Oak Shelter.

Then, we come to site 21 (elated cinematic music should be sounding in your head right now). Site 21 couldn't possibly be a more perfect place to spend a few days camping. There's a short distance to lug in your gear. Make sure to drop your stuff and just look around as you walk into the site. You'll feel as if you've entered a cathedral. The site is majestically framed by statuesque spruce trees and set against a steep cliff wall. As if that's not enough, the Sucker Brook softly splashes by right behind the site. You'll fall asleep to the sounds of the stream as it runs down from the Falls of Lana toward Lake Dunmore.

When I was chatting with the Vermont Youth Conservation Corps members working in the ranger station in early spring, the coveted site 21 was already

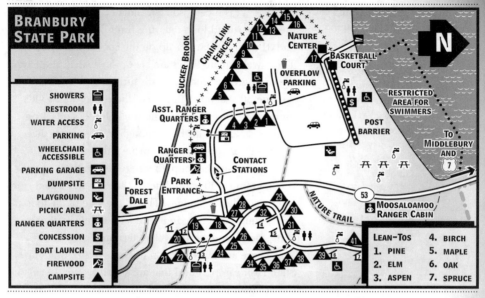

BRANBURY STATE PARK

SHOWERS
RESTROOM
WATER ACCESS
PARKING
WHEELCHAIR ACCESSIBLE
PARKING GARAGE
DUMPSITE
PLAYGROUND
PICNIC AREA
RANGER QUARTERS
CONCESSION
BOAT LAUNCH
FIREWOOD
CAMPSITE

SUCKER BROOK
CHAIN-LINK FENCES
NATURE CENTER
BASKETBALL COURT
OVERFLOW PARKING
RESTRICTED AREA FOR SWIMMERS
ASST. RANGER QUARTERS
POST BARRIER
To MIDDLEBURY AND 7
RANGER QUARTERS
CONTACT STATIONS
To FOREST DALE
PARK ENTRANCE
NATURE TRAIL
53
MOOSALOAMOO RANGER CABIN

LEAN-TOS
1. PINE   4. BIRCH
2. ELM   5. MAPLE
3. ASPEN   6. OAK
           7. SPRUCE

reserved for most of the summer. Plan years in advance, do a sun dance, and try to get yourself some time in site 21. You'll be glad you did!

While most Vermont State Parks have a two-night minimum for reservations, there's a four-night minimum at Branbury State Park. That should be fine though, especially if you get yourself into site 21. Otherwise, consider sites 20, 22, 29, 31, 34, and 41 for the most secluded wilderness experience. Once you land there, you won't want to leave for at least four nights!

Besides being able to fish, paddle, and bask in the sun on the shores of Lake Dunmore, the hiking in and around Branbury State Park is as dramatically beautiful as site 21. There's a nature trail that loops up and over the small cliffs at the back of the wooded side of the campground. There are two hikes in particular that you won't want to miss if you're spending at least a couple of days here: the 1.5-mile, occasionally strenuous hike up to Rattlesnake Point, a rock promontory overlooking the forest and Lake Dunmore; and the relatively easy 1-mile hike up to the Falls of Lana, over which Sucker Brook flows on its way toward site 21 and Lake Dunmore.

GETTING THERE

From Middlebury, Vermont, travel south on US 7, then south on VT 53 until you see signs for the park.

> *This is a spectacularly scenic and isolated campground set deep within the woods of the Green Mountain National Forest.*

THE CHITTENDEN BROOK RECREATION Area, like many campgrounds perched along the spine of the Green Mountains in Vermont, offers a deep-woods atmosphere and easy access to some of the world-class hiking trails that wind through the state.

The 2.5-mile access road (Fire Road 45) into the Chittenden Brook Campground is quite a trip in and of itself. It leads up and over a ridge, with Chittenden Brook running on either side along the way. Farther up, as you near the campground, the road falls off steeply to the right. Even though the forest is dramatically beautiful here, keep your eyes on the road.

Chittenden Brook is one of those campgrounds (and there are certainly plenty in New England) where there isn't a bad site in the place. It's an intimate campground with only 17 sites, which means it can fill up quickly. Once you're there, it's calm and quiet, and it has a delightful sense of solitude.

The whole campground is situated near the ridgeline of the Green Mountains, the course followed by the nearby Long and Appalachian trails. You are at a moderate elevation in the Green Mountains, so the forest isn't quite as towering here. Consequently, lots of light filters down into the sites. There's also the ever-present rush of Chittenden Brook, punctuated by the staccato chirping of the forest birds. It's a profoundly peaceful combination.

Site 1 is down off the road, near the restrooms but set off on its own enough to be fairly well isolated. It's also close to the hand water-pump. Continuing along the campground loop road, sites 2 through 5 are fairly close together, but each has plenty of room. These sites have an open feel, and are probably the least isolated sites in the campground. Still, even these offer a reasonable sense of seclusion.

RATINGS

Beauty: ✪ ✪ ✪ ✪ ✪
Privacy: ✪ ✪ ✪ ✪ ✪
Spaciousness: ✪ ✪ ✪ ✪ ✪
Quiet: ✪ ✪ ✪ ✪ ✪
Security: ✪ ✪ ✪ ✪
Cleanliness: ✪ ✪ ✪ ✪

While it doesn't have a lot of dense forest surrounding it, site 6 is nicely isolated, as it is set off from the other campsites. It's also situated right next to a trailhead between sites 6 and 7 that leads to the Chittenden Brook Trail, the Beaver Pond Trail, and the Campground Loop Trail. You can hike right out of your campsite. Site 7 is larger, so it would be perfect for a group or large family. It's also next to the restroom.

The tent platform for site 8 is set off the campground loop and back in the woods, so this site scores higher on the solitude and isolation scale. Given its location and the trees around the site, you probably won't even be able to see your neighbors. Sites 9 and 10 are right across the campground loop road from each other. Both are pretty, spacious sites surrounded by trees that lend a sense of isolation on either side, although the front of the campsite is open.

Sites 11 and 12 are right next to each other and have a loosely spaced, fairly open forest in between, so these would be good sites if you're with a group large enough to need or want two sites. There's another hand pump for water located across from site 13 and next to site 14.

Sites 13 and 15 are set off from the campground loop road, with a short path leading to the tent platform. These sites not only provide a sense of wilderness and isolation but are also extra scenic since they are set within groves of young deciduous trees, loaded with brilliant green leaves bouncing around in the sunlight.

Sites 16 and 17 are my favorites at Chittenden Brook Recreation Area. In site 16, the tent platform is set off the road, and then from there, the space with the picnic table and fire ring is set down farther still, so both your sleeping spot and hanging-out spot are off on their own. There's also a buffer of woods between sites 16 and 17 and on either side. Site 17 is a bit more level, but still marvelously isolated, quite spacious, and surrounded by a cloak of young trees. It's located near the end of the campground loop road and close to the recycling station. These recycling stations are very much in evidence within the Green Mountain National Forest campgrounds and recreation areas. Bravo to that!

KEY INFORMATION

ADDRESS:	Chittenden Brook Recreation Area Fire Road 45 VT 73 Chittenden, VT 05737
OPERATED BY:	Green Mountain National Forest
INFORMATION:	Green Mountain National Forest Rochester Ranger District 99 Ranger Road Rochester, VT 05767-9431 (802) 767-4261
OPEN:	Memorial Day–Labor Day
SITES:	17
EACH SITE HAS:	Fire ring with grill, picnic table
ASSIGNMENT:	First come, first served
REGISTRATION:	Pay at self-serve fee station
FACILITIES:	Pit toilets, hand water pumps
PARKING:	At sites
FEE:	$10
RESTRICTIONS:	*Pets:* On leash only *Fires:* In fire rings only *Alcohol:* At sites only *Vehicles:* Maximum 2 per site; national forest closed to ATVs *Other:* Quiet hours 10 p.m.–6 a.m.; check out by 2 p.m.; 14-day maximum stay; pack out all trash

MAP

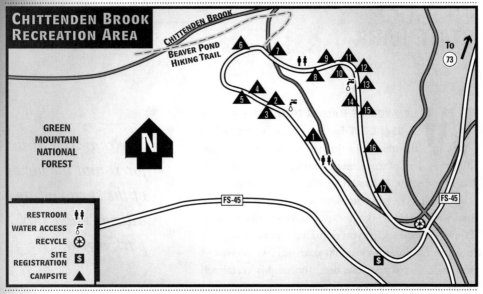

CHITTENDEN BROOK
RECREATION AREA

CHITTENDEN BROOK

BEAVER POND
HIKING TRAIL

GREEN
MOUNTAIN
NATIONAL
FOREST

N

To 73

RESTROOM
WATER ACCESS
RECYCLE
SITE
REGISTRATION
CAMPSITE

FS-45

GETTING THERE

Follow VT 73 to Road 45 and the sign for Chittenden Break Recreation Area which will be on the left if you're heading west on VT 73, or on the right if you're heading east. Follow Road 45 about 2.5 miles to the campground.

This is the place to make base camp if you're planning on exploring portions of the Long Trail or Appalachian Trail. There are trailheads leading right out of the campground. As you drive in on the access road, you'll pass other trailheads also leading off toward the Long Trail.

32
COOLIDGE STATE PARK

WHEN YOU'RE HIKING THROUGH the gentle trails of Coolidge State Park (so named for the nearby birthplace of Calvin Coolidge, 30th president of the United States), you'll come across lots of old stone walls and what's left of foundations. Close your eyes for a moment and imagine what this area was like when the homes of farmers stood here. The land upon which you're hiking and camping looked a lot different just 100 years ago. What was once agricultural land has been thoroughly reclaimed by the forest's persistent growth.

> *The character of the forest and the views of the surrounding hillside make this park a gem.*

The campground at Coolidge State Park is set within a dense, mixed forest of mostly deciduous trees. There's a stately character to the forest, as most of the trees tower 75 to 100 feet overhead. Most of the trees are maple, birch, and pine. The tent sites are generally very spacious, with lots of space and trees between most of the sites, so the sense of seclusion is supreme. The campground is very quiet. The only sounds you'll hear are the woodland birds and the breezes rustling through the trees.

Unlike most other Vermont state parks, there are two distinct areas for most of the lean-tos and the tent sites. The White Birch, Alder, and Poplar lean-tos are the only three mixed in with the tent sites. The White Birch lean-to is located at the head of the tent loop, the Alder across from site 4, and the Poplar off the main campground road.

While it's smaller than the other low-numbered sites, site 1 is well isolated. The main campground road runs behind the site, but you won't notice it once the sun sinks beneath the trees. It's also directly across the campground loop road from site 2, which is framed by a grove of spruce and young deciduous trees. A huge, grand old pine tree guards the entrance to site 2, with branches hanging down redolent of a weeping willow.

RATINGS

Beauty: ✰ ✰ ✰ ✰
Privacy: ✰ ✰ ✰ ✰ ✰
Spaciousness: ✰ ✰ ✰ ✰
Quiet: ✰ ✰ ✰ ✰ ✰
Security: ✰ ✰ ✰ ✰
Cleanliness: ✰ ✰ ✰ ✰

ADDRESS: Coolidge State Park
855 Coolidge State
Park Road
Plymouth, VT 05056

OPERATED BY: Vermont Agency of
Natural Resources,
Department of
Forests, Parks, and
Recreation

INFORMATION: Coolidge State Park
(802) 672-3612
(summer)
(888) 409-7579
(October–May)

OPEN: Memorial
Day–Columbus Day

SITES: 25 tent sites, 35 lean-
to sites

EACH SITE HAS: Fire ring, picnic
table

ASSIGNMENT: First come, first
served; by reserva-
tion: (888) 409-7579

REGISTRATION: At ranger station

FACILITIES: Coin-operated hot
showers, flush toi-
lets, playground, pic-
nic area, dump
station for RVs

PARKING: At sites

FEE: $14 for tent sites,
$21–$23 for lean-tos

RESTRICTIONS: *Pets:* On leash only
Fires: In fire rings
only
Alcohol: At sites only
Vehicles: Parking at
sites only
Other: Reservations
require 4-night mini-
mum stay; check in
after 2 p.m., check
out by 11 a.m.; quiet
hours 10 p.m.–7
a.m.; maximum 8
people per site

There's a fairly well-isolated air about site 3, although it's close to site 2. A decent amount of forest separates the two, and both are very spacious. Site 4 is also spacious, and it's right across the road from the Alder lean-to. The site is framed by a grove of young deciduous trees and a few older spruce. Site 5 is another well-isolated one. It's at least 100 feet from sites on either side, but it is open to the back, and you can see the restrooms behind it. Site 6 is off the camp-ground road. It's spacious and pretty well isolated. There aren't any sites close to you on either side, but it is right across the road from another footpath to the restrooms.

The trailhead for the CCC (Civilian Conservation Corps) Trail is right across from site 7. This is a conve-nient site for easy access to the hiking trails that wind throughout the park, but expect passing foot traffic. Sites 7 and 8 are somewhat close together and up off the campground loop road. Site 9 is very open and has a small grassy area within. It's right next to site 10, so unlike most of the campground, there isn't much pri-vacy between 9 and 10. These two pairs of sites would suit large groups or families.

Site 11 is another open and spacious spot. Site 12 is smaller and more secluded, it's surrounded by a dense grove of young deciduous trees. Site 13 is tucked far off the campground road, so it provides a feeling of isolation, even though it's right next to a short footpath that leads up to the restrooms.

There's a shared entranceway to sites 14 and 15, but there's enough space and forest between the two to afford sufficient privacy. Both sites are spacious and set far off the road. Site 15 offers a fabulous sense of soli-tude, boasting a grassy area, plus a brook.

There isn't much privacy between sites 16 and 17. However, there's plenty of room on either side of both sites, so they're well isolated from the rest of the camp-ground, if not from each other—another possibility for groups. Site 17 is set off the road a bit and has a grassy surface in its center. There are also several maples growing up through the site, and it's framed by shorter deciduous trees—mostly maple and birch—and by ferns at the ground level for an added sense of seclusion.

The ferns give the site a primeval feel and fill in the forest with their brilliant green leaves. When the sunlight filters down on a clear day, the forest looks as if it's glowing green.

Site 18 is a bit smaller than 17 but also has a grassy surface. Site 19 is spacious and there's plenty of forest on either side of the site but not too much privacy from the road. I'm always willing to sacrifice a bit of spaciousness for more forest and a deeper sense of seclusion.

There's a similar character to sites 20 through 23. Site 20 is up off the road. This is a moderately spacious site with a grassy surface. Sites 22 and 23 are across the road from each other. Site 23A is a lug-in site set up off the road. It's almost a part of Site 23, so if you don't know your neighbors in site 23 before your trip, you will before long. Site 23A isn't huge, but it's set way off from the road and the rest of the campground. It is surrounded by a dense, low wall of ferns and a grove of slender, young spruce trees. It has lots of privacy on all sides, save where it abuts site 23.

One of the last sites on this part of the campground loop road is site 24. This is by far the most isolated site within the loop. It's perfectly situated to afford wilderness experience, as it's surrounded by dense forest and is a good distance from its neighbors. It's not the most spacious site, but it's marvelously well isolated.

There's a tradeoff at site 25. It sits way off on its own, but it's located near the point where the campground loop road rejoins the main state park road. It's moderately spacious and well isolated from the other sites, but it is right at that intersection.

Between the tent loop and the lean-to loop, there's a little playground near the ranger station as you enter the park—a good thing to keep in mind if you're camping with little ones. The lean-to loop has very dense forest coverage as well. Most of the lean-tos are quite well isolated from each other, although some are positioned in pairs, like Cherry and Larch, or groups, like Beech, Basswood, and Apple. Between the dense forest and the loose spacing, the individual lean-to sites offer isolation, especially the Sumac, Willow, and Butternut lean-tos. It also bears mentioning that the Cedar lean-to is wheelchair accessible.

The Ash lean-to has an outrageously scenic view of the opposing hillsides and valley. This alone makes it worth keeping the tent packed, and hopping in one of these lean-tos. The Aspen, Box elder, Beech, Basswood, Elm, and Hawthorn lean-tos also share this dramatic view. All these lean-tos face out toward the hills, which would be the first thing you'd see in the morning. I couldn't imagine a nicer way to greet the day.

Once you're up and about, whether you've spent the night in your tent or in a lean-to, there's plenty of great hiking right within the park. Try the 0.75-mile CCC Trail that connects the tent area and the lean-to area for a mellow morning hike. Then try the 1.5-mile trail to the summit of the 2,174-foot Slack Hill and treat yourself to lunch with a commanding view of the surrounding hills.

MAP

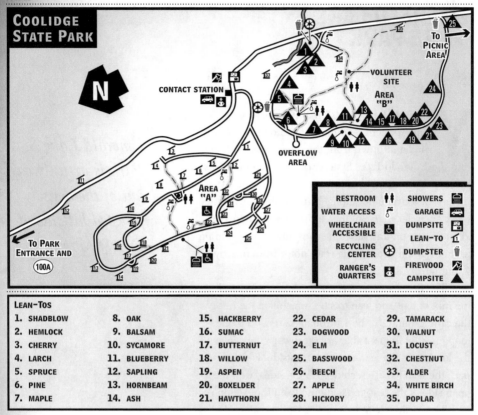

COOLIDGE STATE PARK

N

CONTACT STATION

VOLUNTEER SITE
AREA "B"

OVERFLOW AREA

AREA "A"

To PARK ENTRANCE AND 100A

To PICNIC AREA

RESTROOM	♦♦	SHOWERS	
WATER ACCESS		GARAGE	
WHEELCHAIR ACCESSIBLE	♿	DUMPSITE	
		LEAN-TO	
RECYCLING CENTER	♻	DUMPSTER	
RANGER'S QUARTERS		FIREWOOD	
		CAMPSITE	▲

LEAN-TOS

1. SHADBLOW	8. OAK	15. HACKBERRY
2. HEMLOCK	9. BALSAM	16. SUMAC
3. CHERRY	10. SYCAMORE	17. BUTTERNUT
4. LARCH	11. BLUEBERRY	18. WILLOW
5. SPRUCE	12. SAPLING	19. ASPEN
6. PINE	13. HORNBEAM	20. BOXELDER
7. MAPLE	14. ASH	21. HAWTHORN

22. CEDAR	29. TAMARACK
23. DOGWOOD	30. WALNUT
24. ELM	31. LOCUST
25. BASSWOOD	32. CHESTNUT
26. BEECH	33. ALDER
27. APPLE	34. WHITE BIRCH
28. HICKORY	35. POPLAR

GETTING THERE

Follow VT 100 (the skier's highway) to VT 100A in Plymouth. Follow VT 100A about 2 miles to the sign for the park on the right.

33

EMERALD LAKE STATE PARK

YOU CAN'T HELP BUT NOTICE the steep embankment leading up from one side of the road and down from the other as you drive into the Emerald Lake State Park campground. This place was essentially carved out of the hillside. It makes for a dramatic setting, but consequently, a steep bank encircles many of the camping areas here, so keep an eye on any little ones you may have running around. You'll hear a little road noise from nearby US 7, but hardly any at night.

The first area you'll come to, Area A, has a pleasing mix of tent and lean-to sites, much like the rest of the campground. In the 1-through-12 section of the loop, most of the tent sites are set toward the center of the loop, with the lean-tos on the outside. For the most part, the lean-tos are secluded on the sides, with the open side of the lean-to facing out from the A-loop road.

The Willow lean-to and site 1 are small and adjacent sites. Site 1 is secluded on the sides but open to the road. Willow is set a bit farther back, making it secluded. Cherry is fairly spacious and secluded, as it is set off the road in a dense grove of young maple and beech trees. Both the Pine and Hickory lean-tos are on smaller sites but feel moderately private.

Like the other tent sites in this part of the loop, site 5 is of moderate size but doesn't offer much privacy from the other sites. Site 6 is spacious and open to the road but is a bit more secluded than the other tent sites nearby. The Elm and Alder lean-tos are small and face the main campground road leading to the B and C areas, but they still feel secluded. Site 7 is open to the road, but it does have several large spruce trees growing up through it.

Poplar is on a good-sized site that is fairly private on the sides, but it's a bit open to the road. Site 8 is set up off the road but still has an open feel. It's encircled

> *Emerald Lake State Park is artfully carved out of the densely forested hillside of Dorset Mountain.*

RATINGS

Beauty: ☆ ☆ ☆ ☆ ☆
Privacy: ☆ ☆ ☆ ☆
Spaciousness: ☆ ☆ ☆ ☆
Quiet: ☆ ☆ ☆ ☆
Security: ☆ ☆ ☆ ☆
Cleanliness: ☆ ☆ ☆ ☆

ADDRESS: Emerald Lake State Park
65 Emerald Lake Lane
East Dorset, VT 05253

OPERATED BY: Vermont Agency of Natural Resources, Department of Forests, Parks, and Recreation

INFORMATION: Emerald Lake State Park, (802) 362-1655

OPEN: Memorial Day–Columbus Day

SITES: 69 tent sites, 36 lean-to sites

EACH SITE HAS: Fire ring, picnic table

ASSIGNMENT: First come, first served; by reservation: (888) 409-7579

REGISTRATION: At ranger station at entrance to park

FACILITIES: Day-use area, flush toilets, coin-operated showers, water spigots

PARKING: At sites

FEE: $16–$18 for tent sites, $23–$25 for lean-tos

RESTRICTIONS: *Pets:* On leash only
Fires: In fireplaces only
Alcohol: At sites only
Vehicles: Parking at sites only
Other: Reservations require 2-night minimum stay; check in after 2 p.m., check out by 11 a.m.; quiet hours 10 p.m.–7 a.m.; maximum 8 people per site

by slender beech trees and several large maples and spruce. The Spruce lean-to, as you may imagine, is set within a fairly dense spruce grove, although the lean-to itself is close to the road.

Locust is very spacious and offers an excellent sense of seclusion, set amid a loosely spaced grove of spruce. Larch is also spacious and secluded. It's set way off the campground road within a shimmering, green grove of young beech trees. Birch is on a good-sized site and protected by a grove of spruce, although it's right on the corner of the campground road. It's also right next to the trail that leads to the lake. Beech is a smaller site. It's close to the road but has a decent sense of seclusion, with beech trees (of course) peppering the site.

The sites toward the end of Area A are more secluded and scenic. Site 15 is small but private and open to the sky. Site 16 is very sunny. It's a bit open and encircled by a loose forest of beech and spruce.

There's a line of spruce that frames site 18, which is also spacious and has a canopy of beech overhead. There's a steep bank off to the right of the site that leads down into a small ravine. Site 17 is moderate in size and secluded from the road by several large spruce trees. Site 19 is at the end of the loop. This site is fairly small, but it's nicely enshrouded by maples. It's just open enough to the sky so that plenty of sunlight filters down to the site.

Between the Area A loop and the B loop is a short strip with sites 20 through 23. Even though they're far from the rest of the sites, there's not much of a sense of seclusion from the road or from each other, but if you wanted some sites side by side, these would be just fine.

There's a campground host at site 27 (on the left as you enter Area B) and a small playground next to site 28. Nearby, site 29 and the Tamarack lean-to are both set up for wheelchair access. Both sites 32 and 34 abut the steep hillside behind them, which adds to the sense of seclusion. Site 36 is also isolated and set up against the hillside.

Sites 35, 37, 38, and 39 are in their own little neighborhood. These are spacious sites with a dark canopy of conifers. They're open to each other, but they make for a fantastic quartet of sites. A stone wall runs behind sites 38 and 39, which adds to their privacy. Of this group of sites, site 39 is probably the most secluded.

Sites 43 and 44 are across the road from each other but very well hidden on the sides from neighboring sites. Site 43 is also up against the hillside. Site 49 is spacious, fairly secluded, and set within a grove of young, slender maples. It also has the steep hill against its back, and a trail leading up Dorset Mountain is beside it.

Moving through the lower end of the B loop brings you to the lean-to sites. The Plum, Ginko, and Apple lean-tos are set in a trio. They're nicely secluded on the sides but set close to each other. A bit more road noise from US 7 is noticeable here, but only during the day. Dogwood is quite private, as it's set down off the road at the end of a longer driveway. Sumac is as well, although it's not quite as far off the road. Hazelnut is set off the road on a small rise and is enshrouded in a dark spruce grove.

There are two tent sites in here as well. Site 40 is huge. The bathroom building is behind it, but a small hill creates a sense of seclusion. It's also across from site 41, which is small but private. This site, too, is surrounded by small hills, almost as if it were landscaped, and nestled within a mixed forest of spruce and maples.

Farther up on this part of the loop, there's a trail leading down to the lake across from site 42 and the Sycamore lean-to. The sites and lean-tos here share the ambience of a waterfall in the background.

Moving into Area C, the Yew lean-to is on a small but private site. Sites 50 and 51 are close to each other but beautifully separated from the other sites in this part of the campground. They're both open to the sky and surrounded by young maple and beech trees. Sites 52 and 53 face the steep hill that runs along most of the northern side of the campground. They're open to the road but secluded on the sides. The trail leading down to Emerald Lake is right next to site 53.

Deeper into the Area C campsites, there are many that are rather small, not too private, and close to the restroom. There are also some spacious and spectacularly secluded spots. Set up on a short loop of this part of the campground road and encircled by slender beech, maple, and birch, site 63 enjoys a shimmering green effect when the sun shines through the trees. It's open to this short loop but well secluded on the sides. Site 62 is a bit smaller and more hidden, surrounded by a picturesque mix of spruce and birch. Both of these sites are fairly close to the restroom but are set off by the stand of trees in the center of the loop.

As you near the far end of the campground road, you'll find site 66, which is an absolutely beautiful spot surrounded by a grand, mixed grove of mature beech, spruce, birch, and maple trees. It's open to the sky just enough for a glimpse of the sun and stars. Site 67 is also a large site surrounded by spruce for a cooler, shaded feel and a sense of seclusion. Sites 68 and 69 are at the absolute end of the campground road. They're fairly close to each other but marvelously private, carved out of dense spruce forest. These last few sites share that cool, dark, sylvan feeling. There are many exquisite sites at Emerald Lake State Park, but these more remote sites are among the best.

MAP

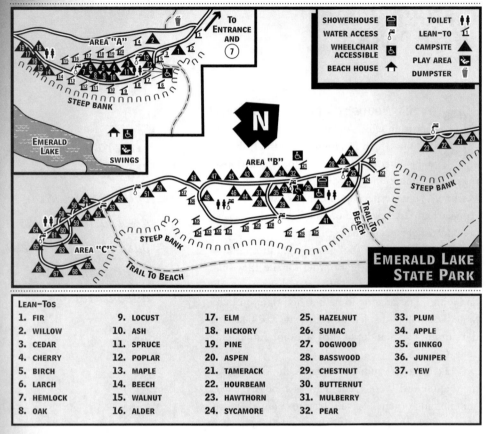

LEAN-TOS

1. FIR	9. LOCUST	17. ELM	25. HAZELNUT	33. PLUM
2. WILLOW	10. ASH	18. HICKORY	26. SUMAC	34. APPLE
3. CEDAR	11. SPRUCE	19. PINE	27. DOGWOOD	35. GINKGO
4. CHERRY	12. POPLAR	20. ASPEN	28. BASSWOOD	36. JUNIPER
5. BIRCH	13. MAPLE	21. TAMERACK	29. CHESTNUT	37. YEW
6. LARCH	14. BEECH	22. HOURBEAM	30. BUTTERNUT	
7. HEMLOCK	15. WALNUT	23. HAWTHORN	31. MULBERRY	
8. OAK	16. ALDER	24. SYCAMORE	32. PEAR	

GETTING THERE

From Interstate 91 north, take Exit 2 and follow VT 30 toward Manchester. Take US 7 north and follow this to the park.

GIFFORD WOODS IS A PERFECTLY SITUATED spot from which to launch your adventures into the Green Mountains and the Killington area. Whether you're here for late-season skiing or mountain biking at Killington, or hiking along Vermont's spine, especially portions of the Appalachian Trail or Vermont's Long Trail, this is a great, centrally located base camp.

The Appalachian Trail passes right through the park, and it forms the right border for site 12 within the campground. I happened to stay there one night and found it fascinating to be perched right on that fabled footpath. Turn left from this site and head for the summit of Katahdin or turn right for Amicalola Falls, Georgia.

Like other Vermont state parks, the site arrangement at Gifford Woods State Park is a loosely spaced combination of tent sites and lean-tos named for tree varieties. There are two distinct areas within the campground, the Upper Loop and the Lower Loop. The whole upper area of the campground is set beneath a truly mixed woodland with deciduous and coniferous trees and old and new forest. Sites 1 and 2 are tucked in together right across from the playground, which is also off the Upper Loop's campground road. These are great if you need a pair of contiguous sites for a larger group. Conversely, you will definitely meet your neighbors if you arrive previously unacquainted.

Site 3 is spacious, but it's right next to the playground, so it's not quite as private and could be noisy if there are a lot of kids on the swings and slide. This would be a great site to secure if you are camping with small kids and plan on spending time at the playground. Besides the playground, kids will like the footpath and self-guided nature tour that winds through the woods behind the playground and picnic area.

> *Gifford Woods State Park is exceptional both as a relaxing destination and as a base camp for Green Mountain hiking adventures.*

RATINGS

Beauty: ✩ ✩ ✩ ✩ ✩
Privacy: ✩ ✩ ✩ ✩
Spaciousness: ✩ ✩ ✩ ✩
Quiet: ✩ ✩ ✩ ✩
Security: ✩ ✩ ✩ ✩
Cleanliness: ✩ ✩ ✩ ✩

KEY INFORMATION

ADDRESS: Gifford Woods State Park
34 Gifford Woods
Killington, VT 05761

OPERATED BY: Vermont Agency of Natural Resources, Department of Forests, Parks, and Recreation

INFORMATION: Gifford Woods State Park, (802) 775-5354 (in season), (888) 409-7579 (October–May)

OPEN: Memorial Day–October 15

SITES: 27 tent sites, 21 lean-to sites

EACH SITE HAS: Fire ring or brick hearth, picnic table

ASSIGNMENT: First come, first served; by reservation: (888) 409-7579

REGISTRATION: At ranger station

FACILITIES: Coin-operated hot showers, flush toilets, playground, picnic area

PARKING: At sites

FEE: $14–$16 for tent sites, $21–$23 for lean-tos

RESTRICTIONS: *Pets:* Dogs on leash only
Fires: In fire rings only
Alcohol: At sites only
Vehicles: Parking at sites only
Other: Reservations require 2-night minimum stay; check in after 2 p.m., check out by 11 a.m.; quiet hours 10 p.m.–7 a.m.; maximum 8 people per site

Sites 4 and 5 are well isolated, with a solid sense of privacy. Site 4 is pretty and private, even though it's set right at the intersection where the one-way, upper campground loop road rejoins itself. Site 5 is tucked off on its own in the woods, set back from the road.

Sites 6 and 7 are set a good distance off the road, but they're quite close to each other. Sites 9 and 10 are right across the campground road from each other. They're more open, so they aren't quite as private. Like sites 1 and 2, this pair would be fine for a group needing two sites.

Site 8 is fairly isolated. It's located next to the Ash lean-to. Site 11 isn't bad, but it's also a bit more open than some of the other sites in the Upper Loop. Site 11 is right across from the Appalachian Trail.

Aside from also being right on the Appalachian Trail, site 12 is otherwise another of Gifford Woods's top-notch tent spots. It has plenty of space and is fairly isolated. Site 13 is a spacious site, set back a bit from the road, but it has a water spigot right outside, so you'll get lots of visitors. If you want to meet a bunch of your campground neighbors, this is the site for you.

The lean-tos are interspersed among the individual tent sites. The Birch lean-to is in a pleasant, isolated spot. This one would be worth getting just for the privacy of the site. Apple is similarly off on its own. Maple and Beech are set right next to each other and would be a fun pair of shelters for larger groups.

Spruce is fairly isolated and on the inside of the loop. Hemlock is across from the frequently visited water spigot at site 13, but it's in the woods a ways, so it's more private. The Elm lean-to also has a decent distance between the site and the road.

Overall, the upper campground sites are quieter than the lower sites. The surrounding forest is thicker, and you're that much farther from VT 100. Still, there are some attractive spots on the lower loop as well. The lower loop includes sites 14 through 27.

Site 27, the first site you come to, is open and quite spacious, but consequently not very private. The same could be said about the first three lean-to sites within this loop: Oak, Walnut, and Poplar. The Willow, Aspen, and Cherry lean-tos are grouped close together

re aren't many trees between these sites. If you're having a camping family
ome other confluence of friends and family, securing either troika of lean-tos
you the perfect venue.

The Fir lean-to is set off on its own, and it's right across from the restrooms. Site 26 is
also conveniently located near the facilities, but it isn't very private. The Alder lean-to is
set up for wheelchair access.

Moving farther along the loop and back into the tent sites, site 25 is smaller but
nicely isolated—a worthwhile tradeoff in my book (so to speak). Actually, sites 21 through
25 are all moderately spaced and well isolated. Next to site 21, there's a short road leading
up to another trio of lean-tos—Cedar, Locust, and Larch. (Larch? I had never heard of that
kind of tree before! It's a hardy, alpine conifer that flourishes at altitudes up to 5,000 feet
and has slender, soft needles that turn somewhat golden in fall.) If you have a very large
group that wants to bunk out in a trio of lean-tos, Gifford Woods State Park is clearly
where you want to be, specifically the Lower Loop, where most of the lean-tos are situated. I sometimes wonder about the naming conventions of these lean-tos. What happens
if they start running out of tree varieties? I can see it: If they built another loop full of
lean-tos in one of the larger Vermont State Park campgrounds, we might end up with
Mangrove, Eucalyptus, and Joshua!

Site 20 is open and spacious but not as private or set into the woods as some of the
others. Sites 15 through 19 are larger sites, but you run the risk of having an RV nearby.
The woods here are moderately dense, but you'll still have an RV in view if it moors next
door. Similarly, site 14 is very open and has plenty of room to spread your wings (or your
tarp and your tent's rainfly), but you'll give up a little privacy.

Perhaps the nicest aspect of Gifford Woods State Park is that you don't have to travel
far outside the park, or even inside the park, before you run across some hiking trails. The
Appalachian Trail runs right through the park and reconnects with the Long Trail approximately 1.5 miles north of the park. Another spectacular sight to see is the seven-acre
stand of old-growth hardwoods, located right across VT 100 from the campground. This
pristine wilderness has some massive sugar maple, beech, birch, and ash trees. Tread
lightly, and enjoy this grand old forest.

MAP

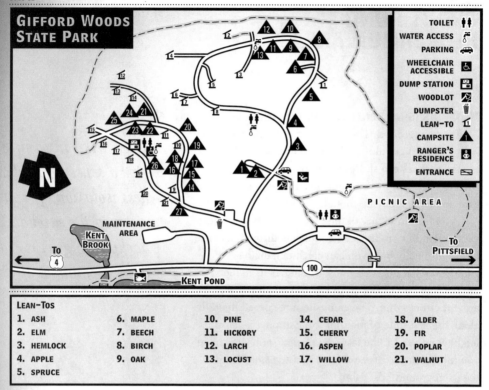

GIFFORD WOODS STATE PARK

TOILET	👫
WATER ACCESS	🚰
PARKING	🚗
WHEELCHAIR ACCESSIBLE	♿
DUMP STATION	🔲
WOODLOT	🔲
DUMPSTER	🗑
LEAN-TO	🏠
CAMPSITE	▲
RANGER'S RESIDENCE	🔲
ENTRANCE	✉

N

MAINTENANCE AREA

KENT BROOK

To **4**

To **PITTSFIELD**

PICNIC AREA

100

KENT POND

Lean-Tos

1. ASH	6. MAPLE	10. PINE	14. CEDAR	18. ALDER
2. ELM	7. BEECH	11. HICKORY	15. CHERRY	19. FIR
3. HEMLOCK	8. BIRCH	12. LARCH	16. ASPEN	20. POPLAR
4. APPLE	9. OAK	13. LOCUST	17. WILLOW	21. WALNUT
5. SPRUCE				

GETTING THERE

Gifford Woods State Park is located right off VT 100, just north of the access road for Killington Ski Area.

THIS IS NO SANITIZED, DRIVE-IN, drive-out campground. The campsites at Grout Pond are spread out along a hiking trail that winds around the western shores of the pond. You have to hike your gear in to your tent site. This extra effort will give you a huge payoff, though.

You hike in to any of the 11 tent and lean-to sites via the Pond Loop Trail. This trail cuts through a dense forest, through which you can catch tantalizing glimpses of the pond as you start out. As its name implies, the Pond Loop Trail brings you all the way around Grout Pond. The campsites are spread liberally along the first mile of the trail. No camping is permitted beyond site 11, the last "developed" tent site. Since you hike in to the sites, parking is in the small lot past the campground host cabin.

Don't expect to happen upon the campsites as soon as you set out from the parking area. The first site is just under a 0.5-mile hike in. Carry a manageable amount of gear, or better yet, have a wagon or some sort of wheeled cart to transport your stuff. If you're hauling gear without wheeled assistance, start out by bringing your tent to stake your claim on your site. These sites are first come, first served. You can't make reservations, so it's a good idea to have a backup plan if they are full.

This is very rustic, primitive camping. There's a true wilderness feel to these sites that is usually experienced by backcountry backpacking trips.

At 0.1 mile down the Pond Loop Trail, you'll come to a trailhead for the 3.2-mile East Trail, the 1-mile hike to the Kelley Stand parking area, and the 2-mile hike to the Somerset Reservoir. Shortly after passing this trailhead, you'll come to another trailhead for the Camp Trail, which follows a shorter loop out from the pond than the winding East Trail. Stay on the Pond Loop Trail to get to the campsites.

These hike-in campsites give a sense of wilderness isolation typically reserved for extended backpacking trips—they are as remote as it gets.

RATINGS

Beauty: ✿ ✿ ✿ ✿ ✿
Privacy: ✿ ✿ ✿ ✿ ✿
Spaciousness: ✿ ✿ ✿ ✿
Quiet: ✿ ✿ ✿ ✿ ✿
Security: ✿ ✿ ✿ ✿
Cleanliness: ✿ ✿ ✿ ✿ ✿

ADDRESS: Grout Pond Recre-
ation Area
Fire Road 262
Arlington, VT 05250

OPERATED BY: Green Mountain
National Forest

INFORMATION: Green Mountain
National Forest
Manchester Ranger
District
2538 Depot Street
Manchester Center,
VT 05255
(802) 362-2307

OPEN: Year-round

SITES: 11 hike-in tent sites
and lean-to sites
around pond, sev-
eral nearby day-use
or trailer sites

EACH SITE HAS: Fire ring with grate,
picnic table, tent
platform or pad

ASSIGNMENT: First come, first
served

REGISTRATION: Register by
occupying site

FACILITIES: Pit toilets

PARKING: At trailhead to
campsites

FEE: Donations accepted

RESTRICTIONS: *Pets:* Dogs on leash
only
Fires: In fire rings
only
Alcohol: At sites only
Vehicles: In main
parking area only
Other: Day-use areas
open 6 a.m.–10 p.m.;
quiet hours are
10 p.m.–7 a.m.; max-
imum 8 people per
site; 14-day maxi-
mum stay

Site 1 is set down off the trail on the shore of Grout Pond. It's an incredibly spacious site where you'll get breezes blowing in off the pond and a decent amount of sunlight filtering through the moderately dense forest. The site is hidden in a very subtle way from the Pond Loop Trail by a stand of trees and a short stone wall. Down in the site, you'll have a clear view of the pond, and access to it for your canoe or kayak.

That brings up another point about getting to your site. Once you've marked your site with your tent, you could go back to your car and haul your gear in, taking four or five (or however many) trips. Or, you could load up your canoe or kayak and paddle to the site. Then you've got your vessel right there at your campsite and can explore the crystalline waters of Grout Pond after you've set up camp. You could also haul your gear inside your canoe or kayak atop a wheeled cart.

The next site on the Pond Loop Trail, site 2, is very isolated from the trail. Standing on the Pond Loop Trail, you can barely see site 2. There's a twist-ing, 50-foot path down to the site, which is a bit smaller than site 1 but just as open to the pond, and extremely secluded.

If privacy is more important to you than being right on the pond, site 3 is a perfect choice. This site is set up in the woods away from the pond. You'll cross a series of short footbridges put there to minimize trail erosion. Please use the bridges; don't step off or around them. The site is set within a very dense forest of deciduous trees, with a lot of maple and beech. It's moderately spacious, but site 1 is clearly the largest at Grout Pond if that's an important factor.

Right across the trail—but extremely secluded from it—on the pond side is site 4. Follow a 50-foot path down toward the pond to the site. It's smaller than site 1 or 2 but very sunny and open to the water.

Just past sites 3 and 4, there's a picnic area next to the pond. If you're waiting for someone to finish pack-ing up before you occupy a site, this is a great spot to rest and have a bite. When I first walked the Pond Loop Trail, I mistook this for a campsite, but it's clearly marked as a no-camping and no-fires area.

Another superbly secluded site is 5, which is up in

the woods on the opposite side of the trail from the pond. The spur trail to the site is approximately 70 feet long. It gets dark early here, as very little evening sunlight penetrates the extremely dense, mostly deciduous forest. The distance from the Pond Loop Trail and the woods encircling site 5 combine to offer a complete sense of solitude.

It may be fairly small, but site 6 is also well isolated from the Pond Loop Trail (being about 25 feet off the trail) and from the neighboring campsites. It's a fairly small site, but it has a tent platform, is very open to the sun, and is encircled by a dense grove of young maple trees.

If you would rather be way off in the woods, check out site 8. This is a lean-to site accessed via a 150-foot spur trail and is set within a grove of moderately spaced beech and ash trees and dense undergrowth.

Site 7 is actually past site 8, and it's located on the pond side of the trail. This is another small site, but it's buffered by dense undergrowth to offer privacy. It's also very sunny and open to the pond. Site 9 is a lean-to in the woods away from the pond in a fairly open part of the forest.

If ever there were a near-perfect site, it would have to be site 10, which is very isolated by virtue of its remote location on the Pond Loop Trail and the distance from its nearest neighbors. It's a medium-sized site set beneath a loose stand of maples and spruce. There's a nice, flat, grass-and-moss-covered area for your tent carved out of the dense undergrowth. There's also a tree hanging over the pond, which adds some character.

There is a complete sense of isolation to site 11. It's on the pond side, about 70 feet from the Pond Loop Trail and distant from any neighbor. This is a moderately spacious site, set within a relatively dense forest of mostly deciduous trees and encircled by dense undergrowth to complete your wilderness camping experience.

These last couple of sites along the Pond Loop Trail—sites 10 and 11—are as secluded and wild as just about any you will find in New England. The layout and character of site 10 make it my favorite. It has a Japanese garden feel to it, with moss cover, artful spacing of the trees, one tree growing out over the pond, and its open flow. From site 10 you have a full view of the pond, and the openness allows you to enjoy the breezes and the sunlight, or the moonlight once dusk has fallen.

When you arrive at Grout Pond, you'll see some sites up near the campground host cabin, near the day-use area. These are likely spots for RVs. Pitch your tent here only as long as you have to wait for one of the pondside sites to open up.

MAP

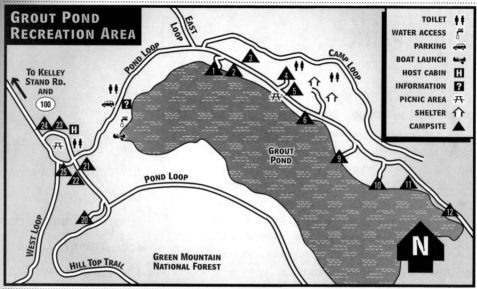

GETTING THERE

From VT 100, take the Stratton/Arlington road in Wardsboro, just north of Mount Snow. Follow this to the brown Forest Service sign for Grout Pond on the left (heading north).

36
HALF MOON STATE PARK

THE CONTIGUOUS **BOMOSEEN** and Half Moon state parks are essentially a string of ponds, marshlands, and abandoned quarry sites, all interconnected by several hiking trails ranging in length from 0.3 to 4.5 miles. From the sheltered enclave of Half Moon Pond, you could hike the Half Moon Pond Trail to the Glen Lake Trail, follow this through Beaver Meadow, and pass Moscow Pond to Glen Lake. From Glen Lake, the Slate History Trail will bring you to Lake Bomoseen.

The campground at Half Moon State Park is divided into two areas along either side of the pond. The loop with sites 1 through 35 is off to the left as you enter the camping area, and the rest of the sites, 36 through 60, are off to the right. Both sides of the campground have sites perched right on the shore of Half Moon Pond. These are the best sites.

As you enter the 1-through-35 loop, sites 1 and 2 sit immediately on your left. They are spacious and set within a loose grove of maples and other deciduous trees. Located right where the campground road splits, site 2 is very open.

Sites 4 and 6 are both situated on the shore of Half Moon Pond. Site 4 is spacious and has a partially grass-covered surface upon which to pitch your tent. It's a bit close to site 6, which is on the left as you look at the pond. Still, this is a key spot if you've brought along a canoe or kayak. You could launch your boat right from your campsite. Site 6 is smaller than site 4, but it's also shadier. Paddlers and anglers should reserve sites 4 and 6, as they're perfectly suited for either activity.

There is a deeper sense of seclusion to site 3. It's set up in the woods off the campground road, opposite but overlooking the pond. Site 5 is too open. The back side faces the restrooms, and the front opens to site 6.

> *Half Moon Pond is pristine, and the campground that wraps around either side provides some spectacular pondside camping.*

RATINGS

Beauty: ✩ ✩ ✩ ✩ ✩
Privacy: ✩ ✩ ✩ ✩
Spaciousness: ✩ ✩ ✩ ✩
Quiet: ✩ ✩ ✩ ✩ ✩
Security: ✩ ✩ ✩ ✩
Cleanliness: ✩ ✩ ✩ ✩

ADDRESS: Half Moon State Park
1621 Black Pond Road
Fair Haven, VT 05743

OPERATED BY: Vermont Agency of Natural Resources, Department of Forests, Parks, and Recreation

INFORMATION: Half Moon State Park, (802) 273-2848 (summer), (888) 409-7579 (October–May)

OPEN: Memorial Day–Columbus Day

SITES: 59 tent sites, 10 lean-to sites, 5 cabins

EACH SITE HAS: Stone hearth, picnic table

ASSIGNMENT: First come, first served; by reservation: (888) 409-7579

REGISTRATION: At ranger station

FACILITIES: Coin-operated hot showers, flush toilets, water spigots, dump station

PARKING: At sites

FEE: $16–$18 for tent sites, $23–$25 for lean-tos

RESTRICTIONS: *Pets:* On leash only
Fires: In fire rings only
Alcohol: At sites only
Vehicles: Parking at sites only
Other: Reservations require 4-night minimum stay; check in after 2 p.m., check out by 11 a.m.; quiet hours 10 p.m.–7 a.m.; maximum 8 people per site

The sites on the forest side of the campground loop road—sites 7, 10, and 11—are very spacious and open, but they still offer mild seclusion because they are surrounded by moderately dense deciduous forest. Sites 8, 9, 12, 13, and 14 are right on the pond but are bunched in close together. They are all super sites, separated by small stands of deciduous trees; however, they're smaller, more closely packed, and less private.

Site 15 is large and well isolated on the sides and back of the site, but it's open to the road. Sites 14 and 16 are right on the pond. Site 16, however, feels jammed in between the other sites. These open sites may not provide as much privacy, but then again, they are on the water. Site 17 is also right on the pond, but it's slightly larger, more private, and right next to the small beach area.

Sites 20 and 21 are well secluded on the sides, if not from the front. Site 19, however, is very open. It's also right next to the restrooms. There's a similar, exposed character to sites 23 and 24. These spacious sites are nestled within a grove of mixed hardwoods.

The 25 through 35 section of the loop generally gives you a choice between smaller pond side sites or larger, open, wooded sites. There's a cool, dark feel to the forest here, as the canopy is high and dense, but at the ground level, the campsites in the low 30s are very open. One plus in this section is a trailhead for the Nature Trail between sites 30 and 31.

Heading off to the right as you enter the campground brings you to its more secluded section with sites 36 through 60. The boat-rental facility is also on this side of the pond. There are several fabulous pondside sites in this area. If you can, try to land in sites 48, 50, 58, or 60—more on them in a moment.

The location of site 36 provides isolation on all sides. It's tucked into the contours of a small hill to the left of the campground road as you head in. There's no pond view, but it's spacious, scenic, and private. The hill on which site 36 is perched is in the center of a small loop where most of the lean-to sites are located, but you can't see them from the site. The seclusion of this site is marvelous.

There's a beautiful, open grove of pine trees

across from site 38. The dark, slender pines poke up through the rich, brown carpet of pine needles, giving a silent, sylvan feel to this site. It's small but very well isolated. Site 37 shares a similar character, although it's a bit larger. It's also right across from the Hazel lean-to. Site 39 is small but secluded and right across from the Ilex lean-to.

Just outside site 40, across the road, there's a short footpath that leads to the pond, so it's the next best thing to being on the water. Site 40 is also isolated and shady, as it's set within a grove of young, mixed deciduous trees. Site 41 is narrow and on the small side, but it's carved out of a grove of young deciduous trees whose brilliant green leaves brighten the whole site.

Sites 42 and 43 sit opposite each other across the campground road. Site 42 is smaller and set in young mixed forest. Site 43 is very spacious and secluded on all sides, but it's open to the road and site 42. There's a similar layout and arrangement to sites 44 and 45. Site 44 is smaller than 45 and set within a grove of conifers and hardwoods. Site 45 is a little bigger and more secluded in a dense coniferous grove.

Site 46 is very spacious and secluded, set off the road in a dense, mixed forest. Sites 47 and 49 are moderately spacious but very open. These two are on either side of an open, grassy area surrounding the water spigot.

The tradeoff of spaciousness and seclusion for a waterside setting is one I am usually quite willing to make. Site 48, for example, is small but right on the pond. There aren't many trees filling in the forest canopy directly overhead, so it has an open view to the sky and easy access to the water.

Site 50 is very spacious and provides a nice sense of seclusion. It's set among towering spruce trees right on the pond. While it's not on the pond and doesn't offer a clear pond view, site 51 does offer excellent seclusion, with dense forest on all sides. It's also up off the campground road.

Just before the boat-launch area is site 52, which is set within a spruce grove and is relatively roomy and private. Site 53 is a bit smaller than 52, and it's very open to the road. Site 55 is of decent size, but it's also open to the road and next to the restrooms and a trailhead for the Glen Lake Trail. It's also directly across the road from the boat-rental facility. You can rent a canoe for $5 an hour, $15 for a half day, or $30 for a full day.

Dense undergrowth and a stand of trees isolate the cabin sites wrapped around the end of a short loop on the campground road. The Butterfly, Caterpillar, Beetle, Cricket, and Dragonfly cabins are grouped together out here, situated within a grove of mixed deciduous and coniferous trees. Their best aspect is the location right on the pond.

Site 60 is also on this short loop. This site is large and set in a loose grove of spruce overlooking the pond. It's between the Tall Timbers cottage and the Caterpillar cabin.

MAP

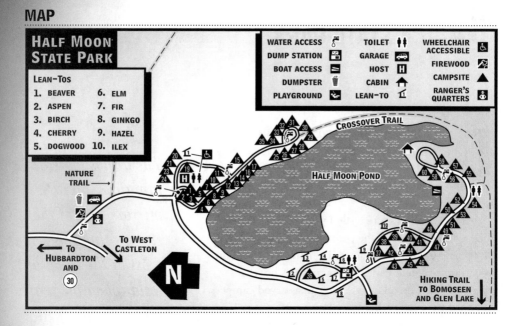

HALF MOON STATE PARK

LEAN-TOS

1. BEAVER
2. ASPEN
3. BIRCH
4. CHERRY
5. DOGWOOD

6. ELM
7. FIR
8. GINKGO
9. HAZEL
10. ILEX

WATER ACCESS
DUMP STATION
BOAT ACCESS
DUMPSTER
PLAYGROUND

TOILET
GARAGE
HOST
CABIN
LEAN-TO

WHEELCHAIR ACCESSIBLE
FIREWOOD
CAMPSITE
RANGER'S QUARTERS

CROSSOVER TRAIL

HALF MOON POND

NATURE TRAIL

To HUBBARDTON AND 30

To WEST CASTLETON

N

HIKING TRAIL TO BOMOSEEN AND GLEN LAKE

GETTING THERE

From VT 4 in Castleton Corners, take Exit 4 for VT 30 north. Follow this to Hubbardton. Turn left on Hortonville Road. Follow this to Black Pond Road. Turn left and follow this to the park.

37

JAMAICA STATE PARK

DON'T EVEN THINK OF COMING HERE without a reservation on one of the river-release weekends. When the West River swells to its banks, the campground at Jamaica State Park swells with whitewater kayakers.

If you want to score a site for one of those biannual weekends (one in the spring and one in the fall), you'll have to plan way ahead. Even for the rest of the year, Jamaica State Park's campground is heavily reserved. They do take first-come, first-served campers, but open sites can be hard to come by. Do yourself a favor and plan ahead for this one.

There are 43 tent sites and 18 lean-tos. Several lean-tos are arranged in a small loop at one end of the campground, but most sit in a line facing the West River. I can only imagine the scene during river-release weekends: Lean-tos packed with camping and paddling gear and the river surging along, dotted with brilliantly colored kayaks and thrilled paddlers.

Generally, the campground and the surrounding park are very quiet. There are no major highways nearby, so there isn't much in the way of road noise. The campsites are situated beneath a forest of moderately spaced towering spruce and shorter, younger hardwoods. The dense undergrowth provides a nice sense of seclusion between most of the individual sites. The sites themselves are spacious and have a hard, sandy surface that's perfect for holding tent stakes.

The loop heading off to the right as you enter the camping area brings you to sites 1 through 11. There's a cathedralesque feel to the forest on this side of the campground, with the towering spruce trees presiding over the woodland. Sunlight and breezes flow easily through the forest to the sites.

Sites 1 and 2 are set back in the woods among the loosely spaced forest. Site 1 is open and fairly spacious.

> *The atmosphere at Jamaica State Park mirrors that of the river: calm and serene most of the time, but wild when the whitewater is up.*

RATINGS

Beauty: ✰ ✰ ✰ ✰ ✰
Privacy: ✰ ✰ ✰ ✰
Spaciousness: ✰ ✰ ✰ ✰ ✰
Quiet: ✰ ✰ ✰ ✰
Security: ✰ ✰ ✰ ✰
Cleanliness: ✰ ✰ ✰ ✰

ADDRESS: Jamaica State Park
285 Salmon Hole
Lane
Jamaica, VT 05343

OPERATED BY: Vermont Agency of
Natural Resources
Department of
Forests, Parks, and
Recreation

INFORMATION: Jamaica State Park
(802) 874-4600 (sum-
mer), (888) 409-7579
(October–May)

OPEN: Late April–
Columbus Day

SITES: 43 tent sites, 18 lean-
to sites

EACH SITE HAS: Fire ring, picnic
table

ASSIGNMENT: First come, first
served; by reserva-
tion (strongly recom-
mended): (888)
409-7579

REGISTRATION: At ranger station

FACILITIES: Hot showers, flush
toilets, water spig-
ots, playground

PARKING: At sites

FEE: $16–$18 for tent
sites, $23–$25 for
lean-tos

RESTRICTIONS: *Pets:* On leash only
Fires: In fire rings
only
Alcohol: At sites only
Vehicles: Parking at
sites only
Other: Reservations
require 4-night mini-
mum stay; check in
after 2 p.m., check
out by 11 a.m.; quiet
hours 10 p.m.–7
a.m.; maximum 8
people per site

Site 2 is larger and set up off the campground loop road. It has an open feel without sacrificing its sense of privacy.

The added elevation of sites 3 and 4 makes them more secluded. These sites, roomy and clean, are set on a small rise off the campground loop road. Site 3 is opposite the volleyball net in the day-use area, which you can see through the woods. It's cool to be close to the action, but it could get noisy during the day. Site 4 is located next to the restrooms. Site 5 is a little smaller than most of the other sites in this loop, but it's off the campground loop road, which adds privacy.

Nearby, the Briar lean-to is set up for wheelchair access. The rest of the lean-tos within this part of the loop are positioned facing out from or perpendicular to the loop road, which increases their privacy.

The lean-tos are spread out beneath the loosely spaced forest and against a good-sized hill that is peppered liberally with loosely spaced pine and spruce and coated in a soft blanket of pine needles. The effect is captivating. The Hackberry and Ironwood lean-tos are at the base of the hill. The forest is open enough here so that there's plenty of room to pitch tents at the lean-to sites.

A spruce grove and a small embankment give site 6 a pleasant sense of privacy from the lean-tos behind the site. However, site 6 is open to the Ironwood and Hackberry sites facing the hill. Site 7 is very spacious and airy but also secluded by a deep spruce grove and young deciduous trees on one side. This is helpful because it's also right next to the restrooms.

The added elevation of site 8 enhances its privacy. This spacious site is set up on a platform off the campground road and surrounded by loosely spaced spruce and dense, young deciduous trees and undergrowth. Site 9 is set at the base of the hill behind the Hackberry and Ironwood lean-tos. This site is very isolated on both sides, but open to site 8 across the road. Site 9 is large, and there's a handsome, open character to the forest here. Site 11 is roomy yet very secluded on all sides, framed by towering spruce trees. Site 10 also is spacious and private.

The campground loop is split by a short road, on

which sites 12 and 13 are located. These sites are roomy but very exposed and close to the road. Site 12 is open to the sky, so the site itself receives lots of sunlight filtered through the forest. The sites don't offer much in the way of privacy, though.

The forest is dense along the larger loop to the left as you enter the campground, which has sites 14 and up. The forest's character adds seclusion and privacy to these sites, most of which are moderately to very spacious. Site 14 is huge but doesn't provide much privacy, as it's very open on the sides. Sites 15 and 16 are both moderate in size and fairly well isolated.

Even though it's right across from the restrooms, site 17 does have dense undergrowth on all sides. It is also set on a small rise, so it strikes a balance between moderate privacy and convenience to the facilities. Site 18 is spacious and open but not too private. Site 19 is a bit smaller and secluded on both sides, but it's open to the road.

There's a deep sense of privacy to site 20 because it's set down off the campground road. There's also a big rock in the center that you could use as a small table. This site is framed by spruce and dense undergrowth. Sites 21, 22, and 23 are all similar in size, shape, and spaciousness. Site 22 is set off the campground road, and site 23 is down off the road. These are all fairly secluded and moderately spacious.

Sites 24 and 25 are close together and a bit smaller than sites 21 through 23. Site 24 is set off the road a bit. Site 27 is huge but very open to the road. This site would be good for a larger group. It's framed on the sides by dense undergrowth and spruce trees, and it abuts the back of site 26. Site 29 is set down off the road and otherwise nicely secluded. It's very spacious and surrounded by dense, young undergrowth broken by towering spruce. Sites 28, 30, and 31 are similar in character in that they are moderately spacious and well isolated on the sides. Site 32 sits off the road in the dense undergrowth. It's smaller but nicely secluded.

If you're camping with kids, site 33 is a good choice, as it's right near the playground. It's also a great site if you plan to do a lot of hiking. There's a trailhead behind the playground that leads you to the gentle, 2.5-mile Railroad Bed Trail that follows the West River to the Ball Mountain Dam, the 2-mile Overlook Trail that takes you up and over the summit of Little Ball Mountain, and the 3-mile Hamilton Falls Trail that brings you to the dramatic, 125-foot cascade of Hamilton Falls.

At sites 38 and above, the forest opens quite suddenly. These sites are separated by narrow stands of spruce and white pine and these are roomy but open. It's up to you to decide how you feel about a site with this character, but I prefer sites that are more densely wooded.

There's a mixed sandy and grassy surface at site 39, which is framed by loose pines and spruce. This site is also right along the day-use parking area, separated by a relatively dense stand of trees.

Sites 39, 40, and 41 are all increasingly vast. These sites would work well for larger groups needing two or three contiguous sites. They're also great for stargazing or sunbathing, as they are wide open to the sky and there's plenty of room to pile up paddling gear for those wild river-release weekends.

MAP

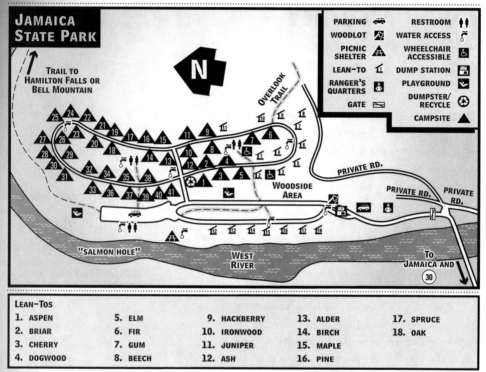

JAMAICA STATE PARK

TRAIL TO HAMILTON FALLS OR BELL MOUNTAIN

OVERLOOK TRAIL

N

PARKING	RESTROOM
WOODLOT	WATER ACCESS
PICNIC SHELTER	WHEELCHAIR ACCESSIBLE
LEAN-TO	DUMP STATION
RANGER'S QUARTERS	PLAYGROUND
GATE	DUMPSTER/ RECYCLE
	CAMPSITE

WOODSIDE AREA

PRIVATE RD.

PRIVATE RD.

PRIVATE RD.

"SALMON HOLE"

WEST RIVER

To JAMAICA AND 30

LEAN-TOS

1. ASPEN	5. ELM	9. HACKBERRY	13. ALDER	17. SPRUCE
2. BRIAR	6. FIR	10. IRONWOOD	14. BIRCH	18. OAK
3. CHERRY	7. GUM	11. JUNIPER	15. MAPLE	
4. DOGWOOD	8. BEECH	12. ASH	16. PINE	

GETTING THERE

Follow VT 30 into Jamaica. Head east on Depot Street for a half mile to the park.

38
MOUNT ASCUTNEY STATE PARK

Windsor

DIFFERENT PEOPLE ASSOCIATE Mount Ascutney with different things. For some, it's the ski area they think of first (although it is not officially part of Ascutney State Park). For others, it may be the hiking. For a select group of people, hang gliding comes to mind. Mount Ascutney is one of the premier spots in New England from which to launch a hang glider. For those activities (well, at least the hiking and hang gliding), spending the night camped out in the state park at the base of Mount Ascutney is a great way to start.

There are two distinct camping areas within Mount Ascutney State Park. Sites 1 through 18 are off to the right as you enter the park. Sites 19 through 39 are in the loop off to the left. The auto road to the summit is directly ahead of you when you enter the park here.

I particularly like the sites in the 1-through-8 loop off to the right. They are spread out, so most provide solitude and seclusion. The forest here is a dense mix of primarily coniferous trees. The only caveat is that this side of the campground is fairly close to VT 44A, so you will hear a bit of road noise during the day but not too much at night.

The first cluster of sites includes sites 1 through 5. The road on this side of the campground is a straight in-and-out, two-way road. The other side has a one-way loop. Site 1 is fairly small and is located right off the campground road. Site 2 is set off the road and is more isolated. Sites 3, 4, and 5 are grouped together, but site 5 has a long driveway leading into it that adds to its privacy. Sites 3 and 4 would be good for a large group, as they are close together. The mixed forest gives the individual sites a shaded solitude.

Site 10 is spacious but open to the road and right across from the restrooms. Sites 9, 11, and 12 are set in

> *Mount Ascutney has an elaborate network of hiking trails, easily accessible from the southern end of the campground.*

RATINGS

Beauty: ✪ ✪ ✪ ✪
Privacy: ✪ ✪ ✪ ✪
Spaciousness: ✪ ✪ ✪ ✪
Quiet: ✪ ✪ ✪
Security: ✪ ✪ ✪ ✪ ✪
Cleanliness: ✪ ✪ ✪ ✪

KEY INFORMATION

ADDRESS: Mount Ascutney
State Park
1826 Back Mountain
Road
Windsor, VT 05089

OPERATED BY: Vermont Agency of
Natural Resources,
Department of
Forests, Parks, and
Recreation

INFORMATION: Mount Ascutney
State Park,
(802) 674-2060
(summer),
(888) 409-7579
(October–May)

OPEN: Mid-May–October 15

SITES: 39 tent sites, 10 lean-
to sites

EACH SITE HAS: Stone hearth or fire
ring, picnic table

ASSIGNMENT: First come, first
served; by reserva-
tion: (888) 409-7579

REGISTRATION: At ranger station

FACILITIES: Coin-operated hot
showers, flush toilets,
water spigots

PARKING: At sites

FEE: $14 for tent sites, $21
for lean-tos

RESTRICTIONS: *Pets:* On leash only
Fires: In fire rings
only
Alcohol: At sites only
Vehicles: Parking at
sites only
Other: Reservations
require 2-night mini-
mum stay; check in
after 2 p.m., check
out by 11 a.m.; quiet
hours 10 p.m.–
7 a.m.; maximum
8 people per site

a small group, much like sites 3, 4, and 5. Site 9 is too open and close to the road. Sites 11 and 12 are tucked around a corner off the campground road, so they offer a deeper sense of privacy. Again, all these sites are a stone's throw from VT 44A through the woods, so at times there will be some road noise.

The next group of sites you'll encounter as you move down the campground road are sites 6 through 8. These three sites are also set in a cluster. Site 8 is near the restroom, which is a good thing for some people and not so good for others. Site 7 sits on a short spur off the campground road. Its added elevation gives it a little more privacy. These sites are all moderately spacious.

As you walk up to site 7, on your right you'll see the short footpath leading to site 6, which is very isolated, with about a 50-foot hike in to it. Site 6 has a fire ring instead of a hearth, which I generally prefer. Although the stone hearths are aesthetically pleasing, the iron fire rings seem to be safer, containing the fire, ashes, and coals on all sides.

The forest surrounding site 6 is relatively dense, but thins directly above the site to let in lots of sunlight during the day and give you a clear view of the sky at night. There are shadowy spruce trees spread on all sides of the site, giving it a pleasant, dark, cool feel, even on the warmest of summer days. There's still a bit of road noise from time to time, which is my only complaint about this otherwise excellent spot.

A dense spruce grove with lots of fern ground cover surrounds site 13, so there's a considerable sense of isolation, but it's still open to the road. Site 14 is small but down off the road, which makes it fairly secluded.

There's a small loop at the end of the campground road where sites 15 through 18 are located. There's a stand of towering spruce trees growing out of the center of the circle. Sites 15 and 16 are large but open to the road. Site 17 is located on a small rise above the campground road. This site is good-sized and fairly secluded. The best site within this loop is site 18. There's about a 25-foot path leading up to it from its parking space. The site is set within a relatively dense grove of mixed deciduous and coniferous trees, but its distance from the road gives it an exquisite air of seclusion.

Now on to the other side of the campground, where the second loop contains sites 19 through 39 and the lean-tos. Site 22 sits near the trailhead for the Futures Trail. From here, you'll have access to a 1-mile hike to Bare Rock Vista, a 3.4-mile hike to the Steam Donkey overlook, a 4.1-mile hike to the junction with the Windsor Trail, and a 4.5-mile hike to the summit of Mount Ascutney.

There's a solitary quality to site 22. It's roomy and buffered on all sides by woods. I like site 22 the best on this side of the campground. Site 21 is also very spacious, but the side of site 21 is the back of site 19. You can see right through one site to the other. Site 20 is spacious and more open than these two, and it's set within fairly dense forest. The arrangement of sites 19 and 21 makes them a good pair for a group.

A low canopy of spruce trees adds to the solitude at site 23. It's a bit on the small side, though. Site 24 is tucked off to the left, and it's also isolated on the sides, but it opens in the back to the sites behind it and to the lean-tos set around an open area. Most of the lean-tos at Mount Ascutney State Park sit in an open field and a loose grove of spruce and maple. The Oak and Beech lean-tos are the most exposed and the least private. The Maple lean-to is set up for wheelchair access and is right across from the restroom and the campground host site. The Pine lean-to is nicely isolated and set within a tall grove of spruce.

Sites 25 and 26 are both moderately spacious and set within a loosely spaced grove of spruce with dense undergrowth. These two sites are secluded on the side but somewhat open to each other. The White Birch and Cherry lean-tos are at the end of a short spur off the campground road. They are close to each other but great for a larger group.

A grove of maples and other mixed deciduous varieties surrounds the spacious site 27, which is open to the sky and set off the campground road. Sites 29 and 31 are spacious, but open to the road. You'll still hear occasional road noise from VT 44A on this side of the campground, especially in this part of the loop.

Set back from the campground road, sites 28 and 30 feel isolated, and site 30 is exceptionally spacious. Site 33 is open to the road but separated from neighboring sites. A loose grove of spruce borders the back of the site, and a wall of deciduous trees and dense undergrowth defines the sides. There's a short footpath right next to this site that leads up to the playground area and the restroom.

There is a slightly longer entryway leading to site 35, buffering it from the campground road. Sites 34 and 37 are across the road from each other but buffered on either side. Site 34 is moderately spacious, while site 37 is huge and very open above.

Site 36 is just like site 34 in size and shape. Site 38 is also similar, but it's a bit larger and very open to the sky. Site 39 is set off the campground road, making it private. It's also set within a dense grove of mixed conifers and hardwoods with lots of underbrush.

Whether it's the hiking or the hang gliding that brings you to Mount Ascutney State Park, a night in one of the campground's secluded sites will be a night well spent.

MAP

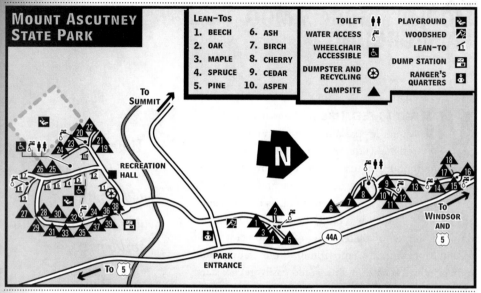

GETTING THERE

Take Interstate 91 to Exit 8.
From there, follow US 5
almost 2 miles to VT 44A.
Follow VT 44A about 1 mile
until you see signs for the
park.

39
MOUNT MOOSALAMOO CAMPGROUND

WANT TO FEEL LIKE you're really out there? Mount Moosalamoo offers an incredibly remote wilderness atmosphere. To get to the campground, you turn off the paved road (actually VT 7), and start heading down a long and winding dirt road. This is called the Goshen Road, as it will eventually lead you to the town of Goshen. Several miles down on the right, you'll come to the road leading into Mount Moosalamoo Campground. If our campground ratings judged seclusion, this would easily get six stars.

Moosalamoo is the Abenaki Indian word thought to mean "the moose departs" or "he trails the moose." The Abenakis frequently traveled through and stayed in this region, and their history and legacy linger.

The entire campground and all of the campsites within are shaded by a mixed forest of hardwoods, with lots of maple and birch. The brilliant green leaves at the height of spring and summer cast a glow over the campground. The forest is young and spaced loosely enough to let generous amounts of light reach the campsites.

There is a total of 19 sites at Moosalamoo. They're set on both sides of the short campground-loop road. The sites are large and spaced well apart with plenty of room at each to accommodate the group limit of eight campers per site. Mount Moosalamoo Campground would also score six stars for site spaciousness if the scale went that high!

The campground host is in site 1, which is off to the left as you enter the campground loop. Behind site 1, you'll catch your first glimpse of the big, open field in the center of the campground. There's also a little arboretum out there with a variety of deciduous and coniferous trees. The sign in front of the arboretum calls it a Backyard Wildlife Habitat. The evergreens

> *When you're camping at Mount Moosalamoo Campground, you are truly out in the wilderness.*

RATINGS

Beauty: ✿ ✿ ✿ ✿ ✿
Privacy: ✿ ✿ ✿ ✿ ✿
Spaciousness: ✿ ✿ ✿ ✿
Quiet: ✿ ✿ ✿ ✿ ✿
Security: ✿ ✿ ✿ ✿
Cleanliness: ✿ ✿ ✿ ✿

ADDRESS:	Mount Moosalamoo Campground VT 32 Ripton, VT 05766
OPERATED BY:	Green Mountain National Forest
INFORMATION:	Green Mountain National Forest Middlebury Ranger District 1007 VT 7 South Middlebury, VT 05753-8999 (802) 388-4362
OPEN:	Memorial Day–Labor Day
SITES:	19
EACH SITE HAS:	Fire ring, picnic table
ASSIGNMENT:	First come, first served
REGISTRATION:	Pay at self-serve fee station
FACILITIES:	Pit toilets, hand water pumps
PARKING:	At sites
FEE:	$10
RESTRICTIONS:	*Pets:* On leash only *Fires:* In fire rings only *Alcohol:* At sites only *Vehicles:* Maximum 2 vehicles per site *Other:* Check out by 2 p.m.; quiet hours 10 p.m.–6 a.m.; maximum 8 people per site; 14-day maximum stay; Green Mountain National Forest is closed to ATVs (woo hoo!)

within were planted in memory of former campground hostess Sarah Foster.

As you get deeper into the campground loop past site 4, the forest becomes denser, and the sites feel even wilder and more isolated. Sites 7, 9, 11, and most of the other odd-numbered sites on the inner side of the campground loop abut the central open field. If you camp on one of the inner loop sites, you'll be able to walk out the back of your site into this field, which is perfect for a game of Frisbee, lying in the sun, or stargazing.

Most of the sites are fairly uniform in size, but sites 10 and 14 are extra large. They each have two picnic tables. Site 16 and 17 are pretty big sites as well, but they are equipped with only one table apiece. Any of these are worth investigating if you're camping with a larger group or family. Site 19 is right next to the arboretum, a pleasant aspect. It's also quite close to the recycling station.

Mount Moosalamoo Campground is small and intimate and has a wonderful sense of remoteness. I can think of only one caveat, although it certainly isn't unique to this campground: Bring whatever bug spray works best for you. You'll be deep in the woods here, and the insects can be ravenous.

There are plenty of hiking trails within easy reach of Mount Moosalamoo Campground. You'll see trailheads for the Mount Moosalamoo and North Branch trails as you enter. The blue-blazed trails are the local hiking trails. The white-blazed trails are the Appalachian Trail and the Long Trail, which overlap through the Moosalamoo region.

There's also a trailhead right outside the campground for the Voter Brook Overlook.

All of these trails intersect other trail networks that wind throughout the forest in this part of Vermont. Try to get your hand on a trail map, because the trail network is extensive, and it wouldn't be too difficult to wander off a bit farther than you intended.

MAP

MOUNT MOOSALAMOO CAMPGROUND

GREEN MOUNTAIN NATIONAL FOREST

Mt. Moosalamoo Trl.

N

To FS-32 AND 7

FS-24

North Branch Trl.

To VOTER BROOK OVERLOOK

VAULT TOILET
WATER ACCESS
PARKING
RECYCLING CENTER
PAY STATION
CAMPSITE

GETTING THERE

Follow VT 7 west, past the Middlebury College Snow Bowl and Breadloaf campus. Turn left on Road #32 (Goshen Road). Follow this dirt road 4 miles and look for the campground signs on the right.

> *There are numerous short hikes in and around Quechee Gorge— you could spend countless hours gazing up into the dramatic formations.*

I N A STATE FULL OF incredible natural spectacles, Quechee Gorge has got to be one of Vermont's most amazing and unique sights. Plunging 165 feet down to the Ottauquechee River (whew, I'm glad they shortened that to name the gorge), Quechee Gorge looks like the scene in Butch Cassidy and the Sundance Kid where Robert Redford and Paul Newman, when cornered by the "good" guys, jump off their perch on a sheer cliff into a raging river.

Seen from the US 4 bridge that passes over it, the gorge's depth looks almost surreal. You'll be able to tell when you're there, even if you miss the signs for the gorge and the state park. There are always a bunch of people who have stopped to look over the bridge.

Just before you get to the gorge (if you're heading north on US 4), you'll come to Quechee Gorge State Park Campground, quietly tucked off on the left opposite the tourist shops selling T-shirts and maple syrup lining the other side of the road. For the most part, the campground is in a loosely spaced forest of conifers without much undergrowth. That factor, combined with the spacing and height of trees, gives the forest a statuesque presence. Visitors feel protected and secluded beneath the forest canopy. The spicy scent of coniferous trees, mixed in with the musty aroma of wood smoke, instantly brings you into the deep wilderness. Olfactory delights abound here.

Overall, the sites are large and somewhat open. You could land a space shuttle in site 2, yet it still feels fairly isolated from the neighboring sites by the forest and a bit of undergrowth. You'll hear some road noise from nearby US 4, but it's not too bad. At night, it's guaranteed to lessen. Also, the road noise is reduced the farther back you go in the campground.

While most of the more spacious sites would be suitable for wheelchair access, site 3 is specifically

RATINGS

Beauty: ☆ ☆ ☆ ☆ ☆
Privacy: ☆ ☆ ☆ ☆
Spaciousness: ☆ ☆ ☆ ☆
Quiet: ☆ ☆ ☆
Security: ☆ ☆ ☆ ☆
Cleanliness: ☆ ☆ ☆ ☆

configured that way. Site 6 is right across from the restroom and shower building. There's a small playground behind the restroom building. Whether or not you want to be close to these is your call.

There's a steep embankment that falls away from the campground behind sites 7 through 14. This is not part of Quechee Gorge per se, but perhaps the river flowed this way many moons ago. This feature of the landscape makes for dramatic scenery, but you'll need to be extra cautious if you have kids running around. A tumble down this embankment would be grim.

The Birch lean-to is also located along the steep drop-off by sites 7 through 14. Additionally, you'll find a horseshoe pit near the Birch lean-to. Didn't bring your own horseshoes? No problem—visit the host site (to the right of the shower building) to check out a set.

There isn't much privacy at site 8, and it's a bit too exposed for my taste. Site 9 is huge and shielded overhead by the forest canopy, although it's very open at the ground level. You find these same characteristics at sites 12 and 10. These two sites are also close to each other, which is particularly appealing for a larger group that might want two adjoining sites. Site 16 is another site that is almost too vast.

The Walnut and Ash lean-tos are located right next to each other, also a good pair for a group large enough to need two. The Hickory and Hackberry lean-tos are also adjacent. With the lean-tos in the Vermont state park campgrounds named for tree varieties, a new species is just one more thing you might learn while camping here.

Another good pair of sites for a larger group would be 18 and 19. These two are very open and close together. What these sites lack in privacy, they make up for in spaciousness. Quite close to a large, open field in the center of the campground, these are good sites for those camping with a tribe of kids who need a place for them to run around and burn off some of their seemingly boundless energy. The swing set and slides are in this field. There is also a trailhead for the Quechee Gorge Trail at the nearby intersection of the campground roads. This short trail is perfect for a quick walk after dinner.

KEY INFORMATION

ADDRESS:	Quechee Gorge State Park 764 Dewey Mills Road White River Junction, VT 05001
OPERATED BY:	Vermont Agency of Natural Resources, Department of Forests, Parks, and Recreation
INFORMATION:	Quechee Gorge State Park, (802) 295-2990 (summer), (888) 409-7579 (October–May)
OPEN:	Memorial Day–October 15
SITES:	47 tent sites, 7 lean-to sites
EACH SITE HAS:	Fire ring, picnic table
ASSIGNMENT:	First come, first served; by reservation: (888) 409-7579
REGISTRATION:	At ranger station
FACILITIES:	Coin-operated hot showers, flush toilets, playground
PARKING:	At sites
FEE:	$14–$16 for tent sites, $21–$23 for lean-tos
RESTRICTIONS:	*Pets:* On leash only *Fires:* In fire rings only *Alcohol:* At sites only *Vehicles:* Parking at sites only *Other:* Reservations require 2-night minimum stay; check in after 2 p.m., check out by 11 a.m.; quiet hours 10 p.m.–7 a.m.; maximum 8 people per site

Set against the woods bordering the central field, sites 20 through 22 are moderately spacious and allow easy access to the field. The Pine lean-to is also located on the field. It is very open and not too private, but it is configured for disabled access. The campground also winds around a bit closer to Route 4 here, so the proximity to the road and the field, can make it a bit noisy.

There will be road noise at sites 23 through 28. Site 23 is very open and lacks some privacy. Site 24 is quite close to the road; inn fact, you can see the store on the other side of Route 4 through the woods. However, site 24 does have a nice amount of dense forest on either side.

Site 26 is huge but wide open. This site is also right next to part of the Quechee Gorge Trail, which is a mere 0.21 miles away. Site 27 is open, spacious, and set within a spruce grove. Site 29 is spacious and open, but the back of the site opens to the field and restroom. Site 30 is set within a grove of mixed deciduous and coniferous trees. This site faces the gorge, so through openings in the forest, there's a view as the gorge drops away below. Site 31 is spacious and set beneath a coniferous grove, so the floor is covered with a blanket of pine needles and leaves upon which you can pitch your tent.

There's a steep drop-off facing sites 31 through 37. The scenery is nothing short of dramatic, but in these sites there are numerous additional reasons to keep a close eye (or a short leash) on the kids. Sites 32 and 34 are quite open and spacious but not as private as the rest. Site 35 is very open. The back of the site opens to the back of the lean-to sites.

At the end of this spur off the campground loop road, site 37 is set in a quiet grove of conifers and offers a nice sense of isolation. Site 37 is an incredible campsite: spacious, framed by conifers, and open to the sky to get lots of sunlight. Site 37 is also right next to the Quechee Gorge Trail, which is a short hike down to the gorge from the campground.

Site 38 is located between the Walnut and Ash lean-tos. It's framed by dense woods, but very open in front. Within the 42-through-47 loop, site 47 is huge and somewhat open in front and above, but there is dense forest on the sides. Site 45 is also huge and has an open feel. It's set within a pine grove. Sites 44 and 46 are a bit smaller but still have a nice isolated feel. Site 43 is huge and open. This site is also set within a grove of pines but is a bit closer to the road and the recycling station.

It's a bit smaller than some of its neighbors, but site 39 is still quite spacious. This site is carved out of a grove of loosely spaced white pines. Site 40 is open and spacious and set within a loosely spaced pines. It's a beautiful site, but it's also on the Route 4 side of the campground, so you'll hear some road noise. Sites 42 and 43 are a bit more open and also closer to the campground loop road, so they're not as quiet as the more secluded sites.

MAP

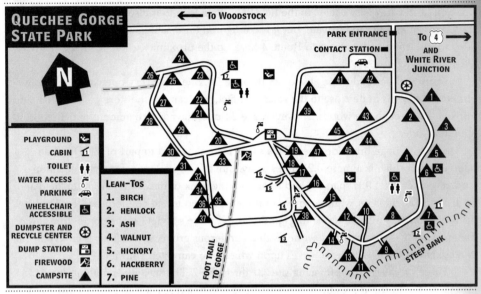

QUECHEE GORGE STATE PARK

To WOODSTOCK ←

PARK ENTRANCE
CONTACT STATION

To **4** →
AND
WHITE RIVER
JUNCTION

N

PLAYGROUND
CABIN
TOILET
WATER ACCESS
PARKING
WHEELCHAIR ACCESSIBLE
DUMPSTER AND RECYCLE CENTER
DUMP STATION
FIREWOOD
CAMPSITE

LEAN-TOS
1. BIRCH
2. HEMLOCK
3. ASH
4. WALNUT
5. HICKORY
6. HACKBERRY
7. PINE

FOOT TRAIL TO GORGE

STEEP BANK

GETTING THERE

From Route 89 in Vermont, follow Route 4 north toward the town of Quechee. The signs for the campground are right before Quechee Gorge itself.

> *Settled high in the Green Mountains, Smugglers Notch Campground has a quiet, secluded feel and easy access to some of the best hiking in Vermont.*

EVER WONDER WHERE THE **"SMUGGLERS"** in Smugglers Notch comes from? Me too. Apparently, when President Thomas Jefferson passed an embargo forbidding trade with Great Britain and Canada in 1807, it was especially hard on the folks living in northern Vermont. Most of those industrious, independent Vermonters kept right on trading with Montreal, moving cattle and other goods up through the narrow passage between the towering, 1,000-foot cliffs. They established a grand tradition of smuggling that continued with abolitionists helping slaves head north to seek liberation in Canada and rumrunners bringing liquor south into the country from Canada during Prohibition.

These days, things are a bit quieter in the notch. The campground at Smugglers Notch State Park is across the road from part of Stowe Mountain Resort ski area, so you get glimpses of the towering mountain through the trees. You're also surrounded by Mount Mansfield State Forest, so the hiking opportunities are virtually limitless. The campground is in a mixed, mostly deciduous forest, with an open field in the center. It is very quiet, especially at night, and even during the warmest periods of summer, the air is crisp and cool this high up in the Green Mountains.

The sites at Smugglers Notch are essentially in two groups—those sites on the inside of the campground loop road, and a handful of hike-in sites on the outside of the road. The rangers have labeled the tent sites and lean-to sites as prime or regular. When you're choosing your site, you can safely follow their assessments. Hermit Island in Maine does a similar thing, ranking sites by location and seclusion.

Most of the lean-to sites on the inside of the loop—Ash, Elm, Beech, and Maple—surround a small open area and loosely spaced trees. These are labeled as reg-

RATINGS

Beauty: ✿ ✿ ✿ ✿ ✿
Privacy: ✿ ✿ ✿ ✿
Spaciousness: ✿ ✿ ✿ ✿
Quiet: ✿ ✿ ✿ ✿ ✿
Security: ✿ ✿ ✿ ✿
Cleanliness: ✿ ✿ ✿ ✿

ular lean-to sites. Also in the lower half of the loop are tent sites 3, 19, and 20. Site 3 is considered a prime site, and it does offer privacy even though it's fairly close to the restrooms.

Tent sites 1 and 2 are nicely secluded from each other and from the road. They're down off the bottom of the campground loop. There will be some sporadic road noise from Route 108 on this end of the campground loop, but practically none at night.

Most of the rest of the lean-to sites are on the outside of the campground loop road. These include the Pine, Hemlock, Spruce, Balsam, and Oak sites. Balsam and Pine are considered prime lean-to sites, and indeed they are set back a bit farther from the road to offer more privacy. Oak is a wheelchair-accessible lean-to site. Tent site 4, which is nearby, is also a wheelchair-accessible site.

The small "village" of hike-in tent sites, including sites 5, 6, 8, 9, 11, 12, and 13, are interspersed with the Larch, Cedar, and Aspen lean-to sites. There are short hike-in trails leading into all of these sites, and a longer trail interconnecting the sites that runs roughly parallel to the campground road. This is a nice collection of spots within a relatively loosely spaced forest of mixed deciduous and coniferous trees.

At the top of the campground loop road, farthest from the ranger station, are most of the prime tent sites. Sites 7, 10, 14, and 15 are on the inside of the campground loop road and are all rightfully considered prime tent sites. The Birch lean-to site is next to site 15. The forest here is a mixed, mostly deciduous forest with lots of beech, birch, and maple. On bright sunny days, the forest seems to glow green, and at night, it offers seclusion for the tent sites.

Sites 16, 17, and 18 are hike-in sites well off to the outside of the campground road. These are some of my preferred spots (and are indeed considered prime sites), as they offer a delightful sense of seclusion. The Cherry lean-to is also off on its own just past site 16. Generally speaking, the prime sites—whether you opt for a tent or a lean-to—are worth the extra couple of bucks. The sense of seclusion you'll gain from scoring one of these prime sites is well worth it.

ADDRESS: Smugglers Notch State Park 7248 Smugglers Notch Road Stowe, VT 05672

OPERATED BY: Vermont Agency of Natural Resources, Department of Forests, Parks, and Recreation

INFORMATION: Smugglers Notch State Park, (802) 253-4014 (summer) or (800) 658-6934 (January–May)

OPEN: Mid-May–October 15

SITES: 20 tent sites and 14 lean-to sites

EACH SITE HAS: Stone hearth and picnic table

ASSIGNMENT: First come, first served: by reservation at (888) 409-7579

REGISTRATION: At ranger station

FACILITIES: Hot showers, flush toilets

PARKING: At sites

FEE: $14–$16 for tent sites, $21–$23 for lean-tos

RESTRICTIONS: *Pets:* On leash only
Fires: In established fireplaces only
Alcohol: At sites only
Vehicles: Parking at sites only
Other: Check in after 2 p.m., check out by 11 a.m., quiet hours 10 p.m.–7 a.m.; 8 person maximum per site; 2-day minimum stay for reservations

MAP

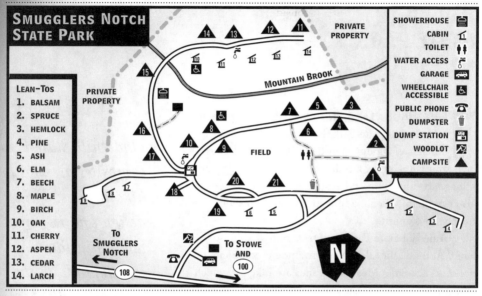

SMUGGLERS NOTCH STATE PARK

PRIVATE PROPERTY

MOUNTAIN BROOK

PRIVATE PROPERTY

FIELD

SHOWERHOUSE	
CABIN	
TOILET	
WATER ACCESS	
GARAGE	
WHEELCHAIR ACCESSIBLE	
PUBLIC PHONE	
DUMPSTER	
DUMP STATION	
WOODLOT	
CAMPSITE	

LEAN-TOS
1. BALSAM
2. SPRUCE
3. HEMLOCK
4. PINE
5. ASH
6. ELM
7. BEECH
8. MAPLE
9. BIRCH
10. OAK
11. CHERRY
12. ASPEN
13. CEDAR
14. LARCH

To SMUGGLERS NOTCH

To STOWE AND 100

108

N

GETTING THERE

Follow Route 100 North to Route 108. Follow Route 108 past Stowe Mountain Resort to the state park on the right, across the road from the northeastern part of the ski area.

Camping at Smugglers Notch puts you right across the road from Mount Mansfield. This is Vermont's highest peak and home to some of the world-class hiking for which Vermont is renowned. There are 35 miles of hiking trails winding up and over Mount Mansfield, so plan your hike and pay attention. It wouldn't do to inadvertently come down on the other side of the mountain.

Test yourself on classics like the aptly named Profanity Trail and Subway, or you can opt for any of a variety of routes that connect to the Long Trail. Even below the summit, this ridgeline hike passes by overlooks with stunning views of the Green Mountains.

42
UNDERHILL STATE PARK

THE AIR IS CLEAR AND COOL as you approach Underhill State Park. Perched on the western flanks of Mount Mansfield, Vermont's highest peak, this is the best place from which to launch your hiking adventures on and around this renowned peak. You can literally begin a hike up Mount Mansfield from your campsite.

Underhill State Park itself feels remarkably isolated. At night, the silence and solitude is complete, the darkness absolute. Most of the sites are hike-ins, which adds to the sense of seclusion.

Sites 8 through 11 are farthest from the rest of the campground. These hike-in sites are up past the park shelter, an open, log cabin–type structure in the day-use and picnic area. Sites 8 through 11 all require a hike of between 50 and 70 feet, so they are well secluded. The only other people you'll see from within one of these sites are your immediate neighbors, and at night, all you'll see are glimmers of their campfire through the moderately dense forest of mostly young deciduous trees, with lots of beech and maples. They are not especially huge sites, especially since much of the center is occupied by the large stone hearth. However, the sense of solitude more than makes up for their modest size.

There is a separate parking area for these hike-in sites, so you won't have to lug your gear quite as far as if you parked down by the ranger station. This parking area is also used by day hikers going up Mount Mansfield, so if it's full when you first arrive, be patient and try again later.

Across the campground road from this small parking area is the Pine lean-to, which is also accessed via a short hike. It would be worth getting this site just for the sense of seclusion. You won't see anyone or anything but the surrounding deciduous forest.

> *Underhill State Park's campsites are mostly hike-in sites. This design and its remote mountainside location add to the campground's wilderness sense.*

RATINGS

Beauty: ✿ ✿ ✿ ✿ ✿
Privacy: ✿ ✿ ✿ ✿
Spaciousness: ✿ ✿ ✿ ✿
Quiet: ✿ ✿ ✿ ✿ ✿
Security: ✿ ✿ ✿ ✿ ✿
Cleanliness: ✿ ✿ ✿ ✿ ✿

ADDRESS:	Underhill State Park P.O. Box 249 Underhill Center, VT 05490
OPERATED BY:	Vermont Agency of Natural Resources, Department of Forests, Parks, and Recreation
INFORMATION:	Underhill State Park, (802) 899-3022 (summer) or (800) 252-2363 (January–May)
OPEN:	Mid-May–Columbus Day
SITES:	11 tent sites and 6 lean-to sites
EACH SITE HAS:	Stone hearth, picnic table
ASSIGNMENT:	First come, first served; by reservation, (888) 409-7579
REGISTRATION:	At ranger station
FACILITIES:	Flush toilets, water
PARKING:	At either of two central parking areas
FEE:	$14 for tent sites, $21 for lean-tos
RESTRICTIONS:	*Pets:* On leash only *Fires:* In established fire rings only *Alcohol:* At sites only *Vehicles:* Parking in either of 2 small lots near groups of sites *Other:* Check in after 2 p.m., check out by 11 a.m.; quiet hours 10 p.m.–7 a.m.; 8 person maximum per site; 2-day minimum stay for reservations

You can also get to sites 8 through 11 by hiking up past the park shelter. On the way up to site 9, you'll pass a water spigot. Fortunately, the site itself is farther up the trail, so you won't have people just walking by on the way to fill their canteens and hydration packs for the hike up Mansfield.

I love these kind of hike-in sites because they really add to the wilderness feel. There are wheeled carts available by the ranger station to help you haul your camping gear into the sites. Sites 6 and 7 are also hike-in sites, spread out along a walking path that winds out from the ranger station in a short loop. These two sites are a bit larger than sites 8 through 10. Site 7 is moderately spacious but fabulously shrouded in dense forest.

Site 6 feels isolated. It has a short wooden retaining wall that keeps the tent platform intact and level. This site is set beneath a grove of tall spruce trees, so there is a deep, woodsy, cool feel to it. The forest is loosely spaced enough that it lets lots of sunlight. This too adds to the unique character of this site. It's relatively close to the restrooms, but not too close.

The Cedar lean-to, on the other hand, is right behind the bathroom building—a bit close for me. Site 5 and the Ash lean-to are also tucked in down behind the Cedar lean-to. Site 5 is set within a moderately dense forest at the edge of the woods and open area in which the Cedar lean-to is situated. Site 5 and the Ash lean-to are at the edge of a fairly steep bank as well, which adds to the character of the sites but requires that you be extra cautious if you're camping here with kids.

There is an open, grassy picnic area right across the parking lot from the ranger station. Sites 1 through 4, and the Maple, Birch, and Beech lean-tos surround this small field. These sites are a bit too exposed, but it is so quiet and dark here at night that it wouldn't matter much as evening fell. These sites also face a steep embankment.

Off to the left at the edge of the picnic area is the tiny Site 4. You'd have trouble pitching a tent designed for more than two people at this site. Sites 1 through 3 are moderately spacious and a bit more set off. Site 1 is set up a bit higher than the others. All three are carved

MAP

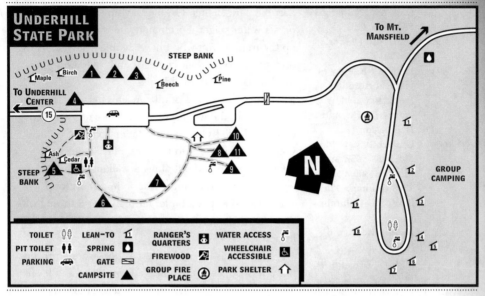

out of fairly dense forest surrounding the open field and the picnic area. Since all of the other sites here are hike-in sites, these are the most easily accessible.

Wherever you land at Underhill State Park, you won't be far from the trails that follow the spine of the Green Mountains and bring you to the highest point in Vermont.

GETTING THERE

Follow Route 15 to Underhill Center. Turn onto Pleasant Valley Road. Follow this through the town of Underhill to Mountain Road. Turn onto Mountain Road and follow the signs to the park.

MASSACHUSETTS

43
BEARTOWN
STATE FOREST

Monterey

BEARTOWN **S**TATE **F**OREST is a beautiful, intimate campground set along the shores of Benedict Pond, a good-sized pond ready to accept anglers, swimmers, and paddlers. There are only 12 sites, but if there were a rating for perfect sites, Beartown would be way out in front.

Camping here is by reservation only (in season), so plan ahead, call ahead, and try to get yourself one of the spectacularly scenic pondside sites. The Appalachian Trail passes right through the forest and next to the campground. If I were hiking the Appalachian Trail, I would think it worth the effort to plan for a night at Beartown State Forest, especially if I could secure site 11.

Sites 1 and 2 are spacious. Site 1 is huge in fact, and it has a large, grassy area where you could place your tent. The sites themselves are surrounded by fairly dense forest. Sites 3 and 4 are in a small grassy field that separates the parking area from the state forest road. These sites are wide open and quite spacious but not very private. They are also close to the pit toilets, which are the only facilities at this primitive campground. Even though sites 3 and 4 are right off the small parking area, they can still offer seclusion, especially since there won't be any road traffic later in the evening.

Site 6 is also a very spacious site. It's just to the left of the restrooms. If you're going to camp closer to the road, though, (i.e. if you couldn't score a pond site), choose site 5. There's a very short lug-in from the parking area, which gives this site a pleasant, isolated feel. It's also set within a dense grove of mixed deciduous and coniferous trees that shield it from the state forest road.

Site 7 is a roomy and private site off to the left as you start to wind down the short road that leads to the pond sites. It is also right across from the water fountain.

> *Whether you're into hiking, biking, paddling, or horseback riding, you won't run out of things to do at Beartown State Forest.*

RATINGS

Beauty: ✪ ✪ ✪ ✪ ✪
Privacy: ✪ ✪ ✪ ✪
Spaciousness: ✪ ✪ ✪
Quiet: ✪ ✪ ✪ ✪ ✪
Security: ✪ ✪ ✪ ✪
Cleanliness: ✪ ✪ ✪ ✪

The dense wall of woods surrounding the site gives it a wilderness feel.

All of the sites have at least one picnic table and a fire ring. From sites 8 and 12, you'll have easy access to the footpath leading to the shore of Benedict Pond. Site 8 is more open than the other sites in the pondside neighborhood. Like site 12, it's near but not directly on the pond.

From site 12, you'll still have a good pond view from your table, but you probably won't see the water through your tent's front flaps. Site 12 is also on a small rise, which gives it good drainage and makes it a better vantage point. Sites 9 through 11 are situated right along the edge of the pond. Site 11 is the primo pond spot. This really is a perfect, dramatically sculpted site. It sits on a small rise that looks out onto the placid waters of Benedict Pond and the rolling hills that frame the water. The pond access trail runs by the right side of the site, but that's no bother. Besides offering a view filled with dramatic scenery, the site is also well isolated. With its pond-facing orientation and the ring of wildflowers and maples surrounding it, this site offers the best of both the pond and the woods.

Since you're bound to spend lots of time just sitting and drinking in the view (and who knows, you may make some new friends happy to share the experience), there are two picnic tables at this site. You could take this site for a week and never have to leave once. You can paddle, swim, and fish right from your campsite. Even doing nothing in a site like this is spectacular.

Sites 9 and 10 have equally dramatic pondside locations. The two individually are a bit smaller than site 11, and they're a bit close together, but this would be a perfect pair for a group, and you couldn't ask for two more-scenic spots. All in all, sites 9, 10, and 11 are classic pondside campsites. It's worth planning way ahead for a few nights in one of these sites.

Beartown State Forest is a very quiet campground, even during the day. The only sounds you'll hear are the woodland birds talking back and forth, the soft splash of a canoe or kayak paddle out in the pond, and perhaps the whiz of a line being cast into the water.

With all this solitude, there's still plenty to do

MAP

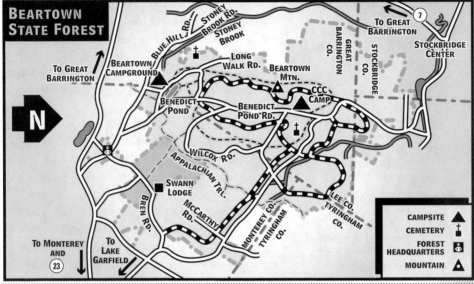

BEARTOWN STATE FOREST

STONEY BROOK RD.
STONEY BROOK

BLUE HILL RD.

To GREAT BARRINGTON

7

To GREAT BARRINGTON

STOCKBRIDGE CENTER

GREAT BARRINGTON CO.

STOCKBRIDGE CO.

To GREAT BARRINGTON

BEARTOWN CAMPGROUND

LONG WALK RD.

BEARTOWN MTN.

N

BENEDICT POND

BENEDICT POND RD.

CCC CAMP

WILCOX RD.

APPALACHIAN TRL.

SWANN LODGE

BREN RD.

McCARTHY RD.

MONTEREY CO.

TYRINGHAM CO.

TYRINGHAM CO.

LEE CO.

TYRINGHAM CO.

To MONTEREY AND

To LAKE GARFIELD

23

CAMPSITE ▲
CEMETERY ✝
FOREST HEADQUARTERS ⊞
MOUNTAIN △

within Beartown State Forest. There's even a larger beach and day-use area up the state forest road before you get to the campground. To hit the hiking trails right from the campground, follow the Benedict Pond Road (the paved road running through the forest and past the campground) to Wildcat Trail, Turkey Trail, Sky Peak Trail, and Airplane Trail. I've never ridden it before, but I've heard from mountain-biking buddies out in this neck of the woods that the Airplane Trail is one you won't want to miss.

All the above trails are multiuse trails, so you'll see hikers and bikers. Be careful, be aware, and share the trails. Horses are allowed on these trails as well, but you might not see as many, since there is a separate bridle trail. The blue-blazed trails are the hiking trails, the red-blazed trail is the bridle trail, and the white blazes indicate the Appalachian Trail. The orange-blazed trails are open to everyone—hikers, bikers, horses, and off-road vehicles.

GETTING THERE

From Great Barrington, follow MA 23 east toward Monterey. Turn left on Blue Hill Road, and follow this to Beartown Road and signs for the park.

> *The Boston Harbor Islands offer a unique combination of wilderness island camping set against the backdrop of the city skyline.*

IT'S A BIT SURREAL to be camping on an island, sitting on a rocky ocean beach, with a view of the Boston skyline. The soundtrack includes the soft crackle of the campfire, the birds and other sounds of the forest, and planes coming in and out of Logan International Airport. After all, you're just minutes from the city.

Make no mistake, though: this is primitive island camping. Despite the fact that you'll probably take a ferry to get there and you can see the city skyline in the distance, you must be 100 percent self-sufficient. Bring all your food, all your water, anything you need to cook with—everything.

Camping on Grape, Bumpkin, or Lovell's island (those being the only 3 of the 34 islands that make up the Boston Harbor Islands that permit camping) is a true island camping experience. Staying here will necessitate a little extra planning, but the payoff is well worth it.

GRAPE ISLAND

The order in which these are presented is roughly my order of preference: Grape Island, Bumpkin Island, and Lovell's Island. On Grape Island, the individual and group sites are spread out along a delightful maze of trails that wind through low scrub brush, wild berries, and a mixed forest of mostly sumac, birch, and pine.

There are also benches and picnic tables situated at strategic spots along the hiking trails. The ocean breezes and views of Boston Harbor and the city skyline are well worth stopping for a moment or two. While Bostonians are sweltering in the city, you'll be nice and cool out on the water. Once the sun dips below the horizon, you may even be tempted to pull on a fleece.

When camping on Grape Island, be sure to explore all the trails. It's a fairly small island, so it

RATINGS

Beauty: ✿ ✿ ✿ ✿ ✿
Privacy: ✿ ✿ ✿ ✿ ✿
Spaciousness: ✿ ✿ ✿
Quiet: ✿ ✿ ✿ ✿
Security: ✿ ✿ ✿ ✿
Cleanliness: ✿ ✿ ✿ ✿

won't really take long. The entire island is filled with spectacularly scenic spots. One trail drops you right down on a rocky beach. Swimming is allowed here, but it's at your own risk.

To get to the individual sites, head off to the right as you come onto the island from the dock. Then turn left at your first opportunity. That trail leads up to the individual sites. The sites here aren't huge, but since you're arriving carrying only what you could bring with you on the boat, that shouldn't pose too much of a problem. Check in with the ranger before proceeding to the sites (especially since they're not all that well-marked), and bring your camping permit.

The first site you'll come to is on the right and is very open and sunny. Across from site 1 on the left is site 2, which is completely shaded by the low dense forest. Overall, the sites on the left side of the trail will feel much cooler on those really still, muggy summer days.

Site 3 is tucked way in on the right. It is located behind the composting toilet, though. You might not want to be too close to that—especially when the wind is right. Site 4 is on the left and is another densely shaded site.

Both sites 5 and 6 are bright, sunny ones, but they're also sheltered from the trail by the forest. Site 7 is also nicely shaded. Site 8 is tucked off to the left and shaded by a grove of young birch trees. Site 9 is another that is partly sunny and partly shaded. It's off to the left and is also sheltered from the trail. Site 10 is well off the hiking trail to the right. This one is also both sunny and shaded. It's set farther back off the trail than are the other sites. The trails that wind through the sites and around the island have a nice, soft, grassy surface.

The group camping sites aren't the big fields you find at inland campgrounds. They're more like a series of nooks and crannies set off the trail. The group sites are to the left when you arrive on the island. Like the individual sites, they aren't well marked, so check with the ranger if you have any questions. Camping is by reservation only, so it's unlikely that anyone will steal your site.

The first part of site 1 has a tent platform. A small

KEY INFORMATION

ADDRESS:	Boston Harbor Islands Partnership 408 Atlantic Avenue, Suite 225 Boston MA 02110
OPERATED BY:	National Park Service and Massachusetts Department of Conservation and Recreation
INFORMATION:	Boston Harbor Islands, (617) 223-8666
OPEN:	Memorial Day– Labor Day
SITES:	26 sites, 4 group sites on 3 islands
EACH SITE HAS:	Picnic table; some have grills
ASSIGNMENT:	By reservation only, call (877) 422-6762 or visit www.reserve america.com
REGISTRATION:	Check in with ranger on island; camping permit required
FACILITIES:	Composting toilets
PARKING:	Park at or near ferry terminals; call (617) 223-8666 for ferry schedules
FEE:	State residents, $8, nonresidents, $10, group camping $25
RESTRICTIONS:	*Pets:* Prohibited *Fires:* Campfires permitted below high-tide line *Alcohol:* Prohibited *Vehicles:* Prohibited *Other:* Pack-in, pack-out policy; 2-week maximum stay; no water or food available on islands

part of the site is tucked in beneath a tree. There's another part of the site across the trail that has a bit more room than the first two parts and is set a bit farther back from the trail. Still another spacious part of the site is set beneath a canopy of trees.

While on Grape Island, explore the ruins of a 19th-century foundation near the dock. The house was occupied by Amos Pendleton, described as "an old hermit with a dangerous temper."

BUMPKIN ISLAND

Bumpkin Island definitely has steeper hills and trails than does Grape—it's a bit easier to navigate in terms of where you're going to find the campsites, though. The low forest and ground cover is also much denser on Bumpkin than on Grape. Most of the campsites are situated along a side trail that extends from the main trail that bisects the island. This main trail was actually paved at one point, as Bumpkin was host to first a children's hospital and then a military training ground.

To the left, you'll find site 1 tucked back off the trail. It's partially shaded and a fairly good-sized site compared to some of the others. Site 2 is to the left as well and is a much smaller site. It's a bit open to the trail to site 4, and to the trail that leads into site 3. Site 4 is on the right and is also open to the trail. Both of these sites are partially shaded by the low, dense forest.

Site 3 wraps around, so it's a bit more secluded. Site 4 is open to the trail and next to another trail leading into site 3. Site 5 is nicely shaded; it's down from the trail to the left. Site 6 is off to the right and is a nice open site next to a sprawling sumac tree. Across the trail is site 7, which is a shadier, slightly smaller site.

On the right side of the trail is site 8, which is a small, circular site that is very sunny, despite being ringed by dense walls of forest. Site 9 is off to the left from a small clearing in the trail. It's set against a couple of good-sized sumac trees. Site 10 is the most secluded of the bunch. It's off to the left of the trail that leads you past all the campsites. This is a larger site as well. It's surrounded by dense shrub and forest yet is also sunny and open to the sky.

Group site 1 would be a good-sized site at a mainland campground. It's open to the sky and ringed by a wall of short sumac, with one defiant clump growing off to the side within the site. Across the trail is the historic site of the Burrage Children's Hospital, which was once a place for crippled children to spend the summer. Group site 2 is well off the central trail, so it is very secluded. It's about the same size as group site 1. There's also big open field designated as a picnic area down on the western side of Bumpkin. This would be a perfect spot for stargazing or tossing a Frisbee around.

Both Grape's and Bumpkin's individual sites are along a relatively short section of trail. I liked the character and sense of seclusion of the Grape sites a bit better. Both islands could benefit from marking the path to the sites better, but both are also fairly small islands, so you can't go too far wrong.

LOVELL'S ISLAND

Bumpkin and Grape are in Hingham Bay, so they're a bit more protected. But Lovell's Island is well out in Boston Harbor. So, there's a bit more noise from marine traffic and Logan Airport. You can hear all that from any of the Boston Harbor Islands, but you're a lot closer when you're on Lovell's. Still, the size and historic aspects of Lovell's, and the dramatic cliffs off the northeastern side of the island, make it well worth checking out. Once you start exploring, you'll easily be able to tune out the sounds of the city.

From the dock, you'll follow a well-worn path of old pavement. I'd wager those paths were paved during World War II when Lovell's was used for coastal gun emplacements. When you reach a fork in the road, the left path will appear to follow the shore of the island while the right path goes up a small hill toward the fort. The campsites are off the left path. Like those at Grape and Bumpkin, the way could benefit from being better marked.

Site 1 on the low road is to the right. It's partially shaded and is set back and down from road, so there's a nice sense of seclusion. Site 2 is also down off the road. Follow a short footpath just past site 1 to reach it. This is a nicely shaded site covered by loosely spaced sumac. Most of these sites have a fire ring, grill, and a picnic table.

Site 3 is also off to the right. It's connected to site 2 by a short footpath. This is a pretty cozy site, but it's very open to the sun and sky. Site 4 is tucked well off the road. This site has a tent platform and a grill and is fairly close to the composting toilet. That may be good for some, not so good for others.

Site 5 must be one of the group sites, as it is quite large. Very spacious and open, it's on the other side of the composting toilet from site 4. It's also conjoined with what appears to be another site with a picnic table and grill: Site 6 is a nicely shaded offshoot and is set off from the open space of site 5. There's one more site on the right side of the road down near the end that is nicely secluded and close to the beach. It's on the small side, but the location is perfect.

A couple of sites appear to be unused. The DCR is rightfully very careful about island conservation, so site placements and numbers probably change here more frequently than on the mainland. This fact, along with the virtually nonexistent site markings, means you should check with the DCR when making your reservation to get exactly the site you're looking for, and check with the ranger on the island to make sure the site you occupy is indeed the site you intended.

MAP

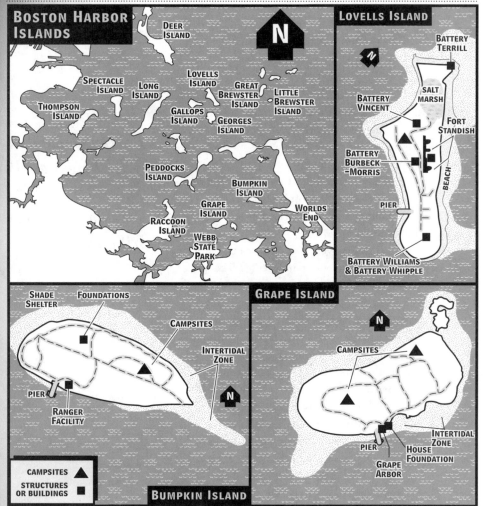

GETTING THERE

Take the ferry from either Marriot Long Wharf in Boston or from Quincy Harbor. The ferries run inter-island loops. Take the south loop from Quincy Harbor for Grape and Bumpkin, and the north loop from Boston or George's Island for Lovell's. Call (617) 223-8666 for ferry information and trip planning.

45
CLARKSBURG STATE PARK

CLARKSBURG STATE PARK is up in the northwestern corner of Massachusetts, right along the Vermont border. The sites at this moderately sized campground are carved out of a dense forest of pine, spruce, and hemlock that gives the woods a dark, cool feeling. Even on the most brilliant, sunny days, the whole campground is immersed in the shade of the verdant forest.

The coniferous trees cover most of the campground with a velvety blanket of pine needles. The sites are spread out along a large, central loop road bisected by a crossroad. Sites 9 through 14 are situated along the crossroad; the rest are on the outer loops.

You can reserve most of the sites. Sites 1, 4, 10, 11, 12, 14, 18, 23, 25, and 29 are the first-come, first-served sites. Those along the inner side of the campground loop and the crossroad have the most densely forested feel. The sites facing Mauserts Pond, although they are still quite a ways back from the water's edge and carved out of the forest, offer a bit more light through the trees and occasional glimpses of the pond.

Sites 1 and 2 are very spacious and have an isolated feeling. Even though the woods here are thick, you can catch a glimpse of Mauserts Pond from site 2. Sites 6 and 7 are pleasant and set down from the road, which adds to their privacy. Sites 10 and 11 are smaller than most of the other sites at Clarksburg State Park, and they are close to the facilities.

Along the stretch of the campground loop where sites 16 through 23 are located, the sites are large and isolated from each other and from the rest of the sites. These are all decent sites for tent camping, as you'll enjoy a sense of solitude here. There are more hardwoods mixed into the forest along this portion of the campground loop road. The brilliant green leaves of the maples in summer brighten the forest.

> *The campground at Clarksburg State Park has a dark, cool, sylvan feel even on the most brilliant summer days.*

RATINGS

Beauty: ✪ ✪ ✪ ✪
Privacy: ✪ ✪ ✪
Spaciousness: ✪ ✪ ✪ ✪ ✪
Quiet: ✪ ✪ ✪ ✪
Security: ✪ ✪ ✪ ✪
Cleanliness: ✪ ✪ ✪ ✪

KEY INFORMATION

ADDRESS: Clarksburg
State Park
1199 Middle Road
Clarksburg, MA
01247

OPERATED BY: Massachusetts
Department of
Environmental
Management

INFORMATION: Clarksburg State
Park, (413) 664-8345
(summer),
(413) 442-8928 (mid-
October–mid-April)

OPEN: Mid-May–
mid-October

SITES: 44

EACH SITE HAS: Fire ring, picnic
table

ASSIGNMENT: First come, first
served or by
reservation:
(877) I-CAMP-MA,
www.reserve
america.com

REGISTRATION: At ranger station

FACILITIES: Flush toilets, beach
area, boat launch

PARKING: At sites

FEE: Massachusetts
residents, $12;
nonresidents, $14

RESTRICTIONS: *Pets:* Dogs on leash
only
Fires: Fire rings only
Alcohol: Prohibited
Vehicles: Maximum
2 per site
Other: Reservations
require 2-night
minimum stay;
campground office
hours 8 a.m.–7 p.m.;
14-day maximum
stay

Moving farther along the one-way campground loop road, you'll come to site 23, which is tremendous. Set way back from the road, it's rather large and has a calming sense of wilderness seclusion. The forest directly overhead is clear, so you'll also get light filtering down and glimpses of the night sky (once you've put your campfire out and your eyes adjust to the dark).

Sites 25 and above are a bit smaller than most of the others, particularly those situated along the outside of the campground loop road, but they're still attractive and offer a private atmosphere, as they're set within the dense coniferous forest. The walls of pine and spruce here form an effective barrier between the individual sites. Site 29 is the exception, but this is a large site well suited for a group or family.

Site 31 is within its own clearing. This is a good spot if you have smaller kids, as it will be easier to keep an eye on them. Site 33 looks much the same but is a bit smaller.

It seems that site 36 has vanished from the Clarksburg State Park campground loop. In its place is a trailhead that leads off in the direction of the Mauserts Loop Trail. Perhaps the site was sacrificed to make a spot for the trailhead—not a bad tradeoff if you ask me.

Finishing up the campground loop road, sites 35 through 44 are smaller than some of the other isolated, larger sites and those along the outer loop. However, thanks to the deep, dense nature of Clarksburg's forest, they still provide privacy and isolation.

Overall, the sensation here is one of being sequestered in a thick forest. There's a hushed silence about the place, even during daylight hours. In the evening, all you're likely to hear is the snap and crackle of campfires.

During the day, you'll definitely want to check out Mauserts Pond. There's a footpath leading to the pond right across from site 25. If you bring a canoe or kayak, it might be easier to head over to the day-use area, which has a boat launch and beach.

There are several fairly lengthy hiking trails winding through Clarksburg State Park. The Mauserts Loop Trail leads from the campground and crosses over Beaver Creek then brings you up toward Vermont.

MAP

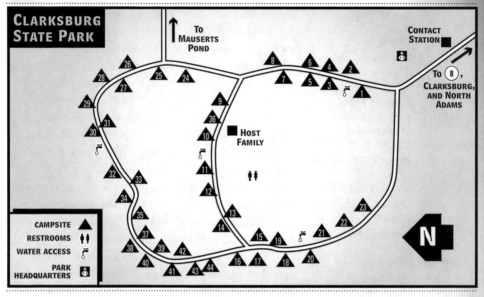

The Horrigan Road Trail veers west about two-thirds of the way to the Vermont border, after which the trail is called (appropriately enough) the Vermont Line Trail. The Bog Trail winds around the northern end of the pond and brings you to the beach and boathouse.

GETTING THERE

Follow MA 8 through Clarksburg heading toward Vermont until you see the signs for Clarksburg State Park on the left.

> *When you're camping at Granville State Forest, you'll fall asleep to the sounds of the forest and the soft whisper of Halfway Brook.*

YOU'LL FIND **GRANVILLE STATE FOREST** in the southwestern corner of Massachusetts. The southern edge of the forest is actually right on the Connecticut border. There used to be two separate camping areas here, Hubbard River and Halfway Brook. The Hubbard River area had a more remote, wilderness feel but it has been closed for several years. If you're interested in this area, contact the ranger station and ask when it may reopen.

The Halfway Brook campsites are a bit farther up the road from where the Hubbard River sites sat. The Halfway Brook sites are nestled within a fairly dense forest of mostly hardwoods. It's a relatively small camping area, with only 22 sites situated deep within the borders of the state forest, so it's nice and quiet here. In the evening, all you'll hear are the birds as they settle down for the night, the soft rush of Halfway Brook, and the crackle of your campfire.

Most of the sites at the Halfway Brook camping area are available by reservation. Only sites 8, 11, 12, 13, and 16 at Granville State Forest are available on a first-come, first-served basis.

Sites 1 through 5 are definitely worth a look if they're available. These are set off from the main campground and face West Hartland Road. Site 1 couldn't be any closer to Halfway Brook, which makes this site particularly attractive. The site sits right next to a small pond formed by the intersection of Halfway Brook and Small Brook. Sites 1 and 2 are very private, as there is plenty of forest between them and the rest of the campground. Adding to the sense of seclusion, sites 1 and 2 are set farther back off the road. Any other sounds you might hear from the rest of the campground are obscured by the light whisper of Halfway Brook tumbling by in the background.

RATINGS

Beauty: ✿ ✿ ✿ ✿
Privacy: ✿ ✿ ✿ ✿
Spaciousness: ✿ ✿ ✿ ✿ ✿
Quiet: ✿ ✿ ✿ ✿
Security: ✿ ✿ ✿ ✿
Cleanliness: ✿ ✿ ✿ ✿

Sites 3, 4, and 5 are also nicely isolated but a bit closer to the rest of the campsites in the main loop. The rear border of these sites abuts the borders of sites 6, 8, and 9 in the main campground loop. These sites are set within more open forest, so they're spacious but a bit less private—even though they're still accessed via West Hartland Road and not via the campground loop. Parking for sites 1 through 5 is also separate from the rest of the campground.

Adjacent sites 6 and 7 are very large. There's a fair degree of privacy between these sites and the rest of the campground, but the forest is loosely spaced between them. This would be a good pair of sites for a larger group. Site 8 is nicely isolated, nestled into the forest right where you turn off the campground road to the parking area. It is surrounded by fairly dense forest, so there is a strong sense of seclusion from the rest of the campground.

The rest of the sites provide a blend of seclusion, spaciousness, and privacy, as they are set amid the dense, mixed forest that shelters the campground. Site 11 is quite secluded. There's a short drive down to the site off the primary parking area in the center of the campground. Sites 10 and 11 are both close to the gently murmuring Halfway Brook.

Sites 12 and 14 are very spacious. They are also set up to be wheelchair accessible, with a wheelchair-accessible parking spot close to site 14. Site 16 is nicely isolated, set at the very end of the campground loop road on the other side of the campground opposite sites 10 and 11. Sites 19, 20, and 21 are all fairly close to each other, and they are a bit more open than some of the sites at Granville State Forest. Sites 15 and 19 are near a small, grassy field, out behind the restrooms. Sites 13 and 21 are bit too open for my taste, and they're situated right on the campground loop road.

There is an elaborate network of hiking trails winding through the rest of the forest. Across the street from the campground are trailheads for the Ordway Trail and the Civilian Conservation Corps (CCC) Trail. From the CCC Trail, you can loop around on the Corduroy Trail, which heads out past the forest headquarters and travels through a wetland before reconnecting

KEY INFORMATION

ADDRESS:	Granville State Forest 323 West Hartland Road Granville, MA 01034
OPERATED BY:	Massachusetts Department of Environmental Management
INFORMATION:	Granville State Forest, (413) 357-6611
OPEN:	Mid-May–mid-October
SITES:	22
EACH SITE HAS:	Fire ring, picnic table
ASSIGNMENT:	First come, first served; by reservation: (877) I-CAMP-MA, www.reserve america.com
REGISTRATION:	At ranger station
FACILITIES:	Flush toilets, hot showers, phone
PARKING:	At sites or in central parking area
FEE:	Massachusetts residents, $12; nonresidents, $14
RESTRICTIONS:	*Pets:* On leash only *Fires:* In fire rings *Alcohol:* Prohibited *Vehicles:* Maximum 2 per site; no ORVs *Other:* Reservations require 2-night minimum stay; office hours 8 a.m.–10 p.m.; quiet hours 10 p.m.–7 a.m; 14-day maximum stay; Hubbard River area remains closed until further notice.

MAP

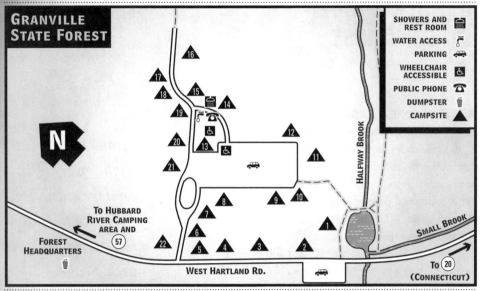

GRANVILLE STATE FOREST

N

TO HUBBARD RIVER CAMPING AREA AND

FOREST HEADQUARTERS

57

HALFWAY BROOK

SMALL BROOK

WEST HARTLAND RD.

TO 20 (CONNECTICUT)

SHOWERS AND REST ROOM
WATER ACCESS
PARKING
WHEELCHAIR ACCESSIBLE
PUBLIC PHONE
DUMPSTER
CAMPSITE

GETTING THERE

From the intersection of MA 8 and MA 57 in New Boston, follow MA 57 west to West Hartland Road. Head south on West Hartland Road until you see signs for the forest and the campground.

with the CCC Trail. The hiking trails on this side of West Hartland Road are fairly flat.

On the same side of the road as the campground, there's the Halfway Brook Trail and the Hubbard River Trail, which leads down to where the Hubbard River Campground used to be. You can also access the Woods Trail, which travels up and over a small ridgeline, and the Ore Hill Trail, which follows the eastern border of the forest. The trails on this side of the road travel either along or up and over Ore Hill. The aforementioned trails are all multiuse trails, so you can hike, mountain bike, and ride horses. Keep this in mind and exercise appropriate caution and courtesy. Even though you might feel like you're out in the middle of nowhere at Granville State Forest, you may find that is just the sensation you were seeking.

47
HAROLD PARKER
STATE FOREST

THE FOREST ENSHROUDING THE CAMPSITES
at Harold Parker is relatively uniform in its
character, at least among the older trees. There
are sections where the undergrowth thins out, and others where it grows so dense it looks primeval. The forest is composed primarily of tall white pines and low
deciduous trees. Huge, open sites characterize most of
the campground.

Sites 7, 8, and 9 are all exposed and close to the
restroom. Site 8 is wheelchair accessible, as are many
others at Harold Parker State Forest. Even though site
10 is moderately spacious, it pales in comparison to the
massive clearing where sites 9 and 11 sit. You could
practically build a house atop this pair of sites.

Site 13 is absolutely enormous, and quite
secluded. Several 80-foot-tall white pine and maple
trees punctuate the site. A low wall of young pines,
which must be the big white pines' progeny, encircles
the site. The younger pines surrounding the site fill in
the forest to offer complete seclusion.

Although it's open to the road and sky, site 14
feels secluded by virtue of its location on the campground road. There are several hiking trails winding
throughout the campground, two of which lead off into
the woods just past site 14.

Site 15 is another massive site. It's set within a
grove of short white pines and is elevated from the
road, which adds privacy. Sites 17 and 19 are small but
set within a grove of white pines. The ground is covered with pine cones and a soft blanket of pine needles. Moderate undergrowth and young white pines
surround these sites.

All these conifers give the forest a wonderful scent
and make it a very quiet place. Usually, all you'll hear
is the wind rushing through the soft needles atop the
forest's elder statesmen. Now is another good time to

> *Harold Parker is
> unique in its feeling of
> remoteness and its
> proximity to Boston—
> great when you need a
> quick escape.*

RATINGS

Beauty: ✪ ✪ ✪ ✪
Privacy: ✪ ✪ ✪ ✪
Spaciousness: ✪ ✪ ✪ ✪ ✪
Quiet: ✪ ✪ ✪
Security: ✪ ✪ ✪ ✪
Cleanliness: ✪ ✪ ✪ ✪

ADDRESS: Harold Parker State Forest 1951 Turnpike Street North Andover, MA 01845

OPERATED BY: Massachusetts Department of Environmental Management

INFORMATION: Harold Parker State Forest, (978) 475-7972 (office), (978) 686-3391 (forest headquarters)

OPEN: Mid-April– mid-October

SITES: 91

EACH SITE HAS: Metal fire box, grill, picnic table

ASSIGNMENT: First come, first served; by reservation: (877) I-CAMP-MA, www.reserve america.com

REGISTRATION: At ranger station

FACILITIES: Flush toilets, water spigots, playground, showers

PARKING: At sites and in 3 additional parking areas

FEE: Massachusetts residents, $12; nonresidents, $14

RESTRICTIONS: *Pets:* On leash only
Fires: In Fire rings only
Alcohol: Prohibited
Vehicles: Maximum 2 per site
Other: Reservations require 2-night minimum stay; quiet hours 10 p.m.–7 a.m; 14-day maximum stay

remind yourself that you're less than an hour from Boston.

Set at the corner of the campground road, sites 21 and 23 are open to the road on two sides. Like sites 17 and 19, they're set in a pine grove, but 21 and 23 are more exposed to the road. Another road just past site 21 leads down to Frye Brook.

The first site within the B loop gives you an idea of what to expect from the rest of the sites in this section. Site B1 is huge, but it's right across from the restroom. Site B3 is similar.

Both sites B5 and B6 are wide open to the road, but they're just far enough from each other on opposite sides of the road to provide some privacy. Sites B7 and B8 are very spacious. B7 is up off the road, and B8 is down from the road. It always seems to rain when I'm camping, so I'd go for higher ground. Site B10 is moderately spacious and isolated at the top of a little hill on the campground road.

There's a uniform, moderately dense character to the forest in this part of the campground. There's also a thick understory of deciduous trees and young pines, with towering white pines filling in the upper layers of the forest.

Site B12 is colossal and punctuated by several massive white pines. B11 is also rather large. Nearby, you can see two sites that were closed for restoration, part of the regular maintenance of this heavily used campground. The forest is slowly and steadily filling in the old sites.

A large, granite boulder guards site B16. This site is also speckled with a stand of towering white pines and is nicely isolated by the boulder and its location along the road. Right across from the G1 group sites, it could get a bit noisy.

While site B18 is much smaller than B16, it has a high degree of privacy, as it's encircled by dense undergrowth. B21 is also a massive, open, sunny site well removed from neighboring sites, and 22 is similarly secluded.

Towering, 100-foot-tall pine trees surround site B23, and a cathedral quality and stately feel prevails in the forest. This site is gigantic and very open. Site B24 is also large (though smaller than B23). Of course, that's like saying Mount McKinley isn't quite as big as Mount Everest.

Sites 29 and 30 are across the road from each other. They're very spacious, but they don't offer much in the way of privacy. Site 28 is like 29 in that it's open to two sides of the road—too open for my tastes. Most of these sites are massive and set among stately white pines. That's certainly the case with site 38.

The few sites along the short C road, including sites C2 through C5, are exposed to each other but very spacious and spread out. On the A-loop road, sites A2 through A6 are roomy but exposed to each other and to the road. Farther up the A loop, sites A7, A8, and A13 are exposed to the restrooms.

Sites A15 and 48 are close neighbors and are open on two sides at an intersection of the campground road. Site 46 is huge—it's a bit secluded by the forest on one side, but it's exposed on the other to site 48.

Site 41 is roomy and surrounded by an understory of young white pines and huge, older white pines and maples. It's secluded by its location, and it's just a bit open to site 44 across the road. Sites 43 and 44 feel a bit more nestled into the forest due to the absence of neighboring sites. A dense understory and huge white pines surround site 45, but the site is small, which gives it a cozy feel.

The loose trio of sites 52, 54, and 56 sits off on its own. The campground road leading past these sites cuts through a dense mixed forest with equally dense understory and ferns filling in the ground cover and thickening up the woods. Sites 52 and 54 are outrageously huge, open, and exposed to the sky.

Then you come to what is most likely the premier site at this campground. Site 56 is unbelievable. It is completely secluded, massive, and encircled by dense, younger white pines, huge maples, and older white pines. It is far from any other site, so the sense of solitude is absolute.

There's a funky bend in the campground road farther down, so even though sites 59, 61, 62, and 63 are moderately spacious, they're all open to this road where it cuts back at almost a 45-degree angle. From this intersection, the sites along the right side of the campground road, including sites 63 and above, face Frye Pond. Sites 61 through 68 are exposed and don't offer much privacy, but they are close to the pond. Site 68 is up off the road, right next to the playground area.

Of the pondside sites, site 69 is the prettiest, set within an open forest that rolls gently down to the shore. The loose pines and maples give this site a dark, cool character.

Sites 79 and 81 are smaller and open to the restrooms, parking area, and basketball net. Sites 85, 86, and 87 are extremely spacious and open. There are more wheelchair-accessible sites in this part of the campground, including sites 61, 74, 77, and 78.

Harold Parker has some of the largest sites I have ever seen, and many are secluded. While this would seem remarkable and welcome at any campground, it's all the more amazing when you consider this campground is closer to Boston than any other profiled in this book.

MAP

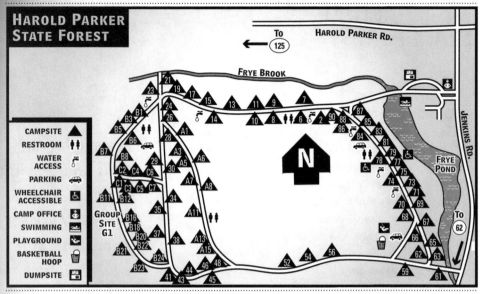

HAROLD PARKER STATE FOREST

To (125) ← HAROLD PARKER RD.

FRYE BROOK

Legend:
- CAMPSITE ▲
- RESTROOM
- WATER ACCESS
- PARKING
- WHEELCHAIR ACCESSIBLE
- CAMP OFFICE
- SWIMMING
- PLAYGROUND
- BASKETBALL HOOP
- DUMPSITE

GROUP SITE G1

FRYE POND

JENKINS RD.

To (62)

GETTING THERE

Follow MA 114 through Middleton into North Andover. Continue several miles until you see Harold Parker Road and signs for the park. Drive through the park, following signs for the campground.

48
MOHAWK TRAIL STATE FOREST

Charlemont

A SENSE OF REVERENCE OVERCOMES you upon entering Mohawk Trail State Forest. The woods here have a "cathedralesque" quality. Take a moment as you drive in to get out of your vehicle. Gaze at the tall, nicely spaced spruce and pine forest towering over you and forming a canopy that preserves both the "wise silence of the forest," to quote Ralph Waldo Emerson, and the delightful scent of conifer.

This is an older-growth forest, as the trees are all at least 100 feet tall, with some considerably taller than that. At the forest floor, the tree trunks are quite massive; there isn't much in the way of an understory, so the forest has an open feel to it. The sunlight filters down through the giant conifers in broken shafts, and most breezes are captured by the long arms of the trees. Parts of the forest are also interspersed with maple, birch, and other hardy deciduous trees and the offspring of the giant evergreens.

The sites in the first cluster are set close together but remain fairly open for such a densely forested area. These sites are clean and spacious but not quite as private as you might expect when you first see the forest.

In the loop with sites 36 through 56 down near the Cold River, you hear the sounds of the forest birds and the rushing water. The sites right along the river are the best. They are set within a beautiful, loose grove of mixed hardwoods and conifers. RVs are allowed in the Mohawk Trail State Forest, but you won't find any in this part of the campground, primarily because they are not able to negotiate the extremely tight turn at the end of the road.

The riverside sites are spectacular. Sites 45 through 48 all sit right on the riverbanks at the end of the loop, so they are even more isolated than the other sites in this cluster. Sites 46 and 47 are the perfect

> *The towering forest at this campground's entrance is breathtaking. If that doesn't get you, wait until you see the campsites along Cold River.*

RATINGS

Beauty: ✩ ✩ ✩ ✩ ✩
Privacy: ✩ ✩ ✩ ✩
Spaciousness: ✩ ✩ ✩ ✩
Quiet: ✩ ✩ ✩ ✩ ✩
Security: ✩ ✩ ✩ ✩
Cleanliness: ✩ ✩ ✩ ✩ ✩

ADDRESS:	**Mohawk Trail State Forest P.O. Box 7, MA 2 Charlemont, MA 01339**
OPERATED BY:	**Massachusetts Department of Environmental Management**
INFORMATION:	**Mohawk Trail State Forest, (413) 339-5504**
OPEN:	**Mid-May– mid-October**
SITES:	**56 sites, 6 cabins, group-camping area**
EACH SITE HAS:	**Fire ring, picnic table**
ASSIGNMENT:	**First come, first served or by reservation: (877) I-CAMP-MA, www.reserve america.com**
REGISTRATION:	**At ranger station**
FACILITIES:	**Flush toilets, water spigots, showers, wheelchair-accessible restrooms**
PARKING:	**At sites**
FEE:	**Massachusetts residents, $12; nonresidents, $14; $25 for group site; $30–$50 for cabins**
RESTRICTIONS:	*Pets:* **Dogs on leash only** *Fires:* **In fire rings only** *Alcohol:* **Prohibited** *Vehicles:* **Parking at sites only** *Other:* **Reservations require 2-night minimum stay; campground office hours 8 a.m.–10 p.m.; quiet hours 10 p.m.– 7 a.m.; 14-day maximum stay**

riverside spots. Across the river from site 47 is the Mohawk State Forest picnic area, but the day-trippers will be gone by the time you're lighting your campfire to cook dinner.

The sites numbered in the 30s are spacious, but they are also exposed and set on a hard, dirt surface. Sites 14 through 22 sit off a short road that leaves the upper campground loop. Sites 15 and 16 are small but sweet riverside sites on the riverbanks, a bit higher than the sites in the 40s and 50s. Site 22, at the end of this small loop, is the key site in this cluster, as it is very spacious and private.

The whole 14-through-22 loop is set in a grove of enormous spruce trees, so there's plenty of shade and that earthy, deep-woods scent. And of course, there's the Cold River rushing right by the campsites, so all your senses are satisfied.

The main section of the campground with sites 1 through 12, and 23 through 33 is a decent section, but the sites offer minimal privacy. There's a developed forest canopy, so this area gets a lot of shade, but the minimal undergrowth doesn't create much sense of seclusion.

When you come to camp at Mohawk Trail State Forest, look for the sites in the upper 40s and lower 50s at the end of the campground and near the Cold River. That's where you'll want to be. If that doesn't work, go for the 14-through-22 loop.

Remember, this is black bear country, so all the appropriate precautions apply to food, garbage, and even clothes upon which you may have spilled food. When you're turning in for the night, hide anything that may retain food scents safely in your car.

MAP

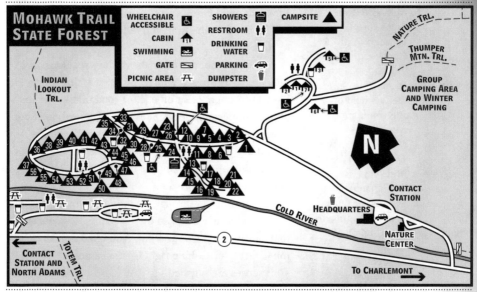

GETTING THERE

Follow MA 2 east from North Adams until you see the signs for Mohawk Trail State Forest on the left.

49

MOUNT GREYLOCK STATE RESERVATION

> *Here you'll be deep in the woods, perched on the mountainside, and close to a massive network of hiking and biking trails.*

YOU WON'T FIND MANY campgrounds with a deeper sense of wilderness and seclusion than the Sperry Road campground on Mount Greylock. This is true, primitive, mountainside camping. Sure, you can still drive your car to the campsite, but you are literally up on the side of a mountain within the deep forest. The campground is 6 miles up the auto road leading to the Bascom Lodge at the summit of Mount Greylock. Bear left off the auto road onto Sperry Road, which leads into the campground.

All these sites feel remote and rustic. There are 34 individual sites and 5 group sites. Most are available by reservation; the rest are first come, first served. The sites here are private and spread out. Some are a bit on the small side, but their rustic nature and deep-wilderness seclusion is perfect. The sites are spread out along the main campground road and a short loop branching off to the left after you enter the campground. Each is nestled within the dense forest of mixed deciduous and coniferous trees.

Located where the short loop heads off the campground road to the left, site 8 is open on both sides. It's less private than the other sites (it has road on two sides), but it's spacious and easily accessible. Sites 6 and 17 are smaller than the others on this loop, but they're still pleasant and surrounded by fairly dense woods. Site 17 lies within a grove of young hardwoods and is close to the pit toilets. Site 18 is set off the road, so the sense of seclusion is intense. Site 21 is very spacious and has a small grassy area for your tent. Site 22 is too open for my taste, but it is close to the restroom, if that's a priority.

Several of the sites farther down the campground road are lug-in sites. These are my favorites, as the wilderness air and privacy predominate. You truly feel as if you have the woods to yourself, even though

RATINGS

Beauty: ✿ ✿ ✿ ✿ ✿
Privacy: ✿ ✿ ✿ ✿
Spaciousness: ✿ ✿ ✿ ✿
Quiet: ✿ ✿ ✿ ✿ ✿
Security: ✿ ✿ ✿ ✿ ✿
Cleanliness: ✿ ✿ ✿ ✿

you're still car camping. Sites 23 and 26 are classic walk-in sites. They require about a 50-foot hike in, making them quite secluded. When you set up in one of these sites, you won't even see your car from your campsite, much less see any neighbors.

Site 30 is small but very isolated and private. Sites 25, 26, 27, and 29 are also lug-in sites that provide a tremendous amount of privacy. Site 28 is right off the road—not quite a lug-in site—but still isolated from its neighbors. The walk-in sites offer the deepest sense of solitude imaginable. You won't see or hear anyone else around you.

Site 33 is another lug-in site on the other side of the road. You can barely see it from the campground road. Overall, Mount Greylock's Sperry Road campground is absolutely silent, save for the natural sounds of the forest and your own campfire.

Sites 34 and 35, at the campground road's end, are also walk-in sites. These are quite spacious and distant from the rest of the campsites. They are remarkably secluded and set within a dense forest of mixed hardwoods and conifers, young and old, so the variety of the forest is visually stunning. After the sun goes down, the thick forest reflects the light from your campfire, making the trees look like a wall surrounding your site.

During the day, there is plenty to do here. Camped right on the side of Mount Greylock, you're in the midst of a giant network of trails for hiking and mountain biking. The Appalachian Trail cuts through here, so you may run into some through-hikers on and around Greylock.

A number of trailheads lead right out of the campground. There's a Nature Trail loop that leads behind sites 13, 14, and the Chimney group site. It eventually intersects the Hopper Trail and the March Cataract Trail. The Hopper Trail starts right next to site 16. Down by the end of the loop with sites 4 and 5, there's the Roaring Brook Trail and the Deer Hill Trail.

Then there's always the classic Thunderbolt Trail on the other side of the mountain, one of New England's earliest ski trails cut by the Civilian Conservation Corps. I've descended only the mighty

KEY INFORMATION

ADDRESS:	Mount Greylock State Reservation P.O. Box 138 Rockwell Road Lanesborough, MA 01237
OPERATED BY:	Massachusetts Department of Environmental Management
INFORMATION:	Mount Greylock State Reservation, (413) 499-4262
OPEN:	Mid-May– mid-October
SITES:	35 sites, 5 group sites
EACH SITE HAS:	Fire ring or stone hearth, picnic table
ASSIGNMENT:	First come, first served; by reservation: (877) I-CAMP-MA, www.reserve america.com
REGISTRATION:	At ranger station
FACILITIES:	Pit toilets
PARKING:	At sites
FEE:	Massachusetts residents, $8; nonresidents, $10
RESTRICTIONS:	*Pets:* On leash only *Fires:* In fire rings only *Alcohol:* Prohibited *Vehicles:* Parking at or near sites *Other:* Reservations require 2-night minimum stay; quiet hours 10 p.m.–7 a.m; 14-day maximum stay

MAP

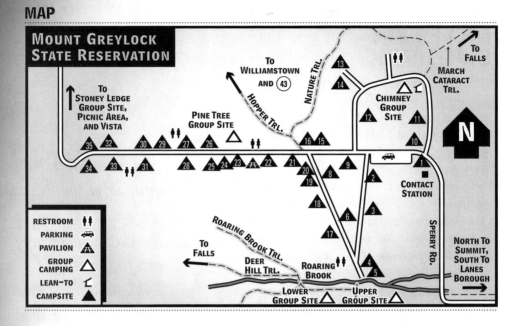

MOUNT GREYLOCK STATE RESERVATION

To WILLIAMSTOWN AND (43)

To STONEY LEDGE GROUP SITE, PICNIC AREA, AND VISTA

PINE TREE GROUP SITE

NATURE TRL.

HOPPER TRL.

CHIMNEY GROUP SITE

MARCH CATARACT TRL.

To FALLS

N

CONTACT STATION

SPERRY RD.

NORTH TO SUMMIT, SOUTH TO LANES BOROUGH

ROARING BROOK TRL.

To FALLS

DEER HILL TRL.

ROARING BROOK

LOWER GROUP SITE   UPPER GROUP SITE

RESTROOM	
PARKING	
PAVILION	
GROUP CAMPING	
LEAN-TO	
CAMPSITE	

GETTING THERE

Follow Routes 7 and 20 north through Lanesborough, then follow signs to the Mount Greylock State Reservation headquarters. The campground is onSperry Road, which is several miles up the auto road heading toward the summit.

Thunderbolt once, and I have somewhat fond memories of the trail. It was in the late winter, so I brought out my telemark skis for the occasion. It was downright ugly—the dense late-winter snow grabbed my skis and refused to let go. The mountain won that day, but it was a blast nevertheless.

50
NICKERSON
STATE PARK

IT'S NO SECRET THAT CAPE COD gets packed during the summer. Just look at Route 3 leading toward the Sagamore Bridge or routes 495 and 25 leading toward the Bourne Bridge on a summer Friday night, and you'll see lines of cars waiting to get on the Cape. What may be a secret though is that you can still find some solitude and wilderness on the Cape. Nickerson State Park is one of those rare, remote spots.

Part of the reason Nickerson is such an incredible refuge is its size: It is huge. At 1,955 acres, with 418 campsites, you can find all sorts of places to quietly lose yourself in the rolling pine forests that blanket the park. This is one of the most densely forested areas on the Cape. The forest itself is beautiful, with loosely spaced balsams, firs, and pines. Once you've decided on a spot to pitch your tent, take a quiet moment for a deep breath. When there's an onshore breeze, you can smell the earthy scent of the coniferous forest and the salty tang of the nearby ocean in the same breath.

There aren't any sites within Nickerson specifically set aside for tent campers, but several of the eight discrete areas lend themselves particularly well to tents. Look for sites in areas 2, 3, 5, or 7. Areas 2 and 3 are about a mile from the main entrance and are in open loops. Each has its own restroom and several drinking-water spigots.

Area 5 is about a half mile from the entrance on the way to Flax Pond. Several of the sites here are open and loosely spaced, especially 12, 14, and 16–18. A few pathways lead off the bluff down to Flax Pond, where you can swim, fish, paddle, or just enjoy a few moments walking along the water.

There are also some loosely spaced sites in Area 7. Of the 46 sites in Area 7, the 27–29 and 30–36 clusters are particularly isolated, especially if you're with a group and can get them all. The sites in the low 30s

> *Nickerson State Park is quite large, but it's also one of the few spots on the Cape where you can find a slice of wilderness for yourself, even during the busy summer season.*

RATINGS

Beauty: ✿ ✿ ✿ ✿
Privacy: ✿ ✿ ✿
Spaciousness: ✿ ✿ ✿
Quiet: ✿ ✿ ✿ ✿
Security: ✿ ✿ ✿ ✿
Cleanliness: ✿ ✿ ✿ ✿

ADDRESS: Nickerson State Park
3488 Main Street,
Route 6A
Brewster, MA
02631-1521

OPERATED BY: Massachusetts
Department of
Environmental
Management

INFORMATION: Nickerson State
Park, (508) 896-3491

OPEN: Mid-April–
mid-October

SITES: 418 throughout
8 areas; 2 group
sites, 6 yurts

EACH SITE HAS: Fire ring, picnic
table

ASSIGNMENT: First come, first
served; by
reservation

REGISTRATION: At main entrance on
Route 6A Monday–
Friday, 9 a.m.–
3 p.m., or call
(508) 896-4615; for
reservations, contact
Reserve America
at (877) I-CAMP-MA,
or www.reserve
america.com.

FACILITIES: Restrooms, hot
showers, pay phone

PARKING: At sites and day-use
areas

FEE: Massachusetts
residents, $15,
nonresidents, $17;
group site $25;
$30–$40 for yurts

RESTRICTIONS: *Pets:* On leash only
Fires: In fire rings
only; do not leave
unattended
Alcoholic: Not allowed
Vehicles: At sites only
Other: Quiet hours
10 p.m.–7 a.m.;
14-day maximum
stay and 2-day
minimum stay

are closest to Higgins Pond. Some of these sites (especially those nearest the water) have sandy areas, so if you have a set of those extra-large tent stakes for securing your nylon dome to loose surfaces, bring them along.

Several sites are available for reservation from late May through early September. These include 24 through 67 in Area 1, 113 through 122 in Area 2, A-83 and 93 through 104 in Area 3, 30 through 78 in Area 4, 16 through 23 in Area 5, 46 through 98 in Area 6, 110 through 144 in Area 6X, and 8 through 17 and 27 through 44 in Area 7. All other sites are first come, first served.

Even if you take the last site in the park (which is not outside the realm of possibility if you come during July and August), you're still in for some sweet tent camping. Even on those sticky summer nights when the weather is hot and muggy, there are often cool breezes blowing through the forest and over the bluffs.

The several kettle ponds (glacial ponds fed by groundwater or precipitation) dotting the park are among Nickerson's main attractions, especially for day-use visitors. Cliff Pond is the largest and is the only pond in which waterskiing is allowed. Nevertheless, it still makes for beautiful paddling and swimming. Electric trolling motors are allowed in Flax Pond, if you want to drop a hook in the water in hopes that you'll find a hungry trout. The others, Higgins Pond, Eel Pond, Little Cliff Pond, Ruth Pond, Keeler's Pond, and Triangle Pond, are just for paddling, swimming, fishing, or pond-gazing.

You could spend days exploring the trails that wind through Nickerson before you crossed them all. You can hike, bike, and rollerblade (on the paved paths), and in the winter you can cross-country ski and snowshoe. It's an amazing network of trails, and even on the busiest summer weekend, you can still discover a little slice of wilderness solitude. Some of the trails end up in the park's neighbor's backyards, so if you find yourself on something that looks like private property, be respectful, turn around, and hike back into the park.

More than 8 miles of the 25-mile Cape Cod Rail Trail pass through the park, making it the perfect launch pad for trips on the trail. You can pedal all the way to Dennis to the west of Nickerson State Park or to South Wellfleet to the east. There are several businesses along the rail trail that rent bikes and helmets, if you didn't bring your own.

The Namskaket Sea Path also runs along the shoreline where Nickerson State Park faces Cape Cod Bay. It extends 2 miles from Linnell Landing in Brewster to Skaket Beach in Orleans. This is well worth exploring, especially at low tide, when you can walk across the mouth of Namskaket Creek. The Namskaket Sea Path passes through an intertidal zone, where you'll see seashells, hermit crabs, seabirds, and all sorts of seaweed and driftwood at the high-water mark.

While you're out there on the ocean side, take some time to explore the Brewster Flats. At low tide, it looks as if you could walk all the way to Provincetown at the end of the Cape. It's especially fun with kids, who tend to notice things adults might otherwise pass by. As peaceful as a stroll along the sandbars of the Brewster Flats can be, make sure you pay attention and exercise caution. When the tide turns and starts coming in, it comes in ferociously fast, rolling up and over the sandbars and advancing on the shore with startling speed. I was caught out there once in February (of all the times to be overtaken by the tide) and came back wet from the knees down.

Whether you spend most of your time at Nickerson State Park hiking the trails, biking along the rail trail, relaxing by the shore of the ocean or by one of Nickerson's ponds, or just enjoying the last embers of your campfire, you'll discover a Cape Cod that isn't quite as crazy and crowded as you had imagined.

MAP

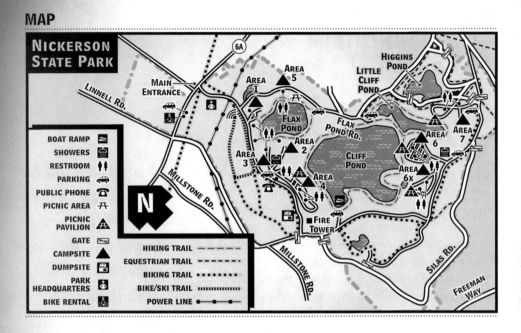

GETTING THERE

Follow Route 6 East to Route 6A West. Follow Route 6A West 1 mile or so to the entrance to the state park and campground on your left.

YOU COULD SEPARATE THE **45** campsites at Savoy Mountain State Forest by character into two very different groups. Most of the campsites are set within the woods bordering the campground, but there are many in a pastoral setting atop a hill covered by an open grassy field, which is punctuated by several large oaks, apple trees, and lilac bushes. This open orchard-like field in the center of the campground affords a nice view of the sky. That unfettered view even extends to most of the sites set into the woods on the outer perimeter of the campground loop road.

The first three sites at Savoy Mountain State Forest are tucked off on their own short road leading off to the right after you pass the ranger station at the campground entrance. Sites 1–3 are quite isolated from the rest of the campground and considerably more private than most of Savoy's other sites, especially site 1, which is located at the end of this short road. Site 3 is very spacious, set off on a slight rise at the beginning of the short road leading down to sites 1 through 3. Sites 1 and 2 are the best sites in this part of the campground, however. They are spacious and isolated from each other and from the rest of the campground and are set in a grove of tall maple trees.

The forest framing the campground at Savoy Mountain State Forest is a dense mix of mostly deciduous trees, so there's lots of shade and privacy. In these sites, light filters down to the forest floor in fractured shards.

The sites on the grassy hilltop at the center of the campground, including sites 34 to 45, are breezy, spacious, and open but not quite as private as the wooded sites. While I'm almost always a fan of more-secluded forested sites, many of these central sites have a fabulous pastoral feel about them: you'll feel as if you were

> *Savoy Mountain State Forest has a fascinating blend of sites, some tucked into the woods, some on a grassy hill, and others nestled among apple trees.*

RATINGS

Beauty: ✩ ✩ ✩ ✩
Privacy: ✩ ✩ ✩ ✩
Spaciousness: ✩ ✩ ✩ ✩
Quiet: ✩ ✩ ✩ ✩ ✩
Security: ✩ ✩ ✩ ✩
Cleanliness: ✩ ✩ ✩ ✩

ADDRESS: Savoy Mountain
State Forest
260 Central Shaft
Road
Florida, MA 01247

OPERATED BY: Massachusetts
Department of
Environmental
Management

INFORMATION: Savoy Mountain
State Forest,
(413) 663-8469

OPEN: Mid-May–Columbus
Day

SITES: 45 sites, 1 group site,
4 cabins

EACH SITE HAS: Fire ring, picnic
table

ASSIGNMENT: First come, first
served; by
reservation

REGISTRATION: At ranger station; for
reservations, contact
Reserve America
at (877) 1-CAMP-MA
or www.reserve
america.com.

FACILITIES: Flush toilets, showers, water spigots

PARKING: At sites

FEE: Massachusetts
residents, $12;
nonresidents, $14;
$25 for group site;
$30–$50 for cabins

RESTRICTIONS: *Pets:* On leash only
Fires: In established
fire rings only
Alcoholic: Not allowed
Vehicles: Parking at
sites only
Other: Quiet hours
10 p.m.–7 a.m.;
14-day maximum
stay and 2-day
minimum stay for
reservations

camping in an orchard. The openness of these sites makes them perfect for some intense stargazing, or even sleeping under the stars. What sites 34 through 45 may lack in seclusion and privacy, they more than make up for in their pastoral setting. Close by are large trees that break up the field, several bunches of brush and wild-flowers. This part of the campground would make a per-fect setting to film a remake of *The Sound of Music.*

On the outside of the campground loop road, sites 29–31 are set within the forest at the edge of the field. They share the benefits of the forest and the field, in that they are open but also feel somewhat secluded.

If these sites had nicknames, site 32 would be called the orchard site, as it is framed with several small apple trees. Site 31 is also nicely isolated with a couple of apple trees holding a vigil at the entrance. If those are the orchard sites, then site 39 is the lilac site: it's set high on the open field right next to a huge lilac bush.

Sites 8–21 are spaced out along the other side of the campground loop road. These sites are close enough to the forest to a sense of solitude, but also face the field for a dramatic view of the hilltop, wildflowers, trees, and a sweeping expanse of sky. Most of these sites also give you a vista of the field on the hilltop from the front of the site and South Pond from the back. The pond isn't too close, but you can catch glimpses of it through the trees. The trail to South Pond Beach starts right between sites 17 and 18.

The spacious site 21 is tucked into a clearing in the dense forest at the end of this part of the camp-ground loop road. Its position at the end of the road and the thick forest encircling the site give you a nice sense of solitude. The forest is also clear directly over-head, giving you a good view of the night sky.

Perched right on the corner where the camp-ground road loops around, site 22 is a bit more open, but is still roomy and nice. Site 23, next door, is large and scenic. A grand old maple hovers overhead, offer-ing a comfortable roof, of sorts.

Nestled into a grove of small apple trees and wild-flowers off the outer perimeter of the campground loop road, site 29 also has an orchard quality. The other sites along this stretch of road are spacious and accessi-

MAP

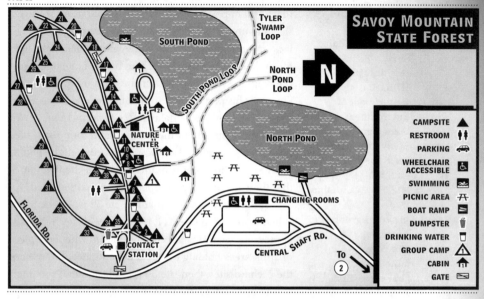

ble but set apart and tucked into the woods enough to offer a bit of privacy.

The day-use area, just down the road from the campground, has a beach and boat launch, giving you access to North Pond. Because of the easier access, expect North Pond to be a bit more crowded than its sibling to the south. While there is a small beach area on South Pond, you can get there only through the campground. Both ponds have excellent hiking trails that loop around them and head off toward the rest of Savoy Mountain State Forest's trail network.

GETTING THERE

Follow Route 2 East into Florida. Turn right on Central Shaft Road and follow the signs to Savoy Mountain State Forest.

> *Tolland State Forest has a bounty of waterfront sites—that magic combination of woods and water.*

THE CAMPGROUND AT TOLLAND STATE FOREST is on a peninsula that juts out into Otis Reservoir. Its closeness to the water means a lot of sites on or near the water. Most of the lakeside sites are set well down off the road, so they also feel secluded. The sites in the high 20s and 30s are the top-notch sites here.

Overall, most of the sites are moderate in size. There are also a few management sites (designated by letters) spread throughout the campground. These are sites that rotate in and out of circulation to minimize impact on the campground overall.

As you enter the outer campground loop, you'll find the lower-numbered sites starting on the right, facing the reservoir. There are also a couple of higher-numbered sites from where the road loops back, so sites 1 and 45 are across the road from each other. Site 46 is also near the entry to the campground. It's a small site and very open to the road, but it's surrounded by beautiful dense forest so it will feel more secluded at night.

Many of the lakeside sites are situated together in groups of three on short driveways that extend down toward the water from the main road. They're set mostly in a loosely spaced forest of pine and hemlock. Sites 2 and 3 are set a bit farther back from the road than site 1. Site 2 is fairly secluded, and site 3 is a bit more so. They're open to each other though. A dense forest isolates these two sites from the road.

RATINGS

Beauty: ✿ ✿ ✿ ✿ ✿
Privacy: ✿ ✿ ✿ ✿
Spaciousness: ✿ ✿ ✿
Quiet: ✿ ✿ ✿
Security: ✿ ✿ ✿
Cleanliness: ✿ ✿ ✿ ✿

Sites 4, 5, and 6 encompass another cluster of sites that are open to each other but nicely secluded from any others. They're set in a fairly dense pine grove so it doesn't feel as open to the lake, but the lake is right there for easy access. Site 7 is well secluded on the sides but feels a bit open to the road.

The next cluster of sites includes sites 8, 9, and 10.

Site 8 is closer to the road and a bit more open to it, but you'll enjoy good views of the lake through the trees. Sites 9 and 10 are set down a bit farther with great views of the lake from both sites, although they're open to each other. They'd be great for a larger group or family.

Another of Tolland State Forest's top-notch sites is site 12. A long driveway leads down to the site, and it's set right on the water. Sites 13, 14, and 15 are up off the lake. Site 16 is the site you'd want in this cluster.

The next troika of sites on the lake side of the campground road includes sites 18, 19, and 20. Of these three, site 18 is up a bit farther off the lake. Sites 19 and 20 are much closer, with commanding views and lake access.

Site 22 is set up a bit higher from the lake, closer to the road and so it has a bit more of an open feel, with sunlight filtering down through the trees. It's also across from the bathroom building. Site 21 is set in a beautiful pine grove but is also open to the road and to the restroom.

There's a long driveway leading into site 23 and a fairly dense forest on either side, so this stellar site has a nicely secluded feel. The fact that it's right on the lake puts it over the top for me. Site 24 has a short driveway into the site and sits on a small rise overlooking the lake.

There's a bit more of an open feel to site 25, but you're on the lake. Sites 27 and 28 share a driveway. Site 27 is nicely secluded in a slightly denser forest. It's a bit farther down from the road and closer to the lake. Sites 29 and 30 are off on their own. Although they're open to the road and the restroom, they're set down off the road and near the lake. That's a tradeoff I'd be willing to make.

There's a small cul-de-sac at the end of the campground road here, with the sites spread out like spokes on a bike. Site 31 is down off the road close to the lake. Sites 32, 37, and 38 are open to the road and to each other, but again, they are right near the water. Sites 33, 34, and 35 are well off the road down close to the lakeshore. This is definitely where you want to be at this end of the campground.

There's a huge rock and stump in the center of

KEY INFORMATION

ADDRESS:	**Tolland State Forest 410 Tolland Road P.O. Box 342 East Otis, MA 01029**
OPERATED BY:	**Massachusetts Department of Conservation and Recreation**
INFORMATION:	**Tolland State Forest, (413) 269-6002**
OPEN:	**Mid-April–mid-October**
SITES:	**92**
EACH SITE HAS:	**Fire ring, picnic table**
ASSIGNMENT:	**First come, first served; by reservation: (877) I-CAMP-MA, www.reserve america.com**
REGISTRATION:	**At ranger station as you enter campground**
FACILITIES:	**Flush toilets, showers, boat launch**
PARKING:	**At campsites**
FEE:	**$12 (MA residents), $14 (nonresidents)**
RESTRICTIONS:	*Pets:* **Dogs on leash only** *Fires:* **In established fire rings** *Alcohol:* **Prohibited** *Vehicles:* **Park at campsites** *Other:* **Reservations require 2-night minimum stay; campground office hours 8:30 a.m.–10 p.m.; 14-day maximum stay**

site 39—a bit of natural landscaping. It's open to the sky and a bit open to the road, but very scenic. Sites 42 and 43 share a driveway; site 43 is nicely isolated. There's a short walk into 43, and it's surrounded on all sides by forest. Site 42 is a bit smaller and more open.

The higher-numbered sites, in the 50s, 60s, and 70s, are in the interior of the peninsula, along Dean Road, Kenny Road, and the Main Road, respectively. Sites 50 and 51 have a bit more privacy than 52 through 55, but they're still fairly open to the road and to each other. Sites 52, 53, 54, and 55 are very open to the road and to each other. They're beautiful sites though, and they're in a quiet corner of the campground.

Sunlight filters down to the forest floor in site 56, which is open to the sky and encircled by towering pines. Site 75 has a similar feel. Sites 57 and 58 are set down off the road and so might grant you a bit more seclusion.

Site 60 is a bit smaller but fairly well secluded. It's surrounded by towering hardwoods and dense undergrowth at the back. Sites 61, 62, 66, and 67 are smaller. They're moderately well secluded on the sides but quite open to the road and to each other. Site 63 is set apart for greater privacy.

If you need a huge site, check out site 64. The tradeoff is that it's very open to the road. Site 65 is a good-sized site and well off on its own, but it's completely open to the bathroom at the back of the site. That's too bad, because it's otherwise awesome. Site 68 is a very spacious site. It's open to the road and the sky above, but there's a dense forest to the back and sides of the site.

Sites 70 and 71 are set well away from other sites but are fairly open to each other. There's a huge white pine in the center of 72. It's a smaller site, though, and very open to the road. Site 73 is also fairly open to the road and located at an intersection, but it's secluded alongside and behind.

There's a spectacular sense of isolation to sites 74 and 75, even though they're close to each other. Site 74 is set back off the road and carved out of the dense forest. It's very picturesque, with shards of sunlight filtering down. Site 75 is smaller and closer to the road but well isolated and scenic. You could almost picture sitting there with the members of the Fellowship discussing how to get into Mordor.

While sites 77 and 76 are off on their own, they're also very open to the road at an intersection of the campground roads. Site 79 is huge site in a majestic stand of towering birch and pine, so it's nicely shaded. It has an open feel, but it's very picturesque.

There's some seclusion, and views and access to the lake with sites 87 and 86. These are set right on the lake at Southwest Bay. Sites 82 and 83 are very open to the road and to each other. These would make a good pair of sites for a larger group. Likewise with sites 80, 81, and 78. The forest is more loosely spaced here, with a bit less undergrowth. This contributes to an open and airy feel but much less privacy.

Sites 89 and 88 offer only moderate seclusion because they're a bit open to the road and to each other. Site 90 is a bit more secluded, and surrounded by a younger forest of smaller trees. Site 91 is a bright, sunny site framed by massive white pines.

There's a funky white pine with multiple trunks just beside site 93, which gives it a unique character. The kid in me couldn't help but imagine what a wild tree house you could build in that tree.

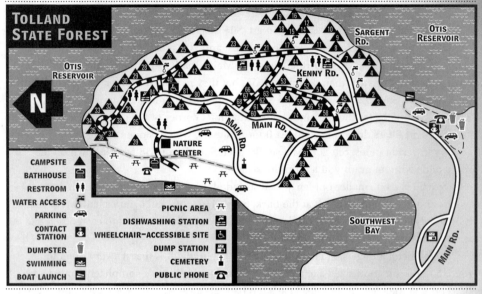

The forest here is fairly dense, for the most part, adding to the sense of seclusion, even for sites that are a bit more open to each other, like sites 52 through 55. There is some boat noise during the day, but it's quiet at night. The juxtaposition of woods and water is always a powerful combination. Do what you can to get a waterfront site when you come to Tolland State Forest. The effort is worth it.

GETTING THERE

From the Mass Pike (US Route 90), take Exit 3 in Westfield. Follow US Routes 10/202 South 3 miles into downtown Westfield. Turn right onto US Route 20 West and continue 6 miles. Turn left onto MA Route 23 West and continue 11 miles through Blandford into Otis. About a half mile past East Otis village, turn left at West Shore Road and follow the signs (West Shore Road becomes Reservoir Road). Turn left at Tolland Road and continue for 2.2 miles to the campground.

> *Washburn Island feels as wild and remote as somewhere in the South Pacific—but getting there is much easier.*

REMOTE, UNCROWDED, QUIET—not words often associated with Cape Cod, especially during the crazy summer season. Washburn Island may change the way you look at the Cape. It certainly did for me. The island is right at the mouth of the Childs River. When you paddle or motor out there, you're never too far from shore. Plus, these are protected waters that rarely get too rough, so it would be a relatively easy trip if you plan to arrive by canoe or kayak, making this is a perfect spot for your first island camping experience.

The beach is long, sweeping, flat, and sandy and opens to a shallow bay with gentle waves. This would be a very safe place for kids to spend the day in and out of the water, which tends to be a bit warmer here as it is so shallow.

The campsites on Washburn Island are all spectacularly secluded. There truly is not a bad site here. This is a pack-in, pack-out camping area, meaning you have to take back all your trash. Also, there are no open fires or fire rings. You'll have to do your cooking on a portable hibachi or camping stove. You'll also have to bring all your own water, as there are no water sources on the island.

Hiking up toward the manager's tent behind the informational signs posted on the beach as you arrive, turn to the right on the trail to get to sites 1 through 6, and left to get to sites 7 through 11. Sites 9 and 11 are the group sites. All are marked (from both the inland side and from the beach,) by small painted stones.

Sites 1 and 2 would be perfect for a group wanting two contiguous spots. Site 1 is a bit smaller than 2, but similar in character in that a dense wall of forest runs behind and alongside, with an open view of the beach to the front.

Up on a small bluff overlooking the beach, site 2 has a truly dazzling view of the bay. There's also a nice sense of seclusion to this site, as it is dense forest and

RATINGS

Beauty: ☆ ☆ ☆ ☆ ☆
Privacy: ☆ ☆ ☆ ☆ ☆
Spaciousness: ☆ ☆ ☆ ☆ ☆
Quiet: ☆ ☆ ☆ ☆ ☆
Security: ☆ ☆ ☆ ☆ ☆
Cleanliness: ☆ ☆ ☆ ☆ ☆

undergrowth run alongside. Site 2 is fairly close to site 1, but both are separated from the rest of the campsites, if not from each other.

Site 3 is a good size. It's relatively close to the bathroom building on the eastern side of the campground, but not too close. As it is a larger site, this would be a good one for a large family or group. Sites 4, 5, and 6 are all fairly open to each other but still quite spectacular. Sites 5 and 6 are moderately spacious, with lots of trees sprinkled throughout. They are both very open to the beach.

Spread out along the southwestern shore of the island, sites 7 through 10 all open to the beach. Sites 7 and 8 are a bit closer to each other, but that certainly doesn't detract from their magnificence. They are still secluded by the forest. They are also perched a bit higher off the beach. Sites 7 and 8 are moderate in size, similar to site 10, which is more isolated.

If stargazing is your thing, check out site 9. This spacious site is very open to the sky and funnels right down to the beach. There is plenty of room to set up your tent anywhere you want within this site. Its size makes it suitable for a larger group or family.

Site 10 feels incredibly remote and is surrounded by 50-foot-tall scrubby white pines and maples. The ground on this site, and most of the others, is a firm, sandy surface covered by a blanket of pine needles. The loosely spaced forest opens to the bay for a million-dollar view of the water and cool sea breezes—a truly magical combination.

Site 11 is a larger group site, and the only site on Washburn Island that isn't right off the beach. Instead it's situated a bit farther inland, within the moderately dense forest. It's

KEY INFORMATION

ADDRESS:	Waquoit Bay National Estuarine Research Preserve P.O. Box 3092 149 Waquoit Highway Waquoit, MA 02536
OPERATED BY:	Massachusetts Department of Conservation and Recreation
INFORMATION:	Waquoit Bay National Estuarine Research Preserve (508) 457-0495
OPEN:	Mid-May–late October
SITES:	9 sites, 2 group sites
EACH SITE HAS:	Incredible beauty
ASSIGNMENT:	By reservation through Waquoit Bay Preserve office or Reserve America at (877) I-CAMP-MA or www.reserveamerica.com
REGISTRATION:	Camping permit required
FACILITIES:	Composting toilets; no water available, so bring plenty
PARKING:	On the beach!
FEE:	Massachusetts residents, $8; nonresidents, $10; $25 for group site
RESTRICTIONS:	*Pets:* Dogs on leash at sites, prohibited on beach *Fires:* No open fires; use portable grills or stoves only *Alcohol:* Not allowed *Vehicles:* Pull your canoe or kayak up on the beach. *Other:* 5 people maximum per campsite, 25 maximum for group site, pack out all trash, check in after 1 p.m., check out by 11 a.m.

WAQUOIT BAY NATURE PRESERVE

RESTROM	♦♦
CAMPSITE	▲
ISLAND MANAGERS	🔱

WAQUOIT BAY

GETTING THERE

From Falmouth, head south on Route 28 and park at the White's Landing boat launch, next to Edward's boatyard. Paddle out of the Childs River, bear left, and follow the shoreline of Washburn Island to the campsites.

also fairly close to one of the two composting toilets on the island. Although it's set back from the shore, you'll still feel some cool breezes blowing in off the water.

The paths within the sites and the hiking trails leading around the island are all very well marked with neatly arranged limbs that have fallen from the trees. Please stay on the paths when walking about the island to preserve the fragile island ecology. You'll also reduce the danger of picking up a tick, which is a real possibility here. Make sure to check yourself and your kids thoroughly. If you find one, don't panic. They have to be embedded for about 24 hours to transmit disease. If you check yourself every day, you should be fine.

The openness to the beach, the incredible views, and the sense of seclusion in most of the campsites here is a powerful combination. The peaceful silence is remarkable, especially for the Cape. Were the pines and beech trees on Washburn Island suddenly replaced by palm trees, you'd swear you were somewhere in the South Pacific.

54
WOMPATUCK
STATE PARK

THERE ARE TWO SIDES to the campground at Wompatuck State Park (WSP)—electric and non-electric. Obviously, the non-electric side is going to be the side with the best tent camping. The forest at WSP is fairly dense with birch, maple, sumac, and pine. Generally, it's nice and quiet—all you'll hear is the breeze rustling through the trees.

The sites are numbered and lettered according to the road they're on. All the N sites, for example, are on the N road. The campground roads are all paved and well marked. Most of the sites are set back from the road at an angle, which helps increase the sense of seclusion.

The non-electric side has the N-through-Y sites. Despite being near an intersection of the campground road, site N2 is well secluded. Although slightly smaller, it has a short berm at the end of the site, which affords some privacy. N3 is also well secluded. Sites N4 and N5 are blocked on the sides yet fairly open to each other.

N19 is another small site that is also well secluded on the sides, even though it's open to an intersection of the campground roads. Similarly, N17 and N18 are very secluded on the sides, although a bit open to each other.

The forest is a bit more open around N17. This site also has an old stone wall running along its border. N15 is a very large site and feels a bit more open as the forest is quite loosely spaced behind. N13 is nicely secluded on the sides, yet somewhat open to the loosely spaced forest toward the back.

Sites N11 and N10 are both fairly private. N11 is a smaller site, but nicely secluded on all sides. Site N10 is surrounded by mixed forest. Site N9 is a slightly smaller site, but the dense mixed forest protects the back and sides.

Moving on to the sites on the O road, site O1 has

> *The dense forest gives the campsites at Wompatuck State Park a cool, verdant feel.*

RATINGS

Beauty: ✿ ✿ ✿ ✿
Privacy: ✿ ✿ ✿ ✿
Spaciousness: ✿ ✿ ✿ ✿
Quiet: ✿ ✿ ✿ ✿
Security: ✿ ✿ ✿ ✿
Cleanliness: ✿ ✿ ✿ ✿

ADDRESS: Wompatuck State
Park
Union Street
Hingham, MA 02043
OPERATED BY: Massachusetts
Department of
Conservation and
Recreation
INFORMATION: Wompatuck State
Park, (781) 749-7160
(in season), 749-7161
(year-round)
OPEN: Mid-April–late
October
SITES: 250 (110 on non-
electric side, 140 on
electric side)
EACH SITE HAS: Fire ring, picnic
table
ASSIGNMENT: First come, first
served; by
reservation: (877)
I-CAMP-MA or
www.reserve
america.com
REGISTRATION: At ranger station
as you enter
campground
FACILITIES: Flush toilets, hot
showers
PARKING: At campsites
FEE: Massachusetts
residents, $12;
nonresidents, $14
RESTRICTIONS: *Pets:* Dogs on leash
only
Fires: In established
fire rings
Alcohol: Prohibited
Vehicles: Park at
campsites
Other: Reservations
require 2-night
minimum stay;
campground office
hours 8 a.m.–
10 p.m.; 14-day
maximum stay

a nice grassy surface. It's a smaller but well secluded. Site O3 is separated by the dense forest. Farther along the O road, the woods get a bit more open, so generally there's less privacy. Sites O4 and O5, for example, have a loosely spaced forest alongside. site O8 has even less seclusion because the forest is so sparse, but it's still a very scenic site.

Site O12 is large. It's also open to the sky, so it's quite sunny during the day. There's a nice sense of seclusion to site O15, as the forest fills in here. It's also set off on the outside of a bend in the campground road. Site O15 is also quite large and private.

The "P" in the P road must stand for primeval, as the area is dense with forest, ferns, and thick pines. Sites P1 and P3 are a good size, but they're a bit open to the road and to each other. P4 is a much smaller site, which also has a fairly open feel. P6 is a nice big site. The forest is fairly loose here, but it's still a secluded site. There's also a little berm blocking the site from the road.

Set in a loosely spaced grove of pines, P8 is a good-sized site. It has a bit of an open feel, though, so you'd probably see your neighbors on the Q road through the forest. P14 is a small site, but it's very well secluded on the sides. Sites P16 and P9 are smaller sites, but a grove of young maple provides privacy. Site P18 is moderate in size and very well secluded, even though it's near a campground road intersection.

Most of the Q sites have an open feel. Q1 and Q2 are both very open to the road and bathroom building at the intersection of the campground roads, so those afford a bit less privacy, although they are convenient to the restroom.

Q3 is a long narrow site, so it's fairly secluded deeper into the site. Site Q4 is much smaller and is framed by towering pines, so it's scenic, even if it's a bit open to the road. Site Q6 is a huge site and fairly secluded alongside and behind, although a bit open to the road. On the other hand, Q5 is much smaller, but more private.

Site Q8 is more secluded still because there's more space between the neighboring sites on that side of the campground road. Site Q7, Q9, and Q10 feel private but are all in very loosely spaced forest.

Even though it's on an intersection, Q17 is fairly secluded on the sides. Site Q19 is a huge site. It's set in a loose forest but still isolated. Sites Q20 and Q21 are a bit smaller and protected on the sides but open to the road. Site Q22 is a good size and very secluded. The site is on a bend in the road. Beyond that is a closed area of the campground.

Along the R road, you'll find a prime site right off the bat. R2 is a beautiful spot, and quite spacious, set in a grove of young white pines with a small berm defining the back of the site.

R3 is small but private. Both R4 and R5 have a much more open feel; R4 is the much larger of the two. Sites R6 and R7 are both secluded on the sides and back, yet open to each other across the road. It is a nice pair if you're camping with a larger group. Likewise with R8 and R9—private yet open to each other across the road. R11 is a smaller site with lots of privacy. It's also much more open to the sky than the other R sites. Site R13 is a medium-sized site with a nice sense of seclusion as there's no site across the road.

Sites R10 through R15 all have a very open feel. They abut the closed area, though, so you won't have as many neighbors. Sites R12 and R17 also have a very open feel as they're set in a young, loosely spaced forest. This is a quiet corner of the campground.

There are a few T-lettered sites at the end of the R road. T1 and T2 are very nicely secluded, being off near the end of the open area of the campground.

The X road is home to a few smaller but private sites. Site X15 is very shaded and secluded on the sides. X13 is a bit smaller, set near what's left of an old stone wall that gives it some character. This is also a very private site. X8 and X11 are fairly open to the road but separated from each other.

Site X6 is a bit smaller, very shaded, and fairly open to the road. It also has the old stone wall defining its edge. Sites X7 and X5 are also small, secluded, and shaded—framed by the towering forest and filled in with dense undergrowth.

On the Y road, Y1 is set within towering pine grove but right across from the restroom. Y4 is much more open to the road and to the bathroom, although it's a good size.

Site Y5 is a moderate-sized site, framed by pines and maples. It's a bit open to the road, but secluded on the sides. Site Y9 is very spacious and open and is framed by the forest, with sunlight filtering through. Y7 is fairly secluded on the sides. Though it feels a bit open at the back, it's mostly open to the forest.

When you come to Wompatuck State Park, be sure to bring your bike—especially if you're a mountain biker. There are literally miles of trails winding through the park that await your exploration.

MAP

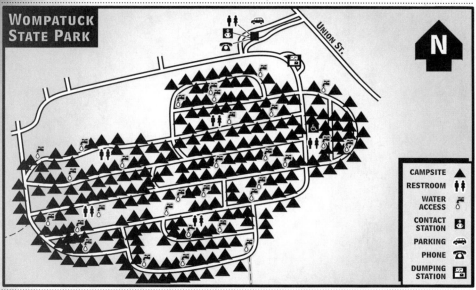

GETTING THERE

From Route 3, take Exit 14.
Then follow Route 228
North about 5 miles to Free
Street. Turn right on Free
Street, and go 1 mile
to the park entrance on
the right.

CONNECTICUT

55
DEVIL'S HOPYARD STATE PARK

IF YOU'RE WONDERING HOW THIS state park came by its name, you're not alone. There are a variety of theories. One thing folks do agree on is that the name refers to the numerous holes bored into the rock at the base of Chapman Falls. The most oft-repeated explanation is that these are the result of the devil hopping from rock to rock to avoid getting his hooves wet, burning holes in the rocks with each hop. If you can think of a better or more entertaining theory, feel free to share it with your fellow campers.

The Chapman Falls Campground at Devil's Hopyard State Park has 21 sites spread out in a wooded grove right near the campground's namesake. The falls provide not only a beautiful spot to relax and enjoy the view right outside the campground, but the constant rush of the water is a welcome addition to the forest's soundtrack.

The 21 wooded sites at this cozy little campground are arranged on either side of the short campground road. The sites are spacious but not too private. A barrier of scrub brush separates the campground from the waters above Chapman Falls on one side; on the other sie the sites abut the woods.

The sites along the water are pleasant. Those at the end of the loop are even nicer, plus they have the added benefit of being a bit more private. Site 8 is one of the most secluded sites in the campground. Sites 10 and 11 are also set off from the rest of the campground but not from each other. This would be a good pair of sites for a group.

Site 15 is desirable, as it's situated right along the water leading to the falls. Sites 16, 17, and 18 are all incredibly peaceful places to camp right along the water. Site 16 is the key spot for anglers—you could fish right from your campsite (for information on fishing licenses, see Appendix C, page 232).

> *Devil's Hopyard is small and scenic, with a cozy group of campsites just a few steps from Chapman Falls.*

RATINGS

Beauty: ☆ ☆ ☆ ☆ ☆
Privacy: ☆ ☆ ☆
Spaciousness: ☆ ☆ ☆ ☆
Quiet: ☆ ☆ ☆ ☆ ☆
Security: ☆ ☆ ☆ ☆
Cleanliness: ☆ ☆ ☆ ☆

KEY INFORMATION

ADDRESS: Devil's Hopyard
State Park
366 Hopyard Road
East Haddam, CT
06423

OPERATED BY: Connecticut Department of Environmental Protection

INFORMATION: Devil's Hopyard
State Park,
(806) 873-8566

OPEN: Mid-April–Labor
Day

SITES: 21

EACH SITE HAS: Fire ring, picnic
table

ASSIGNMENT: First come, first
served; by reservation: (877) 668-1-
CAMP-MA, www
.reserveamerica.com

REGISTRATION: At ranger station

FACILITIES: Pit toilets

PARKING: At sites

FEE: $11

RESTRICTIONS: *Pets:* Prohibited
Fires: In fire rings
only
Alcohol: Prohibited
Vehicles: Maximum
2 per site
Other: Check out by
noon; visitors
allowed 8 a.m.–
sunset; quiet hours
11 p.m.–7 a.m.; no
swimming in river

Because of its small size and remote location, the campground is very quiet except for the welcome sounds of the woodland birds and the light, incessant rushing of Chapman Falls. The loosely spaced forest of mixed deciduous and coniferous trees lets in a lot of light. The forest at the border of the campground and within the rest of the park is much more densely packed.

Chapman Falls is a spectacular series of waterfalls cascading nearly 60 feet, and continuing on as the Eight Mile River. The river flows past the Devil's Hopyard picnic area a bit farther downstream from the campground. This day-use area is popular with anglers. It's also a scenic place to walk around or just relax. Except for the campground, Devil's Hopyard State Park is closed from sunset to 6 a.m.

This area of Connecticut is just north of the town of Lyme. If that name sounds familiar, it should. Lyme has the unique and unwelcome distinction of being home to the first diagnosed cases of Lyme disease. While Lyme disease has been reported in a wider area over the last several years, it's still worth paying extra attention to deer ticks in this area. The nymph (or baby) deer ticks are particularly nasty and are extremely small and difficult to find. This doesn't mean you should stay inside all summer long. Just check yourself very carefully, especially your head and hair. If you do find a tick, don't panic. Generally, the tick has to be embedded for 24 hours to transmit the disease. Just remove the tick completely with a pair of tweezers and sterilize the bite with any antiseptic first-aid ointment.

MAP

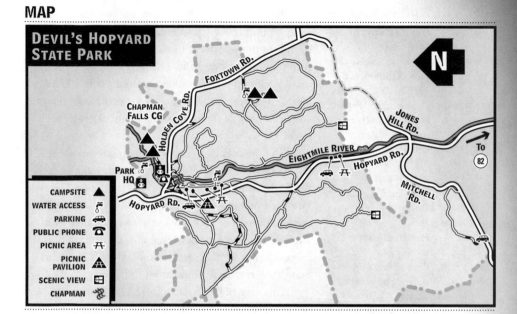

DEVIL'S HOPYARD STATE PARK

N

Foxtown Rd.

CHAPMAN FALLS CG

HOLDEN COVE RD.

JONES HILL RD.

EIGHTMILE RIVER

HOPYARD RD.

To 82

PARK HQ

MITCHELL RD.

HOPYARD RD.

CAMPSITE ▲
WATER ACCESS
PARKING
PUBLIC PHONE ☎
PICNIC AREA ⊼
PICNIC PAVILION
SCENIC VIEW ⊞
CHAPMAN

GETTING THERE

From the intersection of CT 82 and CT 156, follow Hopyard Road north approximately 3 miles. Turn right on Helon Cove Road to the campground.

56
HOUSATONIC
MEADOWS
STATE PARK

> *Between the high forest canopy and the riverside setting, Housatonic Meadows is a beautiful spot.*

THE STATUESQUE FOREST AND THE Housatonic River flowing by make for a dramatic setting at this western Connecticut campground. Many of the sites at Housatonic Meadows are spread along the river banks. There are two main areas within the campground: the Riverside Area off to the left as you enter the campground, and the large loop off to the right, where the majority of the sites are located.

The Riverside sites are very open and set directly on the riverbank beneath a loosely spaced forest of tall conifers. They're also packed in fairly tight. These sites are beautiful. It's a delight to camp next to the river, but you'll be just as close to your neighbors. What the sites offer in peaceful, relaxing scenery and proximity to the river, they lack in seclusion and privacy. You run the risk of being near a trailer or an RV, but you could set up your tent so that the first thing you see and hear in the morning is the Housatonic cascading by.

There are a few sites in the Riverside Area that are more private than the others. Sites 23 and 24, at the end of the Riverside Area road, are the most private in this section. They're at the end of the cul-de-sac, and being off on their own little loop helps isolate them. Sites 1 and 2, at the beginning of the Riverside Area road, also offer a welcome sense of solitude. This is especially true of site 1, which is separated from the rest of the row of sites by a short line of brush.

The forest here is a beautiful mix of tall pines and maples. Closer to the river, it's mostly pines, so there's a deep shade over this part of the campground. The shade of the forest canopy and proximity to the river keep these campsites cool.

While the sites here are close together, they are large and very neat. You might not have much privacy, but you are right on the water. You can fly-cast or launch canoes and kayaks from your campsite,

RATINGS

Beauty: ✿ ✿ ✿ ✿
Privacy: ✿ ✿ ✿
Spaciousness: ✿ ✿ ✿ ✿ ✿
Quiet: ✿ ✿ ✿
Security: ✿ ✿ ✿ ✿
Cleanliness: ✿ ✿ ✿ ✿

although it's probably best to drive upriver and launch from there. Then you can enjoy a leisurely paddle back to the campground. The Housatonic is fairly wide here, and the water moves right along rapidly. It's relatively safe for these activities, but as always, be prudent when entering the river, especially with children. Swimming here is not permitted, as the current is often swift.

The Knob Hill Area is off to the right as you enter the campground. The loop to the left within this area has some very pleasant sites perched high along the riverbank. These sites afford a somewhat obscured view of the river through the forest. They are fairly open but set on the border between the woods and a grove of tall conifers that shade the rest of the sites.

Generally speaking, most of the sites along the left side of this loop (the side facing the river) are the best for tents. These sites are tucked neatly into the forest, and while they're not right on the riverbank like the sites in the Riverside area, they offer more seclusion, and you can still catch glimpses of the river through the loosely spaced forest. You can also walk down through the forest to just sit and watch the river flow by—one of my favorite things to do.

In the first part of the loop on this side, sites 25 through 27 are too exposed, facing the ranger station. Sites 31, 32, and 33 are isolated, set within a dense pine grove. If you're going to erect your tent on this side of the campground, check to see if any of these sites are available.

The farthest end of the loop on this side is called the Pine Bluff Area. The sites numbered in the 80s here are attractive because they face the river and sit on the edge of both the forest and the meadow. They're also more secluded than the other sites in this area, particularly those set within the grassy field. The sites in the meadow (numbered in the 60s, 70s, and 90s) are spacious but not too private. The rest of the Pine Bluff sites are too open, being on a grassy hill without much privacy and no woods separating the camping area from views of CT 7.

The river is clearly the main attraction, but there's also some fun hiking nearby. You can ascend the 1,120-

KEY INFORMATION

ADDRESS:	Housatonic Meadows State Park Campground CT 7 Sharon, CT 06754
OPERATED BY:	Connecticut Department of Environmental Protection
INFORMATION:	Housatonic Meadows State Park, (860) 672-6772 (camp office), (860) 927-3238 (park office)
OPEN:	Mid-April–Labor Day, off-season camping until December 31; call for site and facility availability
SITES:	95
EACH SITE HAS:	Fire ring, picnic table
ASSIGNMENT:	First come, first served; by reservation: (877) I-CAMP-MA, www.reserve america.com
REGISTRATION:	At ranger station
FACILITIES:	Flush toilets, showers, water spigots, pay phone, dump station
PARKING:	At sites
FEE:	$13
RESTRICTIONS:	*Pets:* Prohibited *Fires:* In fire rings only *Alcohol:* Prohibited *Vehicles:* Maximum 2 per site *Other:* Check out by noon; quiet hours 11 p.m.–7 a.m.; no swimming in river

MAP

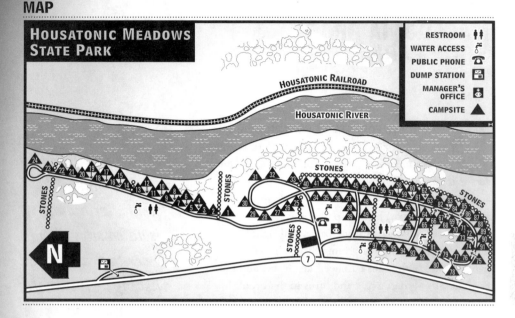

HOUSATONIC MEADOWS STATE PARK

RESTROOM
WATER ACCESS
PUBLIC PHONE
DUMP STATION
MANAGER'S OFFICE
CAMPSITE

HOUSATONIC RAILROAD

HOUSATONIC RIVER

STONES

N

7

GETTING THERE

Follow CT 7 North, approximately 2 miles north of the intersection of CT 7 and CT 4. Look for the campground signs on the right, heading north.

foot-high Pine Knob from the campground. Pick up the trail across CT 7 from the campground, or drive south a short distance to the trailhead. Follow the blue blazes and hike the entire 2.5-mile loop over Pine Knob and Ridge Crest. You'll also be on the Appalachian Trail for a time. The southern leg of this loop follows the Hatch Brook back down to the river, which makes for a cool, relaxing hike.

57

MACEDONIA BROOK STATE PARK

DEEP IN THE FORESTS OF WESTERN Connecticut, Macedonia Brook State Park is grand in both size and character. Following the long access road leading into the campground (or more accurately, *campgrounds,* as there are several distinct areas within the park), you'll pass some stellar picnic areas set beneath the towering forest and right beside the pristine waters of Macedonia Brook. You'll also pass the sites of the Old Furnace, the Gorge, and the Lower Falls. Myriad twists and turns in the brook invite you to spend hours casting a line in the tumbling water to coax out a brook trout.

There are several separate camping areas within Macedonia Brook State Park: Birch, Hickory, Red Pine, Overlook, and Maple. Some of these areas are further subdivided, and they are spread out along the long and winding road leading through the campground. The remote wilderness character of the forest combined with the widely dispersed camping areas give the entire campground a quiet, secluded feeling.

You'll pass the day-use pavilion and volleyball net as you drive toward the camping areas, and the Silver Birch Area is the first group of campsites you'll come to. Sites 1 through 4 in Silver Birch are open sites within a grassy loop right by Macedonia Brook. While these sites don't offer much privacy from one another, they are completely separate from the rest of the campground. Their riverside location is their most compelling characteristic. You could fly-fish right from your site (for information on fishing licenses, see Appendix C, page 232).

The Upper Birch Area includes sites 7 through 12, which are open, spacious, and neat, but not particularly private. They're set on a grassy hillside with sporadic trees, but the whole area is surrounded by dense woods. Many of the sites border forest. The field offers

> *Macedonia Brook State Park is magically scenic, with many isolated sites along the river that are perfect for fishing or just watching the river flow.*

RATINGS

Beauty: ☆ ☆ ☆ ☆ ☆
Privacy: ☆ ☆ ☆ ☆
Spaciousness: ☆ ☆ ☆ ☆
Quiet: ☆ ☆ ☆ ☆ ☆
Security: ☆ ☆ ☆ ☆
Cleanliness: ☆ ☆ ☆ ☆ ☆

KEY INFORMATION

sweeping views of the night sky for an intense stargazing experience. The constant whoosh of the stream rushing by is peaceful and relaxing. There is a water pump between sites 11 and 12, which also have huge stone hearths for your campfire instead of the typical fire ring.

The Lower Hickory Area includes sites 13 through 17. These sites are close to the river and fairly isolated, although the forest is open within this area. Upper Hickory is home to sites 21 and 22. These sites are even more exposed, set on the border between the forest and an open, grassy area.

The Red Pine Loop, with sites 24 through 27, is pleasantly isolated. I especially like this corner of the campground; there's not a bad spot in it. The woods are a bit denser, so these sites offer a great sense of seclusion. There are more deciduous trees mixed into the forest, and the added shade gives these spots a deep-woods feel. Site 24 is tucked off on its own at the top of the loop, and site 25 is nicely isolated.

Perched on the banks of Macedonia Brook, sites 28 and 29 would be well suited for a group wanting to fly-fish. These two sites sit together on a small grassy field right next to the brook. They're exposed, set between the brook and the campground road—but they're actually quite private later in the day, as they're entirely separate from the rest of the campground.

The Overlook Area includes sites 31 through 42. The upper sites on this wide, grassy hillside have a spectacular view of the forest, sky, and the surrounding hillsides of South Cobble and Chase Mountain. While large sites within this loop are not too private.

The Maple Area is quite spread out, and it includes sites 43 through 51. These sites are beautifully isolated in a dense grove of varied tree species. These loops are just past the Overlook Area as you drive along the campground road.

The camping areas within Macedonia Brook State Park seem to offer a choice between seclusion and sweeping views. The sites on the grassy hillsides are more open to breezes, so they are often cooler and less buggy than the sites set deep within the woods.

There are numerous hiking trails winding

MAP

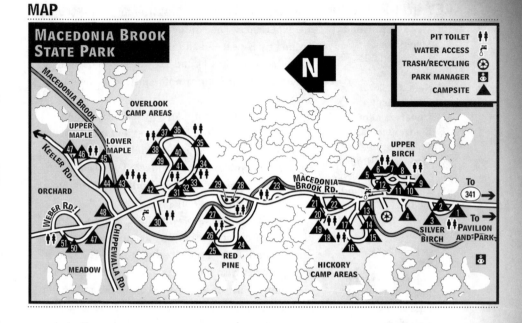

throughout the state park, and there are plenty of places to drop a hook in the water. Most of the trails are called (and marked) simply by colors. The Blue Trail follows a ridgeline to the east of the camping areas. The Yellow Trail intersects the Blue Trail just west of the pavilion. The Green Trail, leading out from the Upper Birch Area, also intersects the Blue Trail. The Orange Trail runs from the Upper Birch Area to the Maple Area. Lastly, the White Trail takes you from the pavilion to the top of nearby Cobble Mountain.

GETTING THERE

From Kent, follow CT 341 north to Macedonia Brook Road on the right. Turn right here and drive until you see signs for the park.

> *Selden Neck has some of the most spectacular and accessible island camping in New England.*

THERE IS ABSOLUTELY NO WAY you'll find an RV at the Selden Neck Campground in Gillette Castle State Park. There are no designated tent-only areas, and no inherent rules or regulations prohibiting them, but until someone invents an RV that floats, Selden Neck is just for tent camping. You can reach the park and the campground only by boat.

This fabulously peaceful little state park is perched on the northern corner of a small island separated from the banks of the Connecticut River by Selden Creek. The campsites are right on the river, and there are no docks, moorings, or facilities other than fireplaces and pit toilets. You'll have to approach the campsite with a small watercraft. Whether you choose a sailboat or motorboat, or better yet, a canoe or kayak, is entirely up to you.

There are four discrete camping areas on Selden Neck: Hogback, Springledge, Quarry Knob, and Cedars Camp, listed roughly in order of my personal preference. The first three areas are situated along the banks of the Connecticut River. The main channel runs down the river right next to Selden Neck, so on a busy summer day, there will be lots of boat traffic, including some ferry boats and sizable powerboats. Consequently, it can be a bit busy during the day, and there may be some chop on the river and splashing up against the banks of Selden Neck. Secure your boat adequately, or pull your canoe or kayak up onto the shore to keep it from getting bashed around—or worse, slipping off into the river without you.

The Hogback, Springledge, and Quarry Knob areas are similar, having small, grassy areas upon which to pitch your tent. You'll be fairly close to the riverbanks, and behind the sites there's a short, steep hill in the center of the island. Hogback is the smallest of these areas, with room for six campers. Springledge

RATINGS

Beauty: ✪ ✪ ✪ ✪
Privacy: ✪ ✪ ✪ ✪ ✪
Spaciousness: ✪ ✪ ✪ ✪ ✪
Quiet: ✪ ✪ ✪ ✪
Security: ✪ ✪ ✪ ✪ ✪
Cleanliness: ✪ ✪ ✪ ✪

accommodates eight campers, and Quarry Knob has room for twelve.

You can really immerse yourself in wilderness and solitude here, despite the fact that you're camping right on the Connecticut River, which can sometimes feel like the maritime equivalent of an interstate. The small, densely forested camping areas, the way they are set off from each other, and the fact that you're on an island all contribute to the atmosphere of isolation on Selden Neck. This becomes even more apparent toward the end of the day as the river traffic quiets down.

The Cedars Camp area attracts a lot of day use, as it's tucked into a corner of Selden Creek off the main branch of the river. If the weather or winds are rough, this would be a good choice because the small beach where you arrive is more protected. It's also a good choice if you happen to be camping with a larger group, as this area of Selden Neck can accommodate up to 20 people.

The nearest boat ramp is the Deep River public boat launch, which is right across the river from Selden Creek and the island on which the campground is located. It's a fairly short paddle in a canoe or kayak, and a snap in a small motorboat or sailboat. The only trouble is parking at the boat launch. Parking right at the boat launch is only for Deep River residents who have purchased a sticker. Get dropped off or park just outside the boat-launch parking area, if there's room.

Keep this in mind as you're preparing for your trip: You are traveling to an island to camp. There are no stores on this island. You need to bring everything with you—all your food, water, and camping supplies. Running out to a store because you forgot batteries or hot dogs is not impossible, but it's not going to be easy. The flip side of that coin is that you must also pack out everything you've used as well as any trash you've generated. The camping areas have pit toilets, but there aren't any garbage cans. Live by the pack-it-in, pack-it-out mantra.

When kayak camping (or taking canoes or other small boats) prepare something you can freeze in Tupperware. By dinner time, your meal will have mostly defrosted. Then just heat it up, and dinner is served.

KEY INFORMATION

ADDRESS: Selden Neck Campground c/o Gillette Castle State Park 67 River Road Haddam, CT 06423

OPERATED BY: Connecticut Department of Environmental Protection

INFORMATION: Contact Gillette Castle State Park, (860) 526-2336

OPEN: May 1– September 30

SITES: 4 sites accommodating 46 people total

EACH SITE HAS: Fire pit, pit toilet

ASSIGNMENT: Reservations required; make at least 2 weeks prior to visit by mail to Gillette Castle State Park Supervisor, address above; include full payment by check or money order made to Treasurer, State of Connecticut

REGISTRATION: Claim your site

FACILITIES: Pit toilets

PARKING: Boats only

FEE: $4 per person per night

RESTRICTIONS: *Pets:* Prohibited
Fires: In ire pits only
Alcohol: At sites only
Vehicles: Boats only
Other: Visitors must leave by 8 p.m.; campers must pack out all trash

Once you make landfall and set up your camp, you'll probably want to take off in your boat to do a little exploring. Selden Creek, which winds its way around Selden Neck Island, is an absolutely delightful area to paddle. The water is often as still as glass, even on days when the wind has churned the main channel of the river into a swirling froth. Selden Creek casually winds around through swampy marsh and overhanging trees past some cliffs and the forested hills of the mainland. At times it feels like you're paddling through a bayou, other times through a northern fjord; but it always feels like you're a million miles from anyone.

There's one important (unexpected) caveat: Beware of the swans. They are beautiful birds, there are plenty of them, and they are fiercely territorial. I have been charged by swans on three separate occasions while paddling through Selden Creek. It's kind of ridiculous from a human's point of view. I was in a 17-foot-long, bright yellow kayak. Still, this stubborn, ornery swan charged me broadside.

Besides the fact that it's always best to view wildlife from a respectful distance so that your presence has as little effect on their behavior as possible, it pays to be mindful of how close you are to the swans. If you get too close and they attack, they could poke a hole in a fiberglass canoe or kayak, or worse yet, break your arm or wrist. Those long, slender necks are solid muscle. If a swan starts posturing, appears agitated, or tucks its wings up into attack mode so it looks like a Romulan Warbird (for you Trekkies out there), simply continue on your way and they'll eventually leave you alone to enjoy the otherwise peaceful and pristine solitude of Selden Creek.

With a campfire crackling in the fire pit, a belly full from dinner, a warm glow on your face from spending the day on and around the water, sit back at your campsite and admire the river as it slows down for the night. Looking west across the river from the Hogback, Springledge, and Quarry Knob sites, you'll have a beautiful view of the opposite riverbank and the top of Gillette Castle. When the weather is right, you're at one of the best spots in Connecticut from which to admire the sunset.

MAP

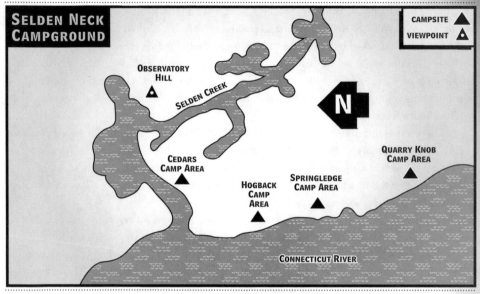

SELDEN NECK
CAMPGROUND

CAMPSITE ▲
VIEWPOINT △

OBSERVATORY
HILL
△

SELDEN CREEK

N

QUARRY KNOB
CAMP AREA
▲

CEDARS
CAMP AREA
▲

SPRINGLEDGE
CAMP AREA
▲

HOGBACK
CAMP
AREA
▲

CONNECTICUT RIVER

GETTING THERE

To Deep River boat ramp, take Exit 4 off Route 9. Follow Route 154 into Deep River. Turn right at the four-way intersection downtown (Route 80 heads off to the left). Follow this road to Deep River boat launch.

RHODE ISLAND

59
FORT GETTY
RECREATION AREA

FORT GETTY RECREATION AREA will appeal to history buffs and anyone wanting to combine a little paddling or beachcombing with their camping experience. It's also a perfect spot to capture some island-camping mystique without actually loading up a boat, canoe, or kayak and rowing off across the water. Set on a windswept bluff near the southern tip of Conanicut Island in the middle of Narragansett Bay, this is a beautiful oceanside campground. Even though this campground is on an island, rest assured you can get there by car. What it lacks in privacy and distance from the nearby flotilla of RVs, it makes up for in salty sea breezes, sunrises and sunsets to die for, rocky beachfronts worth hours of exploring, and a fantastic spot to drop a kayak or a hook in the water.

There is a modest-sized tent-camping area, which is set off as much as possible from where the RVs roam. I say as much as possible because there isn't a whole lot of room within the campground proper. The scenery and setting compensate nicely for the forest density, though. Here's a hint: Once you've found your campsite, set up your tent so the opening faces the bay. That way, when you wake up, your first views will be of the sun rising over the water.

As you drive into the park, the long access road leading into the campground passes a couple of residences, so it feels like you're heading up someone's driveway, but keep on—this road does indeed lead to Fort Getty Recreation Area. You'll come to a pay station in the middle of the road. Check in here, then keep cruising. The road winds around to the right, and the campground is ahead on the left toward the end of the peninsula.

As you drive in, you'll pass the Fox Hill Salt Marsh on your left. This is a great place to walk around or to just find a cozy spot to take in the

> *Fort Getty Recreation Area's campground is fairly wide open, but the panoramic vistas of Narragansett Bay and the sea breezes can't be beat.*

RATINGS

Beauty: ✿ ✿ ✿ ✿
Privacy: ✿ ✿
Spaciousness: ✿ ✿ ✿
Quiet: ✿ ✿ ✿
Security: ✿ ✿ ✿ ✿
Cleanliness: ✿ ✿ ✿ ✿

KEY INFORMATION

ADDRESS: Fort Getty Recreation Area P.O. Box 377 Jamestown, RI 02835

OPERATED BY: Town of Jamestown

INFORMATION: Fort Getty Recreation Area, (401) 423-7211

OPEN: May 15–October 1

SITES: 15 tent-only sites, 105 trailer sites

EACH SITE HAS: Fire ring

ASSIGNMENT: First come, first served

REGISTRATION: At ranger station

FACILITIES: Flush toilets, showers, water spigots, pay phones, boat launch, fishing dock, horseshoe pits, saltwater beach

PARKING: Near sites; additional parking at day-use area

FEE: $20

RESTRICTIONS: *Pets:* Dogs on leash only
Fires: In fire rings only
Alcohol: At sites only
Vehicles: Park near sites

scenery. If you're into birding, you'll particularly enjoy training your eyes and binoculars on the various shore-birds found here.

You'll quickly realize this campground doesn't embody the forest-bound sense of solitude you'll find in most other New England campgrounds, but the waterfront setting can't be beat. The tent-only area is toward the top of the small hill off to the left as you reach the campsites, and includes sites 1 through 14. These sites are all very open and fairly tightly packed, but parking for them is along the periphery, so the site cluster feels like a little tent village.

Right next to the camping area is a big open field; it's a tremendous spot for picnicking, kite flying, Fris-bee throwing—you name it. There's also a sand volley-ball pit nearby. This space for casual play and hanging out reinforces the laid-back, island mentality that pre-dominates at Fort Getty.

Camping with little kids? The rocky beaches sur-rounding the park offer endless hours of rock-hopping and beachcombing. Some of the cliffs and larger rocks are a bit steep, so you'll have to keep a sharp eye on the younger ones, but I can guarantee your kids will be tuckered out after a day spent prowling these rocky shores.

For the historically minded, there are a couple of bunkers remaining from when Fort Getty was an ammunition depot during World War II. These are also cool little spots in which older kids enjoy playing.

Connecticut Island is surrounded by several other small islands. In a place like this, the environment is captivating regardless of the weather. It's brilliant on bright, sunny days, and cool and refreshing when the mainland is sweltering. The stars at night are crystal clear, and you'll see deeper into the universe since there isn't much in the way of light pollution out here. In a fog or light rain, the islands poking in and out of the mist give the place a sense of mystery, as if you'd almost expect to see a pirate ship emerging to bury its sailors' stolen treasures on one of the islands.

If you're planning a family reunion, wedding reception, or some other big bash, you can reserve the Lieutenant Colonel John C. Rembigas Pavilion for

MAP

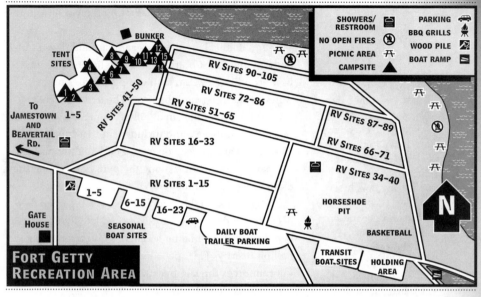

FORT GETTY RECREATION AREA

such functions. This is off to the left of the camp-ground, open field, and volleyball pit; call for more information on reserving the space.

Fort Getty Recreation Area is scenic and centrally located: a perfect base camp for fishing (for information on fishing licenses, see Appendix C, page 232), pad-dling, scuba diving, and beachcombing. It's also an amazing place to fly a kite. Charlie Brown would have loved it—steady winds and few kite-eating trees to be found. Those winds also make Fort Getty Recreation Area the place to be on steamy summer afternoons. While folks camping deep in the forest are sweating bullets and slapping bugs, you'll have a strong, cool breeze keeping your temperature down and the bugs away.

GETTING THERE

Take North Main Street to the south (toward Beavertail State Park). This road will cross Narragansett Road and turn into Southwest Avenue to Beavertail Road. This winds around a sandy beach to the left, and the entrance for the campground is on the right.

Glocester

> *The entire George Washingon Management Area is a lush, dense forest that is quite accessible, yet has a pleasant, remote feel.*

YOU'LL BE TEMPTED to check your map as you drive into the campground at the George Washington Management Area. Did you somehow take a wrong turn and end up in Vermont or New Hampshire? Nope, this is indeed Rhode Island, but it's far from the windswept beaches, sandy soil, and short, scrubby pines and beach roses you might expect of Rhode Island topography. As soon as you enter the campground, you are enshrouded by a canopy of conifers. The tangy pine and balsam scents mixed in with earthy wisps of wood smoke make for quite a welcome.

The entire George Washington Management Area and the contiguous Pulaski Memorial State Forest are both densely wooded areas with a gently rolling forest floor. The area is free of really steep hills, uneven terrain, and heavy undergrowth. This makes for many nice places to pitch a tent. Stop to pay your fee at the ranger station as you drive into the campground, and you're ready to go.

The campground wraps around the shores of Bowdish Lake. Down by the beach area, there's a beautiful stone Recreation Hall built by the Civilian Conservation Corps (CCC). A plaque in front of the building honors the members of the CCC who built the hall. The beach is the perfect spot to go for a quick swim, to spend the day with the kids, or to kick back on a blanket and read a book. You could also drop a hook or a paddle in the water (or both!) if you're so inclined.

Sites 26, 27, and 28 are quite spacious and close to the lake. These are some of the prime spots at the George Washington Management Area campground. The loop with sites 34 thgough 45 is another good area in which to pitch your tent. The sites within this loop are a bit smaller than some of those along the main

RATINGS

Beauty: ✪ ✪ ✪ ✪
Privacy: ✪ ✪ ✪ ✪
Spaciousness: ✪ ✪ ✪ ✪
Quiet: ✪ ✪ ✪ ✪
Security: ✪ ✪ ✪ ✪
Cleanliness: ✪ ✪ ✪ ✪

campground road, but they're nestled within a dense pine grove and fairly close to the lake—both attractive aspects. This loop is the first left off the main road once you're in the campground.

Farther down the road, sites 5 and 6 are well worth investigating. They're good-sized and set off with plenty of space in between them and the other sites. Sites 11 and 14 are right on the border of the campground proper and the rest of the George Washington Management Area. These are also nice sites, as the forest becomes denser on this end of the campground. Site 12 is also particularly secluded.

Follow the main campground road past all these sites, and past the loop for Shelter 1 off to the left and you'll be heading off into the rest of the George Washington Management Area. This is a great area to explore when it's time for a hike or bike ride.

The entire campground has plenty of space and forest for everyone. However, several sites and sections along the main road are a bit too open for my taste. Sites 7, 9, 12, 17, and 18 aren't quite as private as some of the other sites along the main road and those tucked off in the side loops.

If you've come with a large group, or have several members of your group who would rather not sleep on the ground, check out one of the two AMC-type lean-to shelters. These have a wood floor and are open on one side. If you're going for one of the shelters, try to secure Shelter 1. It's up on a small rise at the end of its own loop, offering some privacy. It's at the far end of the campground road, and right on the border between the campground and the rest of the expansive George Washington Management Area.

Shelter 2 is also in a nice spot, quite separate from the rest of the campground at the end of a short road leading off to the right from the main campground road. However, it's right next to a large, open sandy lot that looks like overflow parking. While it may detract a bit from the scenery, if you have a large group all arriving in their own vehicles, you won't have any trouble finding parking. This is the site to choose if you're camping with 100 of your closest friends, all of whom insist on driving their own cars!

KEY INFORMATION

ADDRESS: George Washington Management Area
2185 Putnam Pike
Chepachet, RI 02814

OPERATED BY: Rhode Island Department of Environmental Management, Division of Forest Environment

INFORMATION: Rhode Island Division of Forest Environment, (401) 568-6700, 568-2013

OPEN: Mid-April–mid-October

SITES: 45 sites and 2 shelters for group camping

EACH SITE HAS: Fire ring

ASSIGNMENT: At registration when you pay for permit

REGISTRATION: At pay station near campground entrance or office in recreation hall

FACILITIES: Toilets, water spigots, boat launch

PARKING: At campsites, additional parking available near recreation hall and Shelter 1

FEE: Rhode Island residents, $14; nonresidents, $20; shelters, $35

RESTRICTIONS: *Pets:* Not allowed
Fires: In fire rings
Alcohol: Not allowed
Vehicles: 2 per site
Other: 14-day maximum stay; visitors must be out by 10 p.m.; quiet hours 10 p.m.–7 a.m.

One restriction worth noting is that possession of alcoholic beverages is grounds for expulsion from the campground. They must have had some problems with ebullient revelers in the past, as they seem quite serious about this one. This restriction is clearly stated in several spots in the campground literature. If you like to kick back with a beer or a glass of wine after dinner, wait until the next campground. Try a cup of tea instead.

Another point to ponder is the wildlife. Let them remain wild. Don't feed them or otherwise tempt them by leaving food or dirty dishes around your campsite. The George Washington Management Area campground is wild and scenic, but it's also very accessible. Once otherwise wild animals become acclimated to human's presence, they often have to be relocated or exterminated, and you don't want to be responsible for that. Plus, there are general safety considerations. Raccoons are occasional carriers of rabies, so report any incidences of raccoon or other animal bites or scrapes. It's also not a bad idea to report any strange or aggressive animal behavior.

At 3,500 acres, the George Washington Management Area is big enough to be a one-stop-shopping type of place for outdoor adventure. Bowdish Lake is right there for swimming, fishing, and paddling. The network of trails winding through the George Washington Management Area and Pulaski Memorial State Forest will keep the hikers and mountain bikers in your group busy for days.

The Walkabout Trail, marked by orange and red dots, is an 8-mile hike that passes by Wilbur Pond, a beautiful hemlock grove, and some wetlands. The trail leads right out of the campground. There are several alternate-trail options along the way for those who don't want to go the full 8 miles. The blue dot–marked cutoff makes it a 2-mile hike, and the red dot–marked cutoff makes it a 6-mile hike.

There's a tiny sign at the apex of the roof on the backside of the ranger station that sums up the friendly nature of the George Washington Management Area. Look closely, drive slowly, look up, and you'll see it as you're leaving—"Have a Nice Day"—with the classic yellow smiley face.

MAP

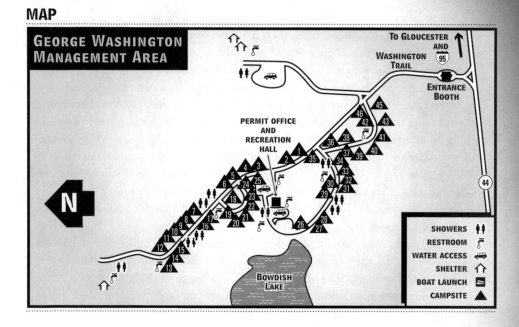

GETTING THERE

From Route 295, follow
Route 44 West through
Greenville and Chepachet
into Glocester. Keep an eye
out for the campground sign
on the right.

APPENDIXES AND INDEX

APPENDIX A
CAMPING EQUIPMENT CHECKLIST

I keep a plastic storage container full of the essentials for car camping—except for the large and bulky items that won't fit—so they're ready to go when I am. I make a last-minute check of the inventory, resupply anything that's low or missing, and take off!

COOKING UTENSILS
Aluminum foil
Bottle opener
Bottles of salt, pepper, spices, sugar, cooking oil, and maple syrup in waterproof, spillproof containers
Can opener
Corkscrew
Cups, plastic or tin
Dish soap (biodegradable), sponge, and towel
Flatware
Food of your choice
Frying pan
Fuel for stove
Matches in waterproof container
Plates
Pocketknife
Pot with lid
Spatula
Stove
Wooden spoon

FIRST-AID KIT
Antibiotic cream
Band-Aids®
Diphenhydramine (Benadryl®)
Gauze pads
Ibuprofen or aspirin
Insect repellent
Lip balm
Moleskin®
Snakebite kit
Sunscreen
Tape, waterproof adhesive

SLEEPING GEAR
Pillow
Sleeping bag
Sleeping pad, inflatable or insulated
Tent with ground tarp and rainfly

MISCELLANEOUS
Bath soap (biodegradable), washcloth, and towel
Camp chair
Candles
Cooler
Deck of cards
Duct tape
Fire starter
Flashlight or headlamp with fresh batteries
Foul-weather clothing
Paper towels
Plastic zip-top bags
Sunglasses
Toilet paper
Water bottle
Wool or fleece blanket

OPTIONAL:
Barbecue grill
Binoculars
Field guides on bird, plant, and wildlife identification
Fishing rod and tackle
Hatchet
Kayak and paddling gear
Lantern
Maps (road, topographic, trails, and so on)
Mountain bike and gear

MAINE

Maine Bureau of Parks and Lands
22 State House Station
Augusta, ME 04333
(207) 287-3821
www.state.me.us

Acadia National Park
Box 177
Bar Harbor, ME 04609
(207) 288-3338
www.nps.gov/acad

NEW HAMPSHIRE

**New Hampshire Department of
Resources and Economic Development**
Division of Parks and Recreation
172 Pembroke Road
P.O. Box 1856
Concord, NH 03302-1856
(603) 271-3628
www.nhparks.state.nh.us

**United States Department of
Agriculture Forest Service**
White Mountain National Forest
P.O. Box 638
Laconia, NH 03247
(603) 528-8721
www.fs.fed.us/r9/white

VERMONT

**Vermont Department of Forests, Parks, &
Recreation**
103 South Main Street
Waterbury, VT 05671-0603
(802) 241-3655
www.vtstateparks.com

Green Mountain National Forest
231 North Main Street
Rutland, VT 05701
(802) 747-6700
www.fs.fed.us/r9/gmfl

MASSACHUSETTS

**Massachusetts Department of
Environmental Management**
251 Causeway Street, Suite 600
Boston, MA 02114-2104
(617) 626-1250
www.state.ma.us/dem

CONNECTICUT

**Connecticut Department of
Environmental Protection**
Bureau of Outdoor Recreation
State Parks Division
79 Elm Street
Hartford, CT 06106-5127
(860) 424-3200
www.dep.state.ct.us

RHODE ISLAND

**Rhode Island Department of
Environmental Management**
Division of Parks and Recreation
2321 Hartford Avenue
Johnston, RI 02919
(401) 222-2632
www.riparks.com

APPENDIX C
FISHING LICENSE
INFORMATION

Note: Rates (unless indicated) are for annual passes for individuals ages 16 and older (younger kids don't need them). Call the same numbers to inquire about hunting licenses.

MAINE
(207) 287-8000
$22 for residents; $53 for non-residents; $24 for a 3-day pass

NEW HAMPSHIRE
(603) 271-3211
$35 for residents; $53 for non-residents; $28 for a 3-day pass

VERMONT
(802) 241-3700
$20 for residents; $41 for non-residents; $20 for a 3-day pass

MASSACHUSETTS
(617) 626-1600
$27.50 for residents; $37.50 for non-residents; $23.50 for a 3-day pass

CONNECTICUT
(860) 424-3000
$20 for residents; $40 for non-residents; $16 for a 3-day pass

RHODE ISLAND
(401) 789-3094
$18 for residents; $35 for non-residents; $16 for a 3-day pass

INDEX

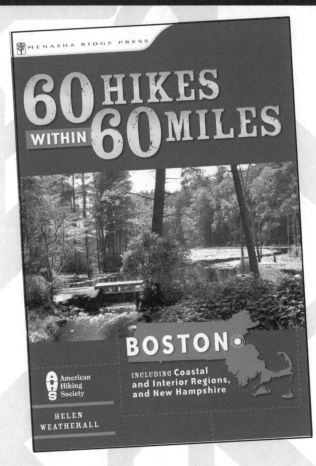

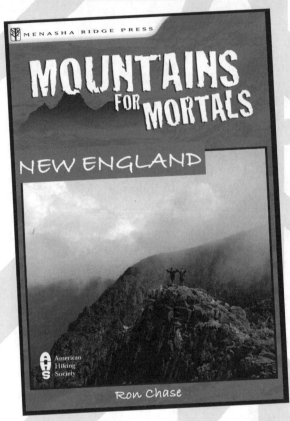